The Price of Freedom Denied

Religious Persecution and Conflict in the Twenty-First Century

The Price of Freedom Denied shows that, contrary to popular opinion, ensuring religious freedom for all reduces violent religious persecution and conflict. Others have suggested that restrictions on religion are necessary to maintain order or preserve a peaceful religious homogeneity. Brian J. Grim and Roger Finke show that restricting religious freedoms is associated with higher levels of violent persecution. Relying on a new source of coded data for nearly two hundred countries and case studies of six countries, the book offers a global profile of religious freedom and religious persecution. Grim and Finke report that persecution is evident in all regions and is standard fare for many. They also find that religious freedoms are routinely denied and that government and the society at large serve to restrict these freedoms. They conclude that the price of freedom denied is high indeed.

Brian J. Grim is senior researcher in religion and world affairs at the Pew Research Center's Forum on Religion and Public Life in Washington, D.C. Dr. Grim is also the co–principal investigator for the international religious demography project at Boston University's Institute on Culture, Religion and World Affairs, where he co-edits the World Religion Database (www.WorldReligionDatabase.org). His findings on international religious demography and religious freedom have been covered by all the major news outlets, including the BBC, CNN, the Associated Press, and Reuters, and he frequently presents to high-level governmental and nongovernmental groups. Dr. Grim has extensive overseas experience. From 1982 to 2002, he lived and worked as an educator, researcher, and development coordinator in China, the former USSR, Central Asia, Europe, Malta, and the Middle East.

Roger Finke is Professor of Sociology and Religious Studies at the Pennsylvania State University and Director of the Association of Religion Data Archives (www.theARDA.com). He has published in numerous social science journals and has co-authored two award-winning books with Rodney Stark: *Acts of Faith: Explaining the Human Side of Religion* and *The Churching of America, 1776–1990*. He is a past president of the Association for the Study of Religion, Economics, and Culture; is a past chair of the American Sociological Association's Sociology of Religion Section; and has served as a member of multiple national and international councils, boards, and committees. He is the 2009 recipient of the Pennsylvania State University President's Award for integrating research, teaching, and service.

CAMBRIDGE STUDIES IN SOCIAL THEORY, RELIGION, AND POLITICS

Editors

David C. Leege, University of Notre Dame
Kenneth D. Wald, University of Florida, Gainesville
Richard L. Wood, University of New Mexico

The most enduring and illuminating bodies of late-nineteenth-century social theory – by Marx, Weber, Durkheim, and others – emphasized the integration of religion, polity, and economy through time and place. Once a staple of classic social theory, however, religion gradually lost the interest of many social scientists during the twentieth century. The recent emergence of phenomena such as Solidarity in Poland; the dissolution of the Soviet empire; various South American, southern African, and South Asian liberation movements; the Christian Right in the United States; and Al Qaeda have reawakened scholarly interest in religiously based political conflict. At the same time, fundamental questions are once again being asked about the role of religion in stable political regimes, public policies, and constitutional orders. The series Cambridge Studies in Social Theory, Religion, and Politics will produce volumes that study religion and politics by drawing on classic social theory and more recent social scientific research traditions. Books in the series offer theoretically grounded, comparative, empirical studies that raise big questions about a timely subject that has long engaged the best minds in social science.

Titles in the Series

Paul A. Djupe and Christopher P. Gilbert, *The Political Influence of Churches*

Joel S. Fetzer and J. Christopher Soper, *Muslims and the State in Britain, France, and Germany*

Jonathan Fox, *A World Survey of Religion and the State*

Anthony Gill, *The Political Origins of Religious Liberty*

Kees van Kersbergen and Philip Manow, editors, *Religion, Class Coalitions, and Welfare States*

Ahmet T. Kuru, *Secularism and State Policies toward Religion: The United States, France, and Turkey*

Pippa Norris and Ronald Inglehart, *Sacred and Secular: Religion and Politics Worldwide*

Dedicated to our wives and families:

Julia Beth Grim

and

Melissa Malika (Ge Tian-en)

Joel Yusup (Ge Tian-ci) and Jamie Lynn

Andrew Nurullah (Ge Tian-fu)

Abigail Adellet (Ge Tian-le)

Terri Finke

and

Matthew, Jill, and Maria

Stacey, Lucas, and Theodore

The Price of Freedom Denied

Religious Persecution and Conflict in the Twenty-First Century

BRIAN J. GRIM
Pew Research Center

ROGER FINKE
Pennsylvania State University

 **CAMBRIDGE**
UNIVERSITY PRESS

BL 640 .G75 2011
Grim, Brian J.
The price of freedom denied

31.00

CAMBRIDGE UNIVERSITY PRESS
Cambridge, New York, Melbourne, Madrid, Cape Town, Singapore,
São Paulo, Delhi, Dubai, Tokyo, Mexico City

Cambridge University Press
32 Avenue of the Americas, New York, NY 10013-2473, USA

www.cambridge.org
Information on this title: www.cambridge.org/9780521146838

© Brian J. Grim and Roger Finke 2011

First published 2011

Printed in the United States of America

A catalog record for this publication is available from the British Library.

Library of Congress Cataloging in Publication data

Grim, Brian J.
The price of freedom denied : religious persecution and conflict in the 21st century / Brian
J. Grim, Roger Finke.
 p. cm. – (Cambridge studies in social theory, religion, and politics)
Includes bibliographical references and index.
ISBN 978-0-521-19705-2 (hardback)
1. Freedom of religion. 2. Religious tolerance. 3. Persecution.
I. Finke, Roger, 1954– II. Title. III. Series.
BL640.G75 2010
323.44′209051 – dc22   2010011467

ISBN 978-0-521-19705-2 Hardback
ISBN 978-0-521-14683-8 Paperback

Contents

Preface: Religions' Shared Experience of Religious Persecution and Conflict   *page* ix

1   Religious Persecution: Pervasive and Pernicious   1

2   Religious Freedom: Broken Promises   25

3   Persecution: The Price of Freedom Denied   61

4   Case Studies: Japan (High Levels of Religious Freedoms), Brazil (Freedoms with Some Tensions), and Nigeria (Partitioned Religion–State Power)   88

5   A Closer Look: China (Religion Viewed as a Threat), India (Social Monopoly), and Iran (Social and Political Monopoly)   120

6   What about Muslim-Majority Countries?   160

7   Do Religious Freedoms Really Matter?   202

Appendix: Testing the Competing Arguments   215

Bibliography   223

Index   239

Preface

Religions' Shared Experience of Religious Persecution and Conflict

Violent religious persecution is nothing new. Nowhere is this clearer than in the prominence that persecution plays in religious rituals and identity. The pronouncement by Moses and Aaron that Pharaoh must let God's people go, recorded in the Old Testament book of Exodus, is reflected in annual commemorations by the three major monotheistic religions originating in the Middle East, namely Judaism, Christianity, and Islam. Each year, the Jewish holiday of Passover commemorates their rapid Exodus from persecution. The Passover is also closely tied with the Christian celebration of both Easter and the Eucharist, and Muslims have historically also commemorated the Exodus from Egypt led by Moses on *Ashura*, the day the Prophet Muhammed initially designated as a day of fasting.[1]

But the significance of violent persecution for the Abrahamic religions is not confined to the Exodus from Egypt. Jews commemorate other persecution and deliverances, ranging from Hanukkah to the World War II Holocaust. Among Christians, many of the most venerated apostles, missionaries, and saints were also persecuted and martyred. The Muslim calendar itself is dated from the Al-Hijra, or Muhammed's migration from Mecca to Medina to escape violent persecution.[2] And today, *Ashura* is primarily associated with commemoration of the martyrdom (at the

---

[1] Shahul Hameed (2007), "Out of Egypt: The Story of Passover in the Qur'an," *Reading Islam: Mohammed and the Message*, http://www.islamonline.net/servlet/Satellite?c=Article_C&cid=1175751840758&pagename=Zone-English-Discover_Islam%2FDIELayout (accessed 5 August 2010).

[2] See http://original.britannica.com/eb/article-9039809/Hijrah.

Supported by a grant from the John Templeton Foundation. The opinions expressed in this book are those of the authors and do not necessarily reflect the views of the Foundation.

hands of other Muslims) of Imam Hussein, whose progeny Shia Muslims regard as the rightful bloodline to succeed the Prophet Muhammed.[3]

The experience of violent persecution is not confined to Abrahamic religions. Religious persecution has touched all major religions.[4] For example, during Diwali, the Festival of Light celebrated by Hindus, Jains, and Sikhs, lighted lamps symbolize the victory of good over evil within every human being. But for Sikhs, the holiday is especially poignant. It is associated with the killing of Bhai Mani Singh, the priest of the Golden Temple – Sikhism's holiest site – on that holiday in A.D. 1737.[5] Singh was arrested for not paying a religious tax and was asked by the judge who had jurisdiction in that part of India to either renounce his faith or face death. Singh refused and suffered brutal limb-by-limb torture as the method of his execution. In the case of the Sikhs, such violent persecution has even become a part of the daily Sikh prayer (*Ardas*):

Those Sikhs, both men and women, who, for the sake of their religion, offered their heads; let their bodies be cut piece by piece; let their heads be scalped off; suffered torture under the body cutting wheel; let their body be sawed through the middle; who sacrificed themselves for the sake of the reformation of the Gurdwaras; but they did not relinquish their religion; who stuck to the principles of "Sikhi" up to their last breath, think of their heroic performance and say "WAHEGURU" [God or Infinite Creator].[6]

Virtually all religions have stories to tell of the faithful being imprisoned, tortured, murdered, and maimed, but how prevalent is violent religious persecution? Barrett and Johnson estimate that more than two hundred million persons have been killed related to their religious affiliation during the past two millennia.[7] We don't have evidence to support or refute this claim, but three familiar twentieth-century examples establish that violent persecution in the recent past not only affected millions, but also continues to be a pressing issue today.

---

[3] Vali Nasr (2006), *The Shia Revival: How Conflicts within Islam Will Shape the Future*, New York: Norton.

[4] Some go so far as to suggest that often religions do not teach people to avoid suffering but, rather, how to make a physical pain, personal loss, or worldly defeat sufferable. See Geertz (1966).

[5] Singh & Singh (1950).

[6] See "ARDAS – THE PRAYER," http://www.gurbaani.com/prayer2.htm (accessed 5 August 2010).

[7] Barrett & Johnson's (2001:227) estimate includes any person killed related to adherence to a religion since each religion's advent: 80 million Muslims killed, 70 million Christians, 20 million Hindus, 10 million Buddhists, 9 million Jews, 2 million Sikhs, 1 million Baha'is, and 11 million from other religions and ethnically based religions.

- At the turn of the past century, there were more than three million Christians in Turkey accounting for more than 20 percent of the total population at the time, but today that community is decimated – at most, some three hundred thousand remain, accounting for only about 2 percent.[8] Most were Armenians who were driven out, killed, or left to die around the time of World War I.[9] This violent persecution, which radically and lastingly altered the religious demography of Turkey, is an extremely controversial topic in Turkey to this day. In 2007, Turkey threatened to curtail U.S. military access to Turkish bases and recalled its ambassador from Washington for consultations in response to the U.S. House Foreign Affairs Committee's approval of a resolution asserting that the Turkish massacre of Armenians nearly a century ago constitutes genocide.[10]

- When the Nazis came to power in 1933, roughly nine million Jews lived throughout Europe. By the end of World War II, it is estimated that six million died or had been executed.[11] The horror of this violent persecution is an indelible part of modern European history, and few in the West deny those atrocities. Ironically, some of the best evidence of this persecution came from the Nazi authorities themselves, who documented through reports, photographs, and film "the public humiliation of Jews, their deportation, mass murder, and confinement in concentration camps."[12] Even still, Holocaust denial occurs today and is supported by at least one head of state, Iranian president Mahmoud Ahmadinejad. In 2005, Ahmadinejad described the Holocaust as "a myth" and suggested that Israel be moved to Europe, the United States, or Canada.[13]

- During China's Cultural Revolution (1966–1976), paranoia toward all who challenged Mao's vision of a revolutionary society led to massive social upheaval throughout the country, displacing and abusing millions. Intellectuals, those with foreign connections or possessions, religious groups, and anyone else charged with being a counterrevolutionary were severely oppressed. Religion was singled out not only

---

[8] World Religion Database estimates.

[9] Dadrian (2003).

[10] See article by Grim & Wike, "Turkey and Its (Many) Discontents," http://pewforum .org/docs/?DocID=255.

[11] See http://www.ushmm.org/wlc/article.php?lang=en&ModuleId=10005143 (accessed 5 August 2010); also see Dawidowicz (1975).

[12] See http://www.ushmm.org/wlc/article.php?lang=en&ModuleId=10007271 (accessed 5 August 2010).

[13] See http://www.cnn.com/2005/WORLD/meast/12/10/iran.israel/index.html?iref= allsearch (accessed 5 August 2010).

because of its supposed foreign connections but also because it promoted loyalties and faith to things in the spiritual realm beyond the control of the revolution. All religious practice was banned and religious leaders and those continuing to practice their faith faced ridicule, exile, imprisonment, torture, and death. Not until the late 1970s were places of worship allowed to reopen.

These examples emphasize that the *physical abuse or displacement of people because of religion* (what we call *violent religious persecution*) is a form of social conflict that is often embedded in larger conflicts within and between societies and countries.[14] Indeed, each case listed happened as societies took radical steps to redefine their national character: Turkey as a nation of Turks with Islam as the binding identity, Germany as an Aryan nation that excluded so-called *Untermenschen* ("inferior people") who were targeted because of their ethnic and religious identities, and China as a revolutionary state that aimed to rid itself of all cultural and religious elements that were considered superstitious or tied to foreign imperialism.

What the first three examples fail to illustrate, however, is that victims and perpetrators of violent religious persecution can quickly alternate. Once again, there is no shortage of examples. Whether it is the war in Bosnia-Herzegovina or the ongoing Palestinian–Israeli conflict, culpability becomes debated and victims can become perpetrators. Perhaps the most prominent example is Iraq. After the overthrow of Saddam Husseim, Shia Muslims quickly went from being targeted to targeting others. The 2009 International Religious Freedom report[15] on Iraq reports that Sunni Muslims have received death threats in Shia neighborhoods, Shia Muslims have received death threats in Sunni neighborhoods, and religious minorities have received threats in both. Nor were these idle threats; the report went on to explain that "in many cases individuals either complied or were killed." Depending on the neighborhood, each group alternated between victim and perpetrator.

---

[14] This definition of *religious persecution* is slightly different from the one used in Grim & Finke (2007) in order to acknowledge that the data on religious persecution used in our analyses include victims of physical abuse or physical displacement. We include victims who are targeted because of their own religious identity or the religiously related motivations of those who perpetuate the violence. Victims are typically targeted because they are the "wrong" religion, but they can also be targeted because they lack religion.

[15] *2009 Report on International Religious Freedom*, http://www.state.gov/g/drl/rls/irf/2009/127348.htm (accessed 5 August 2010).

Certainly, these familiar cases indicate that violent religious persecution was a problem in the past and remains evident in some regions; but still, how prevalent is violent religious persecution today, and what are its root causes?

In the twenty-first century, no religion is held exempt from persecution. Jews remain targets in many regions of the world, not just in Europe. Adherents of minority Muslim faiths have been jailed, deported, and/or killed in Iraq and Saudi Arabia. Hindus remain victims of violent persecution in Bangladesh and elsewhere. Practitioners of Falun Gong, Roman Catholic bishops, Protestant house church leaders, and other religious figures are routinely jailed in China. Adherents of minority religions such as Jehovah's Witnesses are incarcerated in numerous countries. In other countries, such as Belgium, Germany, France, and Singapore, religions that operate freely in many countries are officially condemned as dangerous cults or sects. Christian peace activists have been kidnapped, tortured, and executed in the Democratic Republic of Congo and in Iraq. To be sure, it is the call for social justice by people motivated by their religious convictions that can sometimes trigger their persecution.

In the chapters that follow, we offer a descriptive profile of contemporary violent religious persecution and make an initial effort to explain why it is occurring. We conclude by asking why religious freedom matters and review the evidence that suggests that religious freedom can result not only in less violent religious persecution and less conflict but also in better overall outcomes for societies. The appendix summarizes the empirical tests of the thesis made in this book.

Finally, throughout we use the term "religious freedoms" to mean the freedoms embodied in Article 18 of the 1948 Universal Declaration of Human Rights, one of the foundational documents of the UN: "Everyone has the right to freedom of thought, conscience and religion; this right includes freedom to change his religion or belief, and freedom, either alone or in community with others and in public or private, to manifest his religion or belief in teaching, practice, worship and observance." Accordingly, based on the ability of individuals to change religions, religious freedoms include the right for religious groups to propagate their message within society with the intent of winning new adherents. Also, based on the ability for individuals to manifest his or her religion or belief in teaching, practice, worship, and observance, religious freedoms include that one religion should not seek to control another.

Religious Persecution

Pervasive and Pernicious

On March 20, 2006, Daniel Cooney of the Associated Press reported that "an Afghan man [Abdul Rahman] is being prosecuted in a Kabul court and could be sentenced to death on a charge of converting from Islam to Christianity."[1] The Western world seemed stunned. German chancellor Angela Merkel sought personal assurances from Afghan president Hamid Karzai that the execution would be stopped; Austrian foreign minister Ursula Plassnik promised to "leave no stone unturned to protect the fundamental rights of Abdul Rahman and to save his life"; and Pope Benedict XVI appealed to a "respect for human rights sanctioned in the preamble of the new Afghan constitution."[2] Similar protests and pleas came from scores of other political and religious leaders across North America and throughout Europe.

But the most candid and emotional response came from John Howard, the Australian prime minister. He told an Australian radio network, "This is appalling. When I saw the report about this I felt sick, literally." Howard went on to share his astonishment that this was possible: "The idea that a person could be punished because of their religious belief and the idea they might be executed is just beyond belief."[3]

This book will show that violent religious persecution is neither beyond belief nor uncommon. The prime minister's reactions no doubt reflect the

---

[1] As quoted in an Associated Press article by Daniel Cooney, "Afghan Man Faces Death Penalty for Christian Beliefs," *Philadelphia Inquirer*, March 20, 2006.

[2] Quoted in a BBC story, March 25, 2006, http://news.bbc.co.uk/go/pr/fr/-/2/hi/south_asia/4841812.stm (accessed 5 August 2010).

[3] As quoted by an Associated Press article, "Afghan Judge Resists Pressure in Convert Case," *Washington Post*, March 25, 2006.

thoughts and emotions of many, but they do not reflect global realities. Afghanistan is not the only country to hand down harsh penalties for religious conversion nor is Islam the only world religion to deny others religious freedom. Relying on new sources of data, we will show that despite routine constitutional promises to the contrary, religious freedoms[4] are denied around the globe and violent persecution is pervasive. We will also explain how attempts to regulate religion by supporting a single religion or restricting religions perceived as dangerous frequently lead to violent religious persecution. We will describe how religious cartels, cultural pressures, and the government's regulation of religion are tightly interwoven into an ongoing cycle of violent persecution. Indeed, we will discuss how violent religious persecution is often a form of social conflict that is embedded in or overlaps larger conflicts in society, and as such, is a type of conflict that has consequences for more than just the religious.

The foundation of this book relies on two components, one theoretical and the other empirical. The theoretical component explains why and how persecution is often the consequence of freedoms denied – an argument that began with Voltaire, Adam Smith, and David Hume but has been overlooked in recent times. The empirical component is a new source of information assembled by the Association of Religion Data Archives (ARDA) that reports on religious freedoms and persecution around the globe. In the next sections we introduce these two components and then briefly profile violent religious persecution in the world today.

THE PACIFYING CONSEQUENCES OF FREEDOMS

The dangers of religious pluralities seemingly appear all too obvious. With ever-present religious conflicts around the globe and throughout history, religious plurality seems to be the spark, if not the flame, that leads to raging conflicts within and between countries. Indeed, this apparent relationship serves to motivate and justify states' denying religious freedoms. The concern is that to leave religion unchecked and without adequate controls will result in the uprising of religions that are dangerous to both state and citizenry.

Focusing on violent religious persecution, which is a form of social conflict, we propose just the opposite. Defining *violent religious persecution* as "physical abuse or physical displacement due to religion," we propose that the higher the degree to which governments and societies

---

4 See Preface for definition of "religious freedoms."

ensure religious freedoms for all, the less violent religious persecution and conflict along religious lines there will be. Certainly, in the religiously charged world of the twenty-first century, less religious conflict is in the interests of peace and security for all nations. Our inspiration for this thesis comes from a recent theory on the effects of regulating religious expression and practice, but the intellectual foundation for this reasoning is several centuries old – and probably older.

The Despotism of a Dominant Religion

The groundwork for our thesis is laid out vividly by three of the most prominent scholars of the eighteenth century: Voltaire, Adam Smith, and David Hume. More than two and a half centuries ago François Marie Arouet, aka Voltaire, wrote: "If there were only one religion . . . there would be danger of despotism, if there were two, they would cut each other's throats, but there are thirty, and they live in peace and happiness" (1732). He pointed to the Royal Exchange of London to make his case, noting that the Jews, Muslims, and Christians all willingly traded together and only the bankrupt were treated as infidels. No doubt his confidence that religion could be tamed was in part based on his bold contention that religion would soon disappear.[5] But the despotism of monopoly and the peace of plurality also reflected his own life experiences in France and England. Voltaire experienced the fury of a monopoly religion and its opponents first hand. When growing up in France, Voltaire's older brother, Armand, became a member of the persecuted Jansenists sect, which arose in France in opposition to Jesuit theology within the Roman Catholic Church. Two years later, Voltaire was forced to attend a Jesuit school at the age of ten, and he would later be imprisoned because of his endless attacks on French authorities, including Christianity and the Roman Catholic Church.[6] When he was eventually exiled to England, he marveled that the plurality of sects promoted a peace that was so elusive in France.

A few decades later Adam Smith echoed Voltaire's concerns about religious monopolies and his assurances about plurality: "[The] active zeal of religious teachers can be dangerous and troublesome only where

---

[5] Durant & Durant (1965).

[6] Myers (1985) recounts that when their core reforms were officially condemned by Pope Clement in 1713, and the king was forced to accept the bull in 1714, the movement fell into decline.

there is, either but one sect tolerated in the society, or where the whole of a large society is divided into two or three great sects."[7] He went on to explain, however, that the "zeal must be altogether innocent where the society is divided into two or three hundred, or perhaps into as many [as a] thousand small sects, of which no one could be considerable enough to disturb the public tranquility."[8] For Smith, however, the argument was based on theoretical common sense rather than personal experiences.[9] He explains that if sects are numerous enough, no single sect is large enough to be harmful. The obvious question that follows, of course, is how are the numerous sects generated? For Smith the answer is simple: "[I]f the government was perfectly decided both to let them all alone, and to oblige them all to let alone one another, there is little danger that they would not of their own accord subdivide themselves fast enough, so as soon to become sufficiently numerous."[10] Letting "them all alone" allowed for an open propagating of faith by multiple religions; obliging the religions to "let alone one another" ensured that no single religion would hold control over another. Religious plurality, for Smith, was the natural state of affairs and such plurality resulted in a public tranquility.

David Hume offered a similar observation and concurred that the government must leave the various religions alone and must require all religions to leave one another alone.

If [a magistrate] admits only one religion among his subjects, he must sacrifice, to an uncertain prospect of tranquillity [sic], every consideration of public liberty, science, reason, industry, and even his own independency. If he gives indulgence to several sects, which is the wiser maxim, he must preserve a very philosophical indifference to all of them, and carefully restrain the pretensions of the prevailing sect; otherwise he can expect nothing but endless disputes, quarrels, factions, persecutions, and civil commotions. ([posthumously published in 1780] 1854:223)

Hume brings an important nuance to the discussion by drawing attention to the fact that constraints must be placed on the "pretensions of the prevailing sect." Without such constraints, Hume contends, the dominant religion will seek to control other religions. Thus, Hume and Smith are suggesting that religions must be protected from both the state and one another.

---

[7] Smith ([1776] 1976:314).
[8] Smith ([1776] 1976:314).
[9] Stark (2001:122) recently summarized Smith's argument with the following proposition: "[C]onflict will be maximized where, other things being equal, *a few powerful and particularistic religious organizations coexist*" (italics in the original).
[10] Smith ([1776] 1976:315).

As Voltaire, Smith, and Hume discussed the theoretical principles of religious monopoly and competition, a grand experiment testing these principles was being conducted across the Atlantic. When Thomas Jefferson appealed to his fellow Virginians in 1784 to eliminate religious establishments and assure religious freedoms for all, he pointed to the success of two states without religious establishments: Pennsylvania and New York. He explained that even without a religious establishment social order was maintained and the many sects "perform the office of a Censor" for the others

of various kinds, indeed, but all good enough; all sufficient to preserve peace and order: or if a sect arises, whose tenets would subvert morals, good sense has fair play, and reasons and laughs it out of doors, without suffering the state to be troubled with it.

Jefferson went on to conclude that based on their "experiment," Pennsylvania and New York "have made the happy discovery, that *the way to silence religious disputes, is to take no notice of them*" (italics added).[11] This discovery provided strong support for the predictions of scholars on the other side of the Atlantic.

Although the most immediate concerns of European and colonial writers were the many sects within Protestantism, they did not view the principle as being limited to Protestantism or Christianity. In his autobiography, Thomas Jefferson argued that the bill for establishing religious freedom "was meant to be universal" and included "within the mantle of its protection the Jew and the Gentile, the Christian and Mahometan [sic], the Hindoo [sic], and Infidel of every denomination."[12] He explained that when he wrote the preamble establishing religious freedom in Virginia, the great majority rejected an attempt to make explicit references to Jesus Christ.[13] In his "Memorial and Remonstrance against Religious Assessments," James Madison pointed to a danger in establishing Christianity because the same human authority that establishes Christianity above all other religions can also be used to exclude all Christian sects but one.

Jefferson, Madison, and each of the European scholars mentioned earlier recognized the potential danger of limiting religious practice to a

[11] Jefferson ([1787] 1954:160–161).
[12] Jefferson (2005:71).
[13] Jefferson (2005:71) wrote that any attempts at religious coercion "are a departure from the plan of the holy author of our religion." When an amendment was proposed to change the wording to "a departure from the plan of the Jesus Christ, the holy author of our religion," he reports that "the insertion was rejected by a great majority."

single religion or to two or three competing religions. They argued that not only did this deny the freedoms of individuals, it also threatened the security of the state. This keen insight provides the starting point for our understanding of violent religious persecution – an understanding that can also help dispel what former diplomat and scholar Thomas F. Farr calls a "dangerous disarray and confusion" among many policy makers over how to constructively understand the dynamics of religion and human freedom.[14] Building on the expansive theoretical literature on "religious economies," which we describe in the following section, we will propose that when religious freedoms are denied through the regulation of religious profession or practice, violent religious persecution and conflict will increase. Conversely, the lifting of restrictions on religious profession or practice should result in less persecution and conflict and consequently more peace and security.

Consequences of Restricting Religious Freedom

When James Madison wrote the First Amendment to the United States Constitution, he was well aware that religious groups and their followers needed protections from both the state and dominant religions.

Congress shall make no law respecting an establishment of religion, or prohibiting the free exercise thereof.

The first clause protected minority religions (and the state) from the tyranny of a dominant religion and the second protected religion from the tyranny of the state. As we will review in greater detail in Chapter 2, both the state and dominant religions have motives for restricting religious activity. The state, of course, restricts the freedoms of religions perceived to be a threat to the social order or the ruling regime, but restrictions can also arise from forces beyond the state. Dominant religions (sometimes not even the religion of the majority of the population), in particular, will try to limit the actions of other religions. Together, the state and dominant religions often unite to limit religious freedoms; and such limitations have powerful consequences.

A growing body of research and theory has shown how regulating religion curbs religious activity. Known as a "supply-side" or "religious economies" model, this theory argues that regulations restrict the supply of religion by changing the incentives and opportunities for religious

---

[14] Thomas F. Farr (2008:xi).

producers (religious leaders and organizations) and the viable options for religious consumers (members of religious organizations).[15] That is, religious leaders and their followers face restrictions on the practice and profession of their religion as well as their opportunities to proselytize and convert others to their faith. For religious organizations, these regulations increase entry and operating costs by restricting their ability to form and operate places of worship. For potential adherents, religious choices are reduced and they face inflated costs when joining groups not condoned by the state.

The religious economies model was initially used to explain the surge in religious activity in America in the eighteenth and nineteenth centuries, when the number of religions multiplied and the rate of church adherence increased from 17 percent of the population in 1776 to 51 percent by 1890.[16] The model has since been used to explain religious change around the globe.[17] Anthony Gill,[18] Andrew Chestnut,[19] and others have documented the surge in religious competition and growth in Latin America. After four centuries of a monopoly religion, evangelical Christians burst onto the scene as religious freedoms were granted in the latter half of the twentieth century, with the percentage of evangelicals in the population doubling and tripling over the past thirty years.[20] For example, while Brazil has more Roman Catholics than any other country, it also has more Pentecostals than does the United States.[21] The increase in religious freedoms in Taiwan has been more recent, but no less dramatic. After the 1989 Law on Civic Organizations allowed all religions to exist and removed multiple prohibitions, Yungfeng Lu reports that there was a twelvefold increase in the number of different religious groups in Taiwan (from 83 in 1990 to 1,062 in 2004) and the total number of temples and churches more than doubled.[22] Moving to the post-Soviet countries, Paul Froese found a very similar trend with religious revivalism

---

[15] Finke (1990).
[16] Finke & Stark (1992).
[17] Stark & Finke (2000:218–258).
[18] Gill (1998).
[19] Chestnut (2003).
[20] Although sources vary on the number of evangelicals in Latin American countries, all show a rapid increase. For a more detailed report on the religious demography of Guatemala, Chile, and Brazil, see Pew Forum *Spirit and Power* (2006), http://pewforum.org/Christian/Evangelical-Protestant-Churches/Spirit-and-Power.aspx (accessed 5 August 2010).
[21] Pew Forum (2006), *Spirit and Power*.
[22] Lu (2008). See Kuo (2008) for a discussion on religion and the emergence of democracy in Taiwan.

increasing and atheism declining as regulations were initially lifted.[23] Also, in agreement with the theory, the trend has slowed or even reversed as regulations have returned. Perhaps most convincing, Jonathan Fox and Ephraim Tabory found that "state regulation of religion is significantly and negatively correlated with religiosity" when using a database of 81 nations.[24] This growing body of research has consistently shown how shifts in the freedoms granted explain major religious change.

We extend this argument in two significant ways. First, we increase the scope of the argument. Whereas past work sought to explain levels of religious activity, we seek to explain the level of violent religious persecution. Elaborating on the work of the eighteenth-century scholars, we propose that as religious freedoms increase, violent religious persecution and conflict decline. The freedoms lead to a rich plurality in which no single religion can monopolize religious activity and all religions can compete on a level playing field. Religious grievances against the state and other religions are reduced because all religions can compete for the allegiance of people without the interference of the state.

Not only do these freedoms for all reduce the grievances of religions, they also decrease the ability of any single religion to wield undue political power. When a religious group achieves a monopoly and holds access to the temporal power and privileges of the state, including placing restrictions on other religions, the ever-present temptation is to openly persecute religious competitors and any in society that oppose their interpretations. In contrast, when the state offers identical privileges to all religions and power to none, no single religion can claim the authority of the state. Thus, we propose that to the degree that governments and societies ensure religious freedoms for all, there will be less conflict between religions and less violent religious persecution.

Our second extension is more subtle but equally important. Rather than limit our attention to the state's efforts to restrict freedoms, we look at restrictions that are embedded in the larger culture or in institutions and movements beyond the state. Restrictions on select religions are often mobilized by a dominant religion that either lacks the authority of the state or wants to go beyond the state's actions. Previous work shows that even when religious economies are unregulated by the state, religious cartels form in an attempt to restrict the activities of other religions.[25]

---

[23] Froese (2001, 2004).
[24] Fox and Tabory (2008:245).
[25] Finke & Stark (2005:216–224).

Yet this form of regulation has received little attention. Religions, social movements, cultural context, and institutions beyond the state can all foster actions that lead to persecution. Accordingly, we look at both the *legal* and *social* restrictions that inhibit the practice, profession, or selection of religion.

Including both government and social forces is important for three reasons. First, research has shown that legal restrictions on religion as well as the easing of legal restrictions arise from social origins. Popular religious movements, religious plurality, immigration patterns, political stability, and economic interests have all driven changes in the legal regulations placed on religion around the globe.[26] Jefferson's espousal of the principles of religious freedom might have fallen on deaf ears if religious plurality wasn't a reality and a diversity of immigrants an economic necessity in the young American nation. Second, social restrictions on religion are important to include because the enforcement of any type of legal restrictions relies on social cooperation. For example, William I. Brustein documents the preexistence of widespread anti-Semitism throughout Europe prior to the Holocaust. This anti-Semitism eased the enactment of regulations against Jews and enhanced the enforcement of such regulations.[27] And third, when certain religions are targets of government persecution, this can result in tit-for-tat reprisals between government forces and the group being targeted, especially if the group is or becomes radicalized. For instance, when examining the atrocities of the 1990s in Algeria, Hafez noted that religiously motivated groups operating under repressive regimes became cohesive social forces that in turn restricted and persecuted those who did not support their agendas.[28] As a result, they drew the attention of the government and opened the door for even more persecution. The end result is an ongoing violent religious persecution cycle: restrictions on religious freedoms → persecution → more restrictions → persecution. Understanding both social and government attempts to restrict religious freedoms is essential for explaining violent religious persecution.

We will develop and illustrate this thesis more fully in the chapters that follow, but we should acknowledge that this thesis defies the general consensus of many. Indeed, as we will show in Chapter 3, the implications of Samuel P. Huntington's highly persuasive *Clash of Civilizations*

---

[26] Finke (1990); Gill (2005).

[27] Brustein (2003).

[28] Hafez (2004).

argument contrast sharply with our own.[29] Whereas Huntington calls on countries to avoid conflicts by reaffirming their commitment to a single civilization, we propose that attempts to force religious homogeneity within a country can result in conflict.

Likewise, many view religious regulations as a necessity for controlling social conflict. For instance, we both have had conversations with Chinese government officials who do not question whether religious regulation is good or bad; they simply believe that it is the role of the state to regulate religion. For them, the question is how much regulation is the right amount to maintain a "harmonious society."

As we explore this question throughout the book, we find a close connection between violent religious persecution and conflict. Once a religious persecution cycle is set in motion, persecution can become a constituent element of social conflict that affects more than just the religious communities themselves. Although our focus is on the victims of violent religious persecution, it will become clear that because much of the religious persecution in the twenty-first century occurs at the hands of people in society, violent religious persecution and social conflict often occur in tandem – the victim of violence can sometimes become the perpetrator of more violence leading to a cycle of violence. Furthermore, in Chapter 6 we will discuss how social attempts to restrict religious freedoms underly religion-related terrorism.

The central irony we demonstrate throughout this book is that although governments typically view restricting religious freedoms as a necessity to maintain order and reduce potential violence, the fact is that fewer religious freedoms often results in more violent persecution and conflict. We acknowledge the potential tension of multiple religions residing in the same country, but we draw attention to the violent consequences (often unintended) of religious restrictions. We look at the price of freedom denied.

FROM CLAIMS TO COUNTS:
THE INTERNATIONAL RELIGION DATA INITIATIVE

Claims of violent religious persecution are many. Each week Forum 18 (www.forum18.org) reports on Muslims, Christians, and religious minorities being persecuted in the former Soviet Union. The organization Persecution.org (www.thepersecution.org) details the persecution of

---

[29] Huntington (1993, 1996).

Ahmadiyya Muslims around the globe, paying closest attention to persecution in South Asia and the Middle East. Christian organizations, such as Voice of the Martyrs, Open Doors, and Christian Persecution, list numerous examples each week. The Baha'is, Jehovah's Witnesses, and other minority religions offer frequent claims of persecution and martyrdom around the globe. Many of these groups are vague about numbers, but the Roman Catholic charity Aid to the Church in Need recently estimated that "130,000–170,000 people die each year" from violence directed against Christianity alone.[30]

But the reports come from more than the religious groups claiming to be victims. The media report daily on the fighting between religious factions in Pakistan, Iraq, Nigeria, Sudan, India, and many other countries. The UN Special Rapporteur on Freedom of Religion or Belief annually chronicles claims of violent religious persecution and each country's reaction to such charges. Yet none of these sources provides estimates for all religions in all countries and few offer clear criteria for defining persecution. For this, we turn to a recent data initiative completed by the Association of Religion Data Archives (ARDA) and funded by the John Templeton Foundation.

The International Religious Freedom Reports

In the mid-1990s, a most unlikely alliance of Jews, evangelical Protestants, Catholics, human rights activists, and, later, Buddhists and Baha'is emerged to defend what they described as the "orphan of human rights": religious freedom.[31] Tracing the origin of this informal alliance Allen D. Hertzke notes that, despite drawing attention to the persecution of evangelical Christians abroad, the movement benefited from strong Jewish leadership. Hertzke writes that "[i]ronically, while the American Christian leadership evinced [a] mixed response, Jews have been among some of the most aggressive and effective advocates of persecuted Christians."[32] This broad base of support resulted in a movement with the far-reaching goal of increasing religious freedom for all groups in all countries and key leaders in the movement publishing books on religious persecution around the globe.[33] While the initial legislative campaign focused

---

[30] J. Gyula Orbán, "Violence against Christians in the Year 2001," *Catholic News*, http://www.aidtochurch.org/pdf/violence_0509.pdf (accessed 5 August 2010).

[31] Hertzke (2004:69).

[32] Hertzke (2004:76).

[33] Marshall (1997); Shea (1997).

narrowly on egregious persecution in places like Sudan and China, the focus was greatly broadened in the final legislation to encompass a wider array of violations.

The culminating act of this movement was the passage of the International Religious Freedom Act in 1998, legislation calling for detailed annual State Department reports on religious freedom around the globe. Additionally, the legislation set up a bipartisan commission outside of the State Department for monitoring the collection and reporting of information. The intent was to provide "honest and independent fact-finding" that would *not* be controlled by diplomatic considerations and would expose violations of religious freedoms to the global community.[34] The result has been that each year the State Department's Office of International Religious Freedom now provides detailed reports for nearly two hundred countries around the globe, and the independent and bipartisan U.S. Commission on International Religious Freedom critiques the reports and serves as an official watchdog.

But the International Religious Freedom reports not only review the freedoms allowed, they also report on the freedoms denied and on religious persecution, providing extensive information on people who were tortured, killed, or relocated based on their religion. Loosely structured during the initial years, in 2001 the reports took on the format shown in Figure 1.1. Notice that the reports review the religious freedoms promised in legal codes as well as the actual practice of restricting religious freedoms and the abuses related to religion. This clear distinction between promises and practices will be critical for our discussion in Chapter 2. Moreover, the reports go beyond the formal actions of the government to report on societal attitudes and actions. This allows us to explore how movements, groups, and the larger culture serve to restrict the actions of religious groups. It is also helpful to note that the length of each report varies widely according to the number of documented violations of religious freedom, not according to the size of the country. For example, the 2008 report for Pakistan (pop. 180 million) totals 10,770 words, whereas the 2008 report for Brazil (pop. 190 million) has 1,740 words, the varying lengths reflect the documented restrictions and abuses in each.[35] These reports are now widely regarded

---

34 Hertzke (2004:230).
35 The reports do not have the same information level for North Korea, Libya, and Bhutan because the State Department did not have access to these countries during the reporting period.

Introductory Overview (untitled section)
1. Religious Demography
2. Status of Religious Freedom[†]
   a. Legal/Policy Framework
   b. Restrictions on Religious Freedom
   c. Abuses of Religious Freedom[††]
   d. Forced Religious Conversion
   e. Improvements in Respect for Religious Freedom[‡]
3. Societal Attiudes
4. U.S. Government Policy

[†] Beginning in 2004, the reports contain a section on terrorism.
[††] This section is absent for countries with no reported abuses.
[‡] This section is present only when improvements have been made since the last report.

FIGURE 1.1. Report on International Religious Freedom (for each country)

by international legal scholars and humanitarians as the most extensive and reliable source of information available on religious freedom.[36]

The reports offer several advantages when compared to other sources of cross-national information on religion. First, the reports carefully document the times, places, perpetrators, and numbers of victims of violations of religious freedom that affect persons of any faith, from Ahmadis to Zoroastrians. Second, the data are initially assembled by embassy officials living in the country, not representatives of the local government, the media, or residents with their own vested perspectives; this gives a positive balance between *nearness* (local knowledge) and *remoteness* (objectivity).[37] Third, these embassy officials receive training on gathering the information and follow a standardized reporting format (with similar information included for each country). Fourth, the reports are then vetted by the U.S. special ambassador for religious freedom, who oversees this systematic collection of information for nearly 200 countries. In addition to the primary report from local embassy staff, the ambassador's office consults with many informed sources, including State Department specialists and other government employees, the U.S.

---

[36] For example, on October 30, 2006, at the State Department's commemoration of the 25th anniversary of the UN Declaration on the Elimination of All Forms of Intolerance and Discrimination Based on Religion and Belief, the Cohen Professor of International Law and Human Rights at Emory School of Law, Johan D. van der Vyver, stated that the International Religious Freedom reports "have come to be the most extensive and reliable sources on the state of religious freedom in countries of the world."

[37] Simmel ([1908] 1971).

Commission on Religious Freedom, journalists, human rights organizations, religious groups, local governments, and academics. Fifth, unlike the reports used for some coded conflict data sets, the reports are placed and kept online for critics and supporters to read and evaluate. Foreign governments, researchers, and the general public inspect, criticize, and call for corrections when errors are found. Sixth, and perhaps the most significant advantage already mentioned, the International Religious Freedom Act commissioned an independent, bipartisan commission to "monitor facts and circumstances of violations of religious freedom."[38] Indeed, because the reports are expected to document violations of religious freedom and because the content is held accountable by so many, the reports arguably are sufficiently comprehensive to provide a good estimate of the levels of restrictions and abuses in almost all countries. However, it is very likely that more restrictions and abuses exist than are reported.

Despite the many strengths of the reports, there is an obvious concern that the information is biased by the political interests and assumptions of the U.S. federal government. Georgetown University Islamic scholar John Voll points out that viewing the separation of religion and state as an ideal and "working for an 'unregulated religious context' is itself a form of religious advocacy."[39] After conducting multiple evaluations of the data,[40] our conclusion is that the reports themselves have little systematic bias. For instance, specifically comparing the data coded on social regulation with a variety of other data sources, Brian Grim and Richard Wike concluded that "the [social regulation of religion information] coded from the State Department's annual International Religious Freedom (IRF) reports – as captured by Grim and Finke's 5-item Social Regulation of Religion Index (SRI) – are comparable to relevant findings from public opinion surveys across more than 66 different countries and independent non-government expert opinion for 100 countries."[41]

---

[38] See the *Interim Report of the Advisory Committee on Religious Freedom Abroad*, 1998, http://www.state.gov/www/global/human_rights/980123_acrfa_interim.html (accessed 5 August 2010), or Hertzke (2004:229, 305).

[39] Personal communication, August 10, 2006.

[40] The data we review also hold a high level of agreement with similar cross-national collections. Using dozens of sources besides the State Department reports, but relying on similar measures, the Pew Forum on Religion & Public Life found results that were nearly identical when they coded data for 2007 and 2008. Although Jonathan Fox's (2008) Religion and State project used a different array of measures, when the measures are similar the results are again very close.

[41] Grim & Wike (2009).

THE 2009 INTERNATIONAL RELIGIOUS FREEDOM REPORT
FOR BURMA

There was no change in the Government's limited degree of respect for religious freedom [from 2008 to 2009]. Religious activities and organizations were subject to restrictions on freedom of expression, association, and assembly. The Government continued to monitor meetings and activities of virtually all organizations, including religious organizations. The Government continued to systematically restrict efforts by Buddhist clergy to promote human rights and political freedom. Many of the Buddhist monks arrested in the violent crackdown that followed pro-democracy demonstrations in September 2007, including prominent activist monk U Gambira, remained in prison serving long sentences. The Government also actively promoted Theravada Buddhism over other religions, particularly among members of ethnic minorities. Christian and Islamic groups continued to struggle to obtain permission to repair existing places of worship or build new ones. The regime continued to closely monitor Muslim activities. Restrictions on worship for other non-Buddhist minority groups also continued. Although there were no new reports of forced conversions of non-Buddhists, the Government applied pressure on students and lower-income youth to convert to Buddhism. Adherence or conversion to Buddhism is generally a prerequisite for promotion to senior government and military ranks.

During the reporting period, social tensions continued between the Buddhist majority and the Christian and Muslim minorities. Widespread prejudice existed against citizens of South Asian origin, many of whom are Muslims. Although official religious discrimination was limited, de facto preferences for Buddhism remained.

There continued to be credible reports from various regions of the country that government officials compelled persons, Buddhists and non-Buddhists alike, especially in rural areas, to contribute money, food, or materials to state-sponsored projects to build, renovate, or maintain Buddhist religious shrines or monuments. The Government denied that it used coercion and called these contributions "voluntary donations" consistent with Buddhist ideas of earning merit.

(continued)

Although authorities appear to have moved away from a campaign of forced conversion, there continued to be evidence that other means were being used to entice non-Buddhists to convert to Buddhism. Authorities pressured Christian Chin to attend Buddhist seminaries and monasteries and encouraged them to convert to Buddhism. Christian Chin reported that local authorities operated a high school that only Buddhist students could attend and promised government jobs to the graduates. Christians had to convert to Buddhism to attend the school. An exile Chin human rights group claimed local government officials placed the children of Chin Christians in Buddhist monasteries, where they were given religious instruction and converted to Buddhism without their parents' knowledge or consent. Reports suggested that the Government also sought to induce members of the Naga ethnic group in Sagaing Division to convert to Buddhism through similar means.

Source: http://www.state.gov/g/drl/rls/irf/2009/127348.htm; (a 437-word excerpt from a 6,904-word report) (accessed 5 August 2010).

There does seem, however, to be some bias in how the data are used by government officials.[42] The case of Saudi Arabia serves as an example. Six years before the State Department listed Saudi Arabia as a *Country of Particular Concern*, a designation that permits sanctions against countries with the most egregious violations of religious freedom, the 1998 Interim Report stated that in "Saudi Arabia, where the State religion is Islam and the government is Sunni Muslim, freedom of religion is denied all other religions, including other forms of Islam, such as Shia Islam. Persecution also occurs within the same religion, pitting one group or faction against another of the same religion" (Interim Report 1998).[43] From 2001 to 2005, the opening sentence on the "Status of Religious Freedom" section of the reports states: "Freedom of religion does not exist." The reports go on to explain that "non-Muslim worshippers risk arrest, imprisonment, lashing, deportation, and sometimes torture for engaging in religious

[42] See Grim (2004:47) for a test of the bias and Grim & Finke (2007) for further discussion.
[43] See the *Interim Report to the Secretary of State and to the President of the United States*, January 23, 1998, http://www.state.gov/www/global/human_rights/980123_acrfa_interim.html.

activity that attracts official attention." The annual reports directly point out the government's responsibility: "Government continued to commit abuses of religious freedom." Yet, despite all of these flagrant violations of religious freedom, it was *not until 2004* that Saudi Arabia was listed as a *Country of Particular Concern*. We see this as evidence that what the State Department does *with* the reports is biased by diplomatic considerations more than what is *in* the reports.[44]

Yet, three limitations remain. First, because the International Religious Freedom reports rely on embassies to complete the reports, there is no report on the United States and the reports are more restricted on three countries without U.S. embassies. However, this limitation will not alter our findings. Omitting a single case from the analysis (even if it is the United States) has little effect on the final results. As we have shown in an earlier work, even when we omit twenty-four of the most high-profile cases our key findings remain consistent.[45] Second, although the information on social restrictions is generally consistent with other sources of information, the reports of social abuses of religious freedom may be underreported in countries that strictly limit independent access to information within the country, such as North Korea and Burma. And third, despite providing thousands of pages of text and carefully documenting specific cases in which religious freedoms were denied, the reports offer no summary measures that allow for quick numerical comparisons across countries. This limitation is far more significant, but one that the ARDA's International Religion Data Initiative was able to address. Using an extensive coding instrument chiefly developed by Brian Grim that is available as an online codebook at the ARDA,[46] the ARDA staff recorded information for a long list of items covered by the reports.[47] This provides us with meaningful categories and numerical values that allow us to compare countries and regions. This extensive coding of the International Religious Freedom reports provides a rich new source of cross-national data that we will use to understand religion in the global arena.

[44] For additional statistical support for this conclusion see Grim & Finke (2007).

[45] Grim & Finke (2007).

[46] See "International Religious Freedom Data" at http://www.theARDA.com (accessed 5 August 2010).

[47] All coding was supervised by Brian Grim. The ARDA staff members completing the coding for 2001 and 2005 were Dan McKenrick, Jaime Harris, Catherine Meyers, and Julie VanEerden. Brian Grim, Melissa Grim, and Laura Tach completed all coding for 2003. For the 2003 reports, Brian Grim coded all 196 countries, and two additional raters coded 142 of the 196 countries. For 2001 and 2005, all reports were coded by two raters.

PROFILING VIOLENT RELIGIOUS PERSECUTION

Elsewhere we describe the strict procedures used for coding the reports, document the high level of reliability of the coding, and evaluate the measures produced.[48] Here we present the fruits of our labor. Before we begin, we offer two clarifications. First, although nearly 200 countries were presented in the reports, we will limit most of our attention to the 143 with a population of two million or more. This allows us to focus on countries of sufficient size to act independently on the world stage and provides more meaningful comparisons. Doing this excludes less than 1 percent of the world's population. Second, although we have access to coded data for four different years (ARDA, 2001, 2003, and 2005; and the Pew Research Center's Forum on Religion and Public Life, 2007), much of our statistical analysis in Chapter 3 will be based on the mean or average of the three years of data coded at the ARDA because the Pew Forum used slightly modified question wordings and methodology. By using a summary measure for the three years, we avoid any spikes or aberrations that might have occurred in a single year.[49] In the Appendix we offer a statistical analysis across all four years of the data. We now turn to a brief global overview of religious persecution.

Pervasive and Pernicious

The most striking finding from the new data is that violent religious persecution is pervasive. Of the 143 countries with populations of two million or more, between July 1, 2000, and June 30, 2007, 86 percent (123 countries) have documented cases of people being physically abused or displaced from their homes because of a lack of religious freedom, that is, *religious persecution*. Several of the cases, such as China, Sudan, and Afghanistan, are well known, but the persecution goes far beyond these few countries.

---

[48] See Grim (2004, 2005); Grim & Finke (2006, 2007) ; Grim, Finke, Harris, Meyers, & VanEerden (2006:4120–4127), as well as http://www.thearda.com/Archive/Cross National.asp (accessed 5 August 2010).

[49] The data we review also hold a high level of agreement with similar cross-national collections. Using dozens of sources besides the State Department reports, but relying on similar measures, the Pew Forum on Religion & Public Life found results that were nearly identical when they coded data for 2007 and 2008. Although Jonathan Fox's (2008) Religion and State project used a different array of measures, when the measures are similar the results are again very close.

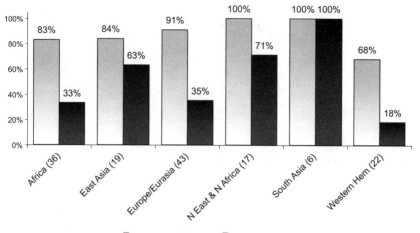

Any Abuse/Displacement ■ > 200 Abused/Displaced

FIGURE 1.2. Percentage of countries with violent religious persecution ($N = 143$) (the total includes all nations with a population of 2 million or more, with the exception of the United States. The State Department does not report on the U.S. or regions under the control of the United States.)

The regional profile in Figure 1.2 illustrates the pervasiveness of violent religious persecution. Persecution is evident in every region of the globe. As expected, the highest rates and most severe levels of persecution are found in the Middle East and South Asia. For the six countries of South Asia and the seventeen in the Middle East and North Africa, violent religious persecution has become the norm. In South Asia, not only has each country experienced high levels of violent religious persecution (more than two hundred cases), but more than one thousand cases also occurred in all six (Afghanistan, Bangladesh, Nepal, Pakistan, India, and Sri Lanka). More than 80 percent of the countries in Sub-Saharan Africa and East Asia reported at least some form of persecution, with the total abused or displaced numbering more than two hundred in more than 60 percent of the East Asian countries. Finally, whereas *high* levels of violent religious persecution are noticeably less frequent for Sub-Saharan Africa, Europe, and the Western Hemisphere (33, 35, and 18 percent, respectively), some level of abuse or displacement related to religion is present in the vast majority of countries in each region.[50]

---

[50] The United States is not included in the reports because the State Department does not report on regions under the control of the United States.

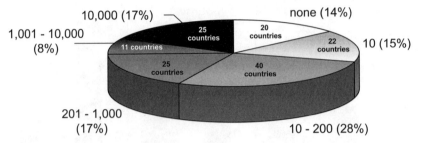

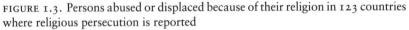

FIGURE 1.3. Persons abused or displaced because of their religion in 123 countries where religious persecution is reported

But violent religious persecution is not only pervasive; it is also pernicious (see Figure 1.3). Of the 123 countries where persecution was reported between July 1, 2000, and June 30, 2007, 36 countries had more than 1,000 people physically abused or displaced. During the time period, the level of persecution reported in 25 countries exceeded 10,000 persons.[51] Even when confined to the most serious acts of persecution, violent religious persecution goes far beyond the obvious examples of China, Sudan, the Middle East, and South Asia. To list only a few, Burma, North Korea, Uganda, Turkmenistan, and Vietnam all had more than 1,000 victims of religious persecution. For some countries, the persecution is an intermingling of religious, ethnic, and regional ties; for others, the persecution is focused solely on religion. With media attention narrowly focused on a handful of cases, the majority of religious persecution goes largely unnoticed.

At first glance the numbers might seem inflated. After all, can the number who are physically abused and displaced based on their religion really be that high and that widespread? The truth, in fact, is that the estimates reported are almost certainly low. As noted, we expect that the numbers and incidences listed in the reports are undercounts. Because embassy staff members are expected to support and verify their counts and because their reports are reviewed by so many with motives to reduce the

---

[51] See *2003 Report on International Religious Freedom* for summary of nations by region (http://www.state.gov/g/drl/rls/irf/2003/index.htm [accessed 5 August 2010]). Also, recall that these annual reports focused on violations that happened *during* the report period, but they also include some violations that continued to have an adverse impact on current religious freedoms. As a result, the numbers used for religious persecution represent a one-year window of time for most nations, but include numbers that have ongoing significance, such as the ongoing displacement of 30,000 people from their communities in Mexico, in part due to conflict between Catholics and evangelicals in the Chiapas region.

appearance of religious persecution, staff members have strong incentives to limit their reports to incidents that are well documented. Moreover, despite having access to multiple sources of information, they will never gain access to all information. Indeed, in countries where freedom of the press is limited and religious groups lack the freedom or the rights to formalize complaints, we would expect the undercount to be higher. Thus the reports offer a more complete and detailed review than any other source, but even these reports underestimate the level of persecution.

Patterns of Persecution

Identifying that violent religious persecution is pervasive and pernicious, however, does not explain why. The research that follows strives to understand the reasons. Why do efforts to control religions and religious persecution often lead to more persecution? Why are religious regulation and violent religious persecution so often involved in a self-perpetuating cycle of violence? And why are rates higher on average in predominantly Muslim countries and other countries where a religion other than Christianity is in the majority? Before we address these questions, we will look at some of the basic results underneath the questions.

Figure 1.2 confirmed that violent religious persecution occurs in all regions of the globe. Yet, even a cursory glance at the regional patterns suggests that persecution is much higher in areas that are predominantly Muslim. Table 1.1 confirms this suspicion, but also indicates that violent religious persecution is not high just in the Muslim world. In countries where Muslims or religions other than Christianity are the majority, religious persecution is reported in 100 percent of the cases. More than 60 percent of Muslim-majority countries and 85 percent of countries

TABLE 1.1. *Religious Majority by Levels of Violent Religious Persecution*

Level of Abuse	Muslim Majority (%)	Other Majority (Atheist, Buddhist, Hindu, Jewish) (%)	No Religion with More than 50% (%)	Christian Majority (%)	World Average (%)
None reported	0	0	25	22	15
1–200 abused or displaced	38	15	42	51	45
>200 abused or displaced	62	85	33	28	43
Total countries	39	13	12	79	143

with majorities other than Christianity have had more than two hundred persons abused or displaced because of religion. These rates are more than twice as high as the rates for Christian-majority countries as well as the rates for countries without a single majority religion (e.g., no religion includes more than 50 percent of the population). At the highest rates of persecution (not shown in Table 1.1), the differences are even more pronounced. Persecution of more than one thousand persons is present in 45 percent of Muslim-majority countries and 60 percent of the "Other Majority" religion countries, compared to 11 percent of Christian-majority countries and 8 percent of countries where no single religion holds a majority.[52]

We must note several specifics about these findings. First, Christian-majority countries, especially those with internal Christian denominational plurality, and those without a majority religion generally have lower levels of violent religious persecution. We will show that for both groups the low level of persecution is associated with high levels of religious freedoms for all religions. Second, the "Other Majority" group of countries has extremely high rates of persecution; but this group is small and heterogeneous, making it inappropriate to draw any conclusions about this as a single category. And third, although violent religious persecution is not confined to countries with Muslim majorities, there are enough countries in this single category (thirty-nine with populations of two million or more) to ask why such countries have higher rates of persecution. As we directly address this sensitive issue in Chapter 6, we will do so by looking at how these higher levels of religious persecution relate to political and legal dynamics in Muslim-majority countries, a number of which face internal conflicts between their own governments and Islamic parties and movements within the countries.

This points to the central question that will be explored throughout this book: Are governments' attempts to restrict or supervise religious activity related to the abuse and displacement of those who are religious? As we will show in Chapter 2, supervising religious activity is a common practice, with nearly two-thirds of the countries having government bureaus for supervising religion. Although many governments argue that supervising religion is a necessity for maintaining order and reducing potential violence (including persecution), we propose that when the supervision restricts religious freedoms, it can fuel violent religious persecution.

---

[52] See Eisenstein (2008) for a recent discussion on the "politics of tolerance" in Christian-majority nations.

TABLE 1.2. *Government Interferes with an Individual's Right to Worship by Levels of Violent Religious Persecution*

Level of Abuse	Government Interferes (%)		
	No	Some Interference	Severe Interference
None reported	45	10	0
1–200 abused or displaced	52	55	16
>200 abused or displaced	3	35	63
Total countries	29	69	57

Table 1.2 offers a glimpse at the strong relationship between a government's denying religious freedoms and persecution. When the government interferes with an individual's rights to worship, the more severe level of persecution (greater than two hundred) increases tenfold (3 to 35 percent) when there is some government interference and more than twentyfold when there is severe interference (3 to 65 percent). Notice that there was at least some instance of interference with this right in the majority of countries, and severe interference in one-third of all countries (fifty-seven). When we looked at other religious restrictions, they all held a similar relationship to violent religious persecution. As regulations increased, religious persecution also increased.

Moreover, we also note that not all restrictions come in the form of negative sanctions. Restrictions can come in the form of favors, or positive sanctions, which can either serve to restrict those religious groups denied government favors or co-opt those religious groups that receive the favors. Table 1.3 shows the strong relationship between violent

TABLE 1.3. *Government Favoritism to Religion by Levels of Violent Religious Persecution*

Level of Abuse	No Obvious Favoritism to Religions (%)	Minimal Favoritism to Religions (%)	Obvious Favoritism to *Some* Religions above Others (%)	Obvious Favoritism to *One* Religion above All Others (%)
None reported	29	24	5	10
1–200 abused or displaced	52	45	45	37
>200 abused or displaced	19	31	50	53
Total countries	21	29	44	49

religious persecution and government's selective favoritism of some religions above others. The more severe level of persecution (greater than two hundred) is present at two-and-one-half times the rate in countries where governments show obvious favoritism to some or one religion above other religions than in countries whose governments show no obvious favoritism to religion (50 and 53 percent, compared with 19 percent).[53]

Yet, despite the strength of the relationship between violent religious persecution and government policies and actions that restrict religion, we need to understand why it exists. Chapter 2 will reveal that religious freedoms are routinely promised, yet frequently denied. So, what are the motives for denying these freedoms, and what are the avenues through which they are denied?

---

[53] See Chapter 7 for further discussion of the relationship between government favoritism of religion and violent religious persecution and conflict.

2

Religious Freedom

Broken Promises

When Abdul Rahman was charged with converting from Islam to Christianity, the apparent contradictions of the Afghan constitution were gradually revealed. The Afghan judge explained that "[w]e are not against any particular religion in the world. But in Afghanistan, this sort of thing is against the law. It is an attack on Islam."[1] In contrast, representatives from across the globe claimed that the new Afghan constitution promised religious freedom for all.[2] The president, Hamid Karzai, was no doubt painfully aware that supportive evidence could be garnered for both sides. Article 2 of the constitution proclaims that all religions "are free to exercise their faith and perform their religious rites within the limits of the provisions of law" but Article 3 explains that "no law can be contrary to the beliefs and provisions of the sacred religion of Islam." Afghanistan is not the only country to pronounce religious freedoms with one statement, only to deny them in the next. We find that promises of freedom were frequently denied.

This chapter will try to uncover how and why religious freedoms are denied. First, we review the promise and practice of religious freedom. Using our coding of the International Religious Freedom reports, we

---

[1] As quoted in an Associated Press article by Daniel Cooney, "Afghan Man Faces Death Penalty for Christian Beliefs," *Philadelphia Inquirer*, March 20, 2006.

[2] For example, on March 23, 2006, in "For Afghans, Allies, a Clash of Values," Pamela Constable reported that "R. Nicholas Burns, the [U.S.] undersecretary of state for political affairs, said that the Afghan constitution 'affords freedom of religion to all Afghans' and that the U.S. government hoped for a 'satisfactory result' of the case." She went on to explain that the case "continued to draw protests from the governments of Italy, Germany, Canada and other NATO nations" as well.

25

document that religious freedoms are consistently promised, yet frequently denied. Next we will attempt to address how: If freedoms are so consistently promised, how are they denied? Here we document how promised freedoms give way to administrative discretion or fall prey to "higher" priorities. Finally we turn to why: Why does the state hold motives for denying religious freedoms? Why do other religions and other social movements hold such motives? We propose that when religious freedoms are viewed through the lens of competing state and religious interests, the state and social and religious groups hold strong motives for limiting religious freedoms. Like free speech and many civil liberties, religious freedoms can be viewed as inconvenient luxuries for a state desiring social control and a dominant religion seeking to prevent heresy.

THE PROMISE OF FREEDOM

Despite being described as the "orphan of human rights,"[3] religious freedom is widely acknowledged and consistently promised in international documents. Perhaps the most prominent example is article 18 http://www.un.org/en/documents/udhr/index.shtm#a18 of the United Nations' Universal Declaration of Human Rights:

Everyone has the right to freedom of thought, conscience and religion; this right includes freedom to change his religion or belief, and freedom, either alone or in community with others and in public or private, to manifest his religion or belief in teaching, practice, worship and observance.

When combined with article 2, which promises that none of the human rights in the Declaration can be denied based on a person's religion, religious freedoms seem assured.[4] Adopted by the General Assembly of the United Nations on December 10, 1948, the articles on religious freedom have served as a model for many, including article 9 of the European Convention on Human Rights.

The Universal Declaration of Human Rights also served as the basis for the UN's 1966 treaty: the International Covenant on Civil and Political Rights (ICCPR). Going into effect on March 23, 1976, and ratified by 160 nations, the ICCPR was intended to serve as a source for legal obligations and to more fully specify the human rights outlined in the Universal Declaration. Although some debate the improved clarity in the area of religious freedoms, the ICCPR did result in the appointment of

---

[3] Hertzke (2004:69).
[4] Taylor (2005).

a Human Rights Committee for monitoring such freedoms.[5] Composed of eighteen members and meeting three times each year, the committee reviews each state's report on compliance with the treaty and calls attention to any notices it receives on human rights violations. The result is a public dialogue on human rights between the committee and each state.

The UN's support of religious freedoms was still further strengthened when the General Assembly passed the Declaration on the Elimination of All Forms of Intolerance and of Discrimination Based on Religion or Belief in 1981. Devoted to religious freedoms, this resolution resulted in two additional supports. First, the eight articles of the 1981 declaration provided far more detail on the international expectations for religious freedoms. Second, the 1981 declaration led to the appointment of a Special Rapporteur on freedom of religion or belief in 1986.[6] Using the declaration as the standard, the Special Rapporteur is charged with examining violations of religious freedom, transmitting appeals to states guilty of such violations, conducting fact-finding visits, and submitting annual reports.[7] Like the more general Human Rights Committee reports, this has resulted in an expansive public dialogue and yet another attempt to monitor religious freedoms.

But the promises of religious freedoms are not confined to international documents. Our coding of the International Religious Freedom reports allows us to offer a profile of the promises made in country constitutions. Under the Legal/Policy Framework section, each report states whether there is a constitutional or legal guarantee of religious freedom and the government's support of these freedoms. As shown in Figure 2.1, the vast majority of countries offer assurances of religious freedom in their constitutions. Eighty-three percent of the countries with a population of more than two million offer promises of religious freedom in their constitutions. Another 8 percent, some without constitutions, hold laws providing such assurances.[8] Only 9 percent, or thirteen nations, fail to offer promises of religious freedom. If judged by the promises of country constitutions, the international campaign for religious freedoms

---

[5] For a more detailed review and assessment, see Evans (1997). Also see http://www2.ohchr.org/english/bodies/hrc/members.htm (accessed 5 August 2010).

[6] The full text of the UN resolution can be found in Taylor (2005:368–372) or at http://www2.ohchr.org/english/issues/religion.htm (accessed 5 August 2010).

[7] Taylor (2005); Evans (1997); Office of the United Nations High Commissioner for Human Rights, http://www2.ohchr.org/english/issues/religion/index.htm (accessed 5 August 2010).

[8] For example, the United Kingdom does not have a constitution, but it has multiple laws providing for religious freedom.

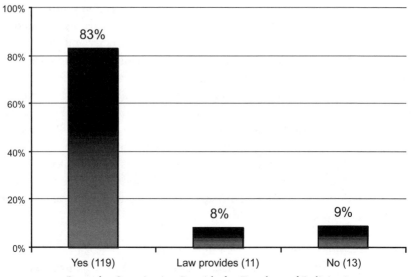

FIGURE 2.1. Does the Constitution Provide for Freedom of Religion?

would appear highly effective. The crucial question, however, is how these promises translate into practice.

Based on the evidence, the simple and obvious answer is that they don't. After reviewing the constitutional and legal promises of religious freedom, the International Religious Freedom reports went on to list laws and other legal actions that denied religious freedoms. As shown in Figure 2.2, legal violations of freedoms promised were routine. Of the 130 countries promising religious freedom, 86 percent (112 countries) have at least one law denying a religious freedom and 38 percent have four or more such restrictions. Of the thirteen countries *not* promising religious freedom, all have four or more. Once again, these rates might seem inflated at first glance. As with persecution, however, they are probably low. In fact, hiding the subtle restrictions placed on such things as building and operating places of worship and denying freedom of expressing religious beliefs in the public square are no doubt easier than hiding open physical persecution. Despite the comprehensiveness of the reports, there can be little doubt that they miss many of the local and regional laws restricting religious freedoms. Yet, even this incomplete count clearly documents that states routinely deny religious freedoms. Moreover, a recently completed study on constitutional clauses and religious legislation by Jonathan Fox also confirms our findings. He concluded that "while constitutional clauses influence the extent of religious

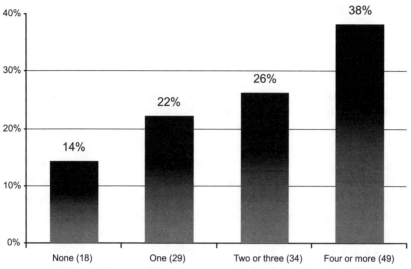

FIGURE 2.2. Laws Restricting Religious Practice for 130 Countries Promising Religious Freedom in 2005

legislation, this influence is limited" and that "nearly all states" have religious legislation.[9]

Our conclusions on the gap between promise and practice are confirmed by multiple other sources as well. Not only do a host of human rights and religious advocacy groups confirm these findings, the UN's Special Rapporteur on freedom of religion or belief also offers very similar conclusions.[10] At the close of her 2007 report, Asma Jahangir wrote that the implementation of the 1981 declaration "is far from being a reality" and "there still is a huge gap between rhetoric and practice in many instances."[11] She went on to express concern over the number of "urgent appeals" and "allegation letters" on the denial of religious freedoms that receive no response from governments. In her 2006 report she complained that the number of countries refusing to offer her an invitation to visit is

---

[9] Fox (2009).

[10] We rely most heavily on peer-reviewed research, the International Religious Freedom reports, and UN reports. But there are many advocacy groups (e.g., Forum 18, Voice of the Martyrs, Open Doors, and Christian Persecution) that provide information on the religious freedoms denied and multiple minority religions (e.g., Ahmadiyya Muslims, Baha'is, and Jehovah's Witnesses) that offer detailed descriptions of the restrictions they face.

[11] Asma Jahangir, 2007, "2007 Report of the Special Rapporteur on Freedom of Religion or Belief," United Nations' Human Rights Council, Fourth Session, Item 2, http://www2 .ohchr.org/english/issues/religion/annual.htm, p. 16 (accessed 5 August 2010).

increasing. She noted with special concern that after "numerous requests and reminders," Indonesia and the Russia Federation refused to grant her an invitation.[12] In 2009 she concluded that "discrimination based on religion or belief preventing individuals from fully enjoying all their human rights still occurs worldwide on a daily basis."[13] Thus, despite the many assurances of religious freedoms in country constitutions, as well as in the declarations, covenants, and resolutions of the UN, the wide chasm between promise and practice remains.

Public dialogue with the Special Rapporteur's office and the open debates leading up to the UN resolutions on religious freedom have revealed the very different standards and definitions used for religious freedom. Defining religion and what constituted religious beliefs was a difficult and often unresolved task when developing the resolutions, but setting the definitional boundaries for religious freedom was the most highly contentious. Controversy consistently centered on religious choice and the freedom of individuals to change religions.[14] For many Muslims, the idea that it could be legitimate to abandon Islam was both foreign and dangerous. Understanding these differences is crucial for understanding why the religious freedoms promised in UN treaties are so consistently denied in Muslim-majority countries. We will address this in greater detail in Chapter 6; here we briefly introduce a couple of the key areas of tensions between Sharia (Islamic) law and the religious freedoms outlined by the UN.

Some Islamic scholars have argued that Sharia law is not only compatible with religious freedom but also supportive of such freedoms. Mohammad Hashim Kamali, professor of law at the International Islamic University of Malaysia, argues that "freedom of belief" lies at the very foundation of Islam and writes that "the Qur'ān has explicitly declared freedom of religion a norm and principle of Islam." Quoting the Quran

---

[12] Asma Jahangir, 2006, "2006 Report of the Special Rapporteur on Freedom of Religion or Belief," United Nations' Commission on Human Rights, Sixty-Second Session, Item 11, http://www.ohchr.org/english/issues/religion/annual.htm, p. 9. She also noted that Egypt, Eritrea, Kyrgyzstan, Turkmenistan, and Uzbekistan failed to offer a requested invitation in 2006. The 2007 report included Cuba, Ethiopia, India, Lao People's Democratic Republic, Malaysia, Mauritania, Pakistan, Saudi Arabia, Serbia and Montenegro, and Yemen as not responding to her requests for an invitation.

[13] Asma Jahangir, 2009, "Report of the Special Rapporteur on freedom of religion or belief," Human Rights Council, Tenth Session, Item 3, http://daccess-dds-ny.un.org/doc/UNDOC/GEN/Go8/101/61/PDF/Go810161.pdf?OpenElement (accessed 5 August 2010), page 20.

[14] Evans (1997); Taylor (2005).

he explains that "there is to be no compulsion in religion" and that all must have the freedom of belief.[15] Yet, understanding the meanings used for *religious freedom* and *freedom of belief* requires that we step back and understand how they are defined by Islamic scholars. Earlier we noted the apparent contradiction in the Afghanistan constitution, but for those familiar with various applications of Sharia law at the state level, article 2 of the Afghan constitution (stating that no law can be contrary to Islam) is viewed as confirming the obvious rather than contradicting article 1. In this case, all freedoms are filtered through the lens of Islamic law, and no law can defy the law of Islam. Although this seems a contradiction to Westerners, to many Muslims the rule of law within Islam is not only a source of pride (pride that the realm of Islam was governed by rules when the caprice of kings governed much of the world), but also a fundamental characteristic of the religion. As Philip K. Hitti observes,

Islamic law followed the Jewish precedent. It thereby differed from Christianity, whose founder [Jesus Christ] concerned himself more with things spiritual than legal. Paul, founder of Gentile Christianity, was equally spiritually minded. In the [Muslim] mind religious law, secular law, and theology were inextricably mixed. Religious law (*Sharia*, literally "a watering place") was an integral part of the word of Allah incarnate. It coexisted with him.... Of the roughly six thousand verses [in the Quran], some two thousand are strictly legislative.[16]

Christian scriptures and theological tradition recognize the role of government authorities in regulating civil society. Augustine, Aquinas, and numerous passages from the Christian New Testament all point to the authority of the state in the use of physical force for safeguarding the public good.[17] In contrast, Muslims look to Sharia as a way to safeguard society from corruption, social ills, and even colonial and foreign encroachments. Islam began as a movement opposing a corruptly regulated society in Mecca, and the community of faith sought to supplant that corrupt civil authority. Rather than look to the state to correct the injustice of persecution, for example, the legitimate response was to fight

---

[15] Kamali (1997:89, 99).

[16] Hitti (1970:41–42).

[17] The Bible acknowledges that *government authorities* are agents of "wrath to bring punishment on the wrongdoer" (Romans 13:4b, New International Version). Augustine argues that Christians may kill without incurring the guilt of murder if they represent "public justice or the wisdom of government" (1952:142). Aquinas states that support from the sovereign of the state is one of the three conditions for a so-called just war (1952:578).

"until there is no persecution," according to the Quran.[18] Although many Muslims have come to accept a distinction between civil and religious law, and in Muslim-majority countries such as Turkey Sharia currently has no civil jurisdiction, tensions between Islamic law and the religious freedoms of UN resolutions typically center on two key areas: apostasy (renunciation of faith) and blasphemy (defamation of God or that which is sacred).

There are multiple schools of thought in Islamic law, but all treat apostasy and blasphemy as serious offenses, with some interpretations of Islamic law penalizing both with death – especially in cases in which treason to the community of Muslims is evident. And, although Kamali and many other Islamic scholars have argued for limiting the offences included, raising the standards of evidence, and sharply reducing penalties, these offences remain serious concerns in all branches of Sharia law.[19] Regarding apostasy, the assumption of Sharia law remains: once individuals embrace Islam, they are Muslim for life. The apostasy of choosing another religion or abandoning Islam is inconceivable and dangerous to the community as a whole, not just to the soul of the individual. Blasphemy, any open contempt or ridicule of God (Allah), the Prophet Muhammed, or Islam, is especially censured, and the censorship is applied to Muslim and non-Muslim alike. Some monotheistic non-Muslims, especially those referred to as "People of the Book," hold the status of dhimmi[20] and are exempt from some aspects of Sharia law, but none receive an exemption from blasphemy.

The limitations on religious freedom are clearly evident when we return to data used in Figures 2.1 and 2.2. Of the countries with provisions for Sharia law and populations greater than two million, fifteen of twenty-two countries (68 percent) make promises of religious freedom in their constitutions or other legal codes. This is less than the 87 percent for the world as a whole, but still far more than half. Of the fifteen promising religious freedom, however, fourteen have *four* or more laws restricting religious practice in some way.

But those applying Sharia law are far from the only countries to offer differing definitions of religious freedoms. Indeed, most countries passing laws that deny religious freedoms are countries without Sharia law. Crucial decisions for any state to make are centered on deciding how far

---

[18] Quran 2.193a, M. H. Shakir's English interpretation.
[19] Kamali (1997).
[20] Dhimmi is a status frequently granted to non-Muslims, especially Jews and Christians. The status holds many legal and social limitations but allows them to practice their religion within specified restrictions.

human rights extend, when they can be compromised, and how they are defended. Balancing religious freedoms with other individual freedoms and with public welfare is an inevitable challenge of the state. Before we address *why* freedoms are denied, we want first to explore *how* freedoms are denied and who denies them. The state is an obvious source. Armed with the capacity to regulate behavior and holding priorities that can conflict with defending freedoms, the state may allow religious freedoms to fall victim to state regulations. But the state is not the only source. Indeed, the state's ability to deny freedoms often relies on cultural and social supports of the society as a whole.

THE REALITIES OF REGULATION

Many actions targeted at restricting religious freedoms are subtle and seemingly harmless to most. Because regulations are most frequently aimed at religious minorities, most restrictions are noticed by only a few. Even laws that can potentially reach a much wider segment of the population are often differentially enforced. As we will show in the examples that follow, the laws denying religious freedoms often allow for substantial discretion by administrators, and enforcement of the laws is often subject to the social pressures of the local culture.

Many nations have government bureaus or agencies that are charged with monitoring religion. Indeed, religious bureaus operate in six of ten countries, and in 2006–2008,[21] 20 percent of such bureaus acted coercively toward religious groups. Because these bureaus are designed to protect the interests of the state, and often the interests of a dominant religion, their most frequent targets were and are minority religions. Because they often have broad discretionary authority at the local level and are often given latitude to enforce vaguely defined political and social norms, their enforcements can be capricious and sometimes harsh. As expected, the bureaus were standard practice in states with Sharia law provisions, but the rates remain high for every region of the globe. For example, bureaus were mentioned in more than 75 percent of the European country reports, and coercive in more than one in four instances. The recent history of France offers one example of how the bureaus can be used to restrict religious freedoms.

After members of the religious group Order of the Solar Temple committed mass suicide in 1994, strong anticult movements arose both within and outside European governments. German scholar Hubert Seiwert

---

[21] Pew Forum, *Global Restrictions on Religion*, 2009.

reports that "even serious newspapers only marginally escaped the general hysteria."[22] Although most inquiries would later conclude that the new religions posed no danger to state or society, several European countries took strong action, especially France, Germany, and Belgium.[23] For France, the actions were immediate and ongoing. The National Assembly appointed a commission headed by Alain Gest to study cults and sects and, by late 1995, the Gest Commission offered a detailed report. The report devoted more than one hundred pages to explaining the potential dangers of cults to the individual and society, and identified 173 dangerous cults in France alone. The government's Observatory on Sects/Cults was created in 1996 and was reorganized into the Interministerial Mission in the Fight against Sects/Cults in 1998 and into the Interministerial Mission of Vigilance and Combat against Sectarian Aberrations (MIVILUDES) in 2002.[24] The authority of these agencies was further strengthened when the 2001 About-Picard law placed increased restrictions on "cult-like movements" and eased the process for dissolving such groups.[25] Although the Council of Europe, the French Human Rights League, the Catholic Church, and the United Nations Special Rapporteur expressed concern that the legislation violated human rights, both the legislation and the ongoing monitoring remained.[26]

The case of France illustrates several points that are common to many bureaus regulating religion. First, the danger of being regulated is vague and often ill defined. Despite the efforts of the special commission appointed to study religious cults, two agencies charged with combating cults, and legislation aimed at restricting cults, a definition for cults or sects was never offered. Instead, the About-Picard legislation and the Gest Commission listed several vague traits or qualities to help identify cults: pressuring individuals, requiring substantial financial

---

[22] Seiwert (2003:369).

[23] Seiwert (2003:370).

[24] France recently established a separate agency for monitoring religions around the globe. In August 2008, *Foreign Affairs* announced the establishment of a Religion Poll. The Religion Poll will follow international religious trends, monitor the positions religions take on a wide range of issues, and be active in diplomacy.

[25] *2001 Report on International Religious Freedom* http://www.state.gov/gldrl/irf/rpt/index.htm (accessed 5 August 2010).

[26] *2001 Report on International Religious Freedom*; Asma Jahangir, 2007, "2007 Report of the Special Rapporteur on freedom of religion or belief: Addendum summary cases transmitted to Governments and replies received," United Nations' Human Rights Council, Fourth Session, Item 2, http://www2.ohchr.org/english/issues/religion/annual.htm (accessed 5 August 2010); Duvert (2004).

contributions, encouraging antisocial behavior and speech, and cutting members off from their families.[27] Such traits could easily be applied to any number of other close-knit social groups, from college fraternities to social and political movements – and perhaps a few sports clubs as well.

But if a definition was absent and the defining traits were vague, the Gest Commission's list of 173 sects and cults was clear. The dangerous groups were identified, which included the third largest Christian group in France – Jehovah's Witnesses – as well as Soka Gakkai; Scientologists; and multiple evangelical, Adventist, and Pentecostal groups.[28] Of the thirty-six largest groups, ten were classified as "Evangélique." A popular journalist described the religious groups as an American "Trojan Horse" invading France.[29] Ten years later, when Prime Minister Jean-Pierre Raffarin requested that the list no longer be used, the government's MIVILUDES published a guide for public servants and local authorities on how to identify and combat the "dangerous" sects. The MIVILUDES president insisted that they must continue to fight against "sectarian abuses" and highlighted three concerns: protecting children from being recruited, curbing the demand for alternative medicines and healing, and preventing the use of humanitarian aid to bolster a sect's image and to proselytize.[30] Once again, no clear definition would surface and the danger of the groups seemed more amorphous than ever.

The vague definition leads to a second point that is common to religious bureaus. Because the religious dangers being regulated are vaguely defined and typically enforced at local levels, the laws give local authorities broad discretion in how they should be interpreted and enforced. In her 2007 report, the UN's Special Rapporteur exhorted the state to be more vigilant in monitoring state-sponsored agencies and activities that threatened to violate religious freedoms, especially the schools.[31] Armed with vague definitions and charged with fighting sectarian abuses, local officials within France were waging campaigns that quickly denied the

---

[27] *2001 Report on International Religious Freedom.*
[28] Alain Gest and Jacques Guyard, 1995, "Report Made in the Name of the Board of Inquiry into Sects," December 22, http://www.cftf.com/french/Les_Sectes_en_France/cults.html#page76 (accessed 5 August 2010).
[29] Larry Witham, 2001, "France Determines Jehovah's Witnesses Are Not a Religion," *Washington Times* (national weekly edition), July 6–12, p. 21.
[30] *2006 Report on International Religious Freedom.*
[31] Asma Jahangir, 2007, "2007 Report of the Special Rapporteur on freedom of religion or belief: Addendum summary cases transmitted to Governments and replies received," United Nations' Human Rights Council, Fourth Session, Item 2, http://www2.ohchr.org/english/issues/religion/annual.htm (accessed 5 August 2010).

freedoms of religions deemed as dangerous sects. Like religious bureaus around the globe, the regulation of religion soon reflected the zeal of local officials and the pressure of local groups.

Finally, the vague definitions and wide-ranging discretion of local officials allow for the majority of regulations to be targeted at religious minorities. The 2001 report on France stated bluntly that "[l]ocal authorities often determine the treatment of religious minorities."[32] When the About-Picard bill was about to be passed in 2001, reports surfaced that evangelical clergy were "afraid to speak up" and succumbed to the perceived threat of local government action and public pressure.[33] The 2004 legislation prohibiting students or employees from wearing conspicuous religious symbols in public schools was viewed as targeting Muslim women from wearing the *hijab*, or head covering.[34] Public rhetoric against the burqa, a head-to-toe covering for women, escalated in the summer of 2009, with French president Nicolas Sarkozy stating to a gathering of French legislators at Versailles that the "burqa is not a religious sign, it's a sign of subservience, a sign of debasement. I want to say it solemnly: it will not be welcome on the territory of the French Republic."[35] Regardless of the intent, the burden of the legislation and proof that the burqa or hijab is a valid religious symbol rested on minorities. But the religious minorities of France are not alone. When regulations arise and religious freedoms are denied, religious minorities (and sometimes even religious majorities) are frequent targets.[36]

One of the mechanisms most frequently used to regulate religious groups is the simple requirement of registration. Nine of ten countries ask religions to register with the state for one reason or another. This seemingly benign practice is little more than a formality in some countries, imposing no serious hardships on the groups registering. For other countries, however, the threat of revoking registration serves as a warning for the recognized religions, and the denial of registration prevents other religions from getting a foothold. In still other countries, the requirements for registration are so high or so specific that few can

---

[32] *2001 Report on International Religious Freedom.*

[33] Larry Witham, 2001, "France Determines Jehovah's Witnesses Are Not a Religion," *Washington Times* (national weekly edition), July 6–12, p. 21.

[34] Nine months after passage of the legislation, cases of aggression against women wearing headscarves were reported (European Monitoring Centre on Racism and Xenophobia, 2006:73–75).

[35] Jamey Keaten, 2009 "Sarkozy: Burqas Are 'Not Welcome' in France," *Huffington Post*, June 22, http://www.huffingtonpost.com/2009/06/22/sarkozy-burqas-are-not-we_n_218920.html (accessed 5 August 2010).

[36] For additional discussion on religion and state issues in France, see Kuru (2009).

qualify.[37] Once again, there is no shortage of examples. Of the ninety percent of nations requiring registration, we found that the requirements resulted in problems for or discrimination against certain religious groups in six of ten cases, and in four of ten countries, registration requirements were clearly discriminatory.[38]

Russia and most of the former Soviet countries serve as examples. Following the breakup of the Soviet Union, virtually all of the new countries struggled with the issue of religious registration. Following is a brief overview of how registration has opened or restrained religious activity in Russia.

In October 1990, the Supreme Soviet abandoned the official Soviet ideology of scientific atheism and passed legislation guaranteeing freedom of conscience and legal status for all religious communities. This new legislation, the Law on Freedom of Religions, opened the door for a host of new religious groups, including a flood of evangelicals and Pentecostal groups. Even the often persecuted Jehovah's Witnesses were welcomed. Receiving an official legal registration on March 27, 1991, the Jehovah's Witnesses held a series of conventions throughout Russia and neighboring areas, reporting a total attendance of 74,000.[39] But as the new groups' audience and membership grew rapidly and began to provide competitive alternatives to the Russian Orthodox Church, support for allowing virtually all groups to register began to wane.[40]

In 1997, the same year the Jehovah's Witnesses opened a major administrative center outside of St. Petersburg, the Russian parliament passed the complex law On Freedom of Conscience and Associations by a vote of 358 to 6. Contradicting the Russian constitution, which states that all religions are equal under the law, this bill established two categories of religious institutions: traditional organizations and nontraditional groups. The traditional organizations received full legal privileges and tax exemptions. The nontraditional groups, which included Catholic, Baptist, and sectarian Russian Orthodox groups operating separately from the Russian Orthodox Church, were denied full privileges and were required

---

[37] Even some countries with otherwise low levels of religious regulation can have high registration demands. In Angola, for example, the Ministries of Justice and Culture grant legal status to a group only if it has at least 100,000 members according to the 2006 *Report on International Religious Freedom.*

[38] Pew Forum, 2009, "Restrictions on Religion in the World: 2009," www.PewForum.org (accessed 5 August 2010).

[39] For a historical account as reviewed by the Jehovah's Witnesses, see http://www.jw-media.org/rights/russia.htm (accessed 5 August 2010).

[40] For an overview of these changes see Froese (2008); Wanner (2004). For evidence on the growing interest in religion during the early 1990s see Greeley (1994; 2002).

to undergo an annual registration.[41] Along with being cumbersome and time consuming, this registration procedure proved highly restrictive, with many regional authorities within Russia passing even harsher legislation against the "new" sects.[42]

The burdens and threats of reregistering following the 1997 law have proved to be many. In particular, Muslims, Jehovah's Witnesses, the Salvation Army, the Church of Scientology, Seventh-Day Adventists, the Church of Jesus Christ of Latter-day Saints (Mormons), and Pentecostals have all faced extensive challenges, with several requiring court action to avoid "liquidation." When a 1999 amendment to the 1997 law required all groups to reregister or be dissolved, the Ministry of Justice dissolved approximately 980 groups by May 2002.[43]

But even a successful reregistration was no guarantee that it would not be revoked in selected locations. After multiple attempts, the Jehovah's Witnesses were reregistered, but in 2004 the Moscow Golovinskiy Intermunicipal District Court found Jehovah's Witnesses to be a "threat to society" and revoked the organization's registration in Moscow. Not only did this ban its activities in Moscow, it also resulted in landlords across Russia revoking rental agreements with Jehovah's Witnesses. The Salvation Army and others are facing similar challenges that are still not fully resolved. Defined as a "militarized organization," the Salvation Army was not allowed to reregister in Moscow and was officially "liquidated." The Russian Constitutional Court ruled against this decision in 2002, the European Court of Human Rights (ECHR) ruled against the decision in 2006, and the Russian Ministry of Justice restored the Salvation Army's central office registration in 2006, yet the Moscow branch was not reregistered until April 2009.[44] For Muslim mosques and small congregations without international support, the challenges for registration are even greater. Forum 18 reported in 2005 that thirty-nine of the forty-seven mosques in the Stavropol region were denied registration.[45]

---

[41] Wanner (2004:738) indicates that legal privileges included the ability to own property, distribute literature, run radio and television programs, and conduct services in alternative locations such as hospitals and prisons.

[42] Froese (2008); Wanner (2004:738–739).

[43] The Ministry of Justice claimed that all dissolved groups were defunct, but members of the groups claimed otherwise in the *2006 Report on International Religious Freedom*.

[44] *2001 Report on International Religious Freedom Report*; *2009 Report on International Religious Freedom*.

[45] Geraldine Fagan, 2005, "Russia: Unregistered Religious Groups," *Forum 18 News Service*, April 14, http://www.forum18.org/Archive.php?article_id=543 (accessed 5 August 2010).

TABLE 2.1. *Government Restriction of Religious Freedom*

Does the government interfere with an individual's right to worship? (percent of countries)	
No	34
Some interference	40
Severe interference	26
Are foreign missionaries allowed to operate? (percent of countries)	
Allowed or not mentioned	55
Restricted	41
Prohibited	4
Is proselytizing limited? (percent of countries)	
Not mentioned	59
Limited for some	30
Limited for all	11
Does government policy contribute to the generally free practice of religion? (percent of countries)	
Yes	48
Exceptions mentioned	12
No	40

Furthermore, once religious groups are registered with the government, the possibility for intrusive government oversight increases. For instance, Geraldine Fagan of Forum 18 reports that orders signed by Russia's justice minister Aleksandr Konovalov in 2009 greatly expanded the Ministry's Expert Council for Conducting State Religious-Studies Expert Analysis powers, "allowing it to investigate the activity, doctrines, leadership decisions, literature and worship of any registered religious organisation and recommend action to the Ministry."[46]

Although our attention has focused on the registration of religious groups, a restriction that is easily documented and discussed by many, religious bureaus and other government agencies also restrict religious activity in multiple other ways. Table 2.1 lists a few of those we coded from the International Religious Freedom reports. Nearly two-thirds of the countries interfered with the individual's right to worship, and more than 40 percent of the reports mentioned that proselytizing and foreign missionaries are restricted. In practice, we found that less than half (48 percent) of the countries had government policy that contributed to

[46] Geraldine Fagan, 2009, "RUSSIA: Widespread Protests at New 'Inquisition,'" *Forum 18*, June 2, http://www.forum18.org/Archive.php?article_id=1303 (accessed 5 August 2010).

the "generally free practice of religion." Even this list only scratches the
surface of the various regulations used by government agencies, and the
most pervasive controls go beyond government regulations.[47]

BEYOND GOVERNMENT REGULATION

Government agencies are not the only institutions restricting civil liberties. For example, prior to the Civil Rights Act of 1964, unequal hiring
practices and segregation were promoted by social movements and cultural pressures as well as U.S. legal codes. The activities of the Ku Klux
Klan and other movements were the most visible and violent, but the
larger cultural pressures were more ubiquitous and unrelenting. Even
after legal codes changed, the pressures continued for many years, and in
some social sectors they continue today.[48]

For many countries, restricting religious freedoms relies on similar
social supports. Other religions, social movements, and the culture as
a whole can serve to deny religious freedom. In fact, the government's
ability to regulate religion relies heavily on other social forces. When
local social groups and beliefs support legal codes, this eases regulatory
actions, reduces monitoring costs, and increases effective enforcement.
This social and cultural regulation is evident in the enforcement of most
legal codes, but for some legal codes, such as religion, the enforcement
often goes far beyond the formal regulations.

The most vocal advocates for denying religious freedoms are often
other religions. The established or dominant religions frequently call on
their followers as well as local agencies or institutions to deny the religious
freedoms of others. As shown in Table 2.2, we found that in 75 percent of
the countries established or existing religions try to shut out new religions.
Many have commented that the Russian Orthodox Church was a driving
force behind the more restrictive legislation passed in 1997, but they often
fail to notice that the church was effectively promoting tighter restrictions
even before the formal legislation was passed.[49] Shterin and Richardson
note that the restrictions of the 1997 legislation "could already be seen in

---

[47] When the formal provisions of law prove unworkable, as is often the case with the 1997
   Russian legislation, officials resort to differential enforcement of building codes or the
   denial of property rights to curtail the activities of minority religions. For examples in
   Russia, see "Russia: Religious Freedom Survey, April 2007," *Forum 18 News Service*,
   April 26, 2007, http://www.forum18.org/Archive.php?article_id=947 (accessed 5 August
   2010).

[48] Berry (2009).

[49] Shterin & Richardson (1998).

TABLE 2.2. *Social Restrictions on Religious Freedom*

Established or existing religious try to shut out new religions (%)	
No	25
Yes	75
Societal attitudes toward other or nontraditional religions (%)	
Tolerant	16
Isolated discrimination	15
Negative	69
Extent of assertive religious social movements (%)	
None	59
Flashes of activity	6
Regional activity	16
National activity	18

reality before the new law was adopted." The Russian Orthodox Church already held a favored position with local authorities, and they estimated that one-third of the regions in Russia had passed local laws or regulations that violated the religious freedoms promised in the 1990 legislation.[50]

The social pressures are also evident in the example offered at the beginning of this chapter. When Abdul Rahman was being tried in Afghanistan for converting to Christianity, the harshest demands came from clerics, placing the Afghanistan government between insistent international demands for his release and loud local outcries for his execution. On March 25, 2006, the *Washington Post* reported that senior clerics in Kabul reissued their support for prosecuting Rahman and warned that "they would incite people to kill him unless he reverted to Islam." Three days later, when Rahman was released and the case was dropped, the *Post* reported that "hundreds of clerics, students and others chanting 'Death to Christians!'" marched in the streets protesting the decision.[51] This example, no doubt, represents one extreme of the social pressures placed on restricting religious freedoms, but we nonetheless find that social pressures for restricting religious freedom are routine.

Table 2.2 shows that social attitudes toward other religions were reported as discriminatory or negative in 74 percent of the country reports. Although these totals fail to report on how many within each country favor discriminatory action, a nationally representative sample of France illustrates how widely the concern can spread. Conducted in 2000, the survey found that 73 percent of the respondents viewed sects

---

[50] Shterin & Richardson (1998:324–325).
[51] As quoted by an Associated Press article, "Afghan Judge Resists Pressure in Convert Case," *Washington Post*, March 25, 2006.

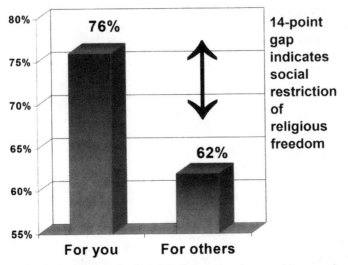

FIGURE 2.3. Support for "My" Religious Freedoms and Support for the Religious Freedoms of "Others."

as a "very considerable threat" or "quite a threat" to democracy and 86 percent favored prohibiting selected sects such as the Church of Scientology and the Order of the Solar Temple.[52] Once again, the totals reported from our coding in Table 2.2 represent only the countries where negative attitudes were mentioned and clearly underreport discriminatory attitudes. Even these totals, however, illustrate that support for denying religious freedoms is common.

A ten-nation survey conducted by the Pew Forum in 2006 illustrates that respondents are highly concerned about religious freedoms, *if the freedoms are their own.*[53] In nine out of ten of the countries, large majorities consider it "very important" to live in a country that protects "my" religious freedom. The only country where a large majority did not agree was South Korea, where only 42 percent strongly agreed, but an additional 49 percent agreed that it was "somewhat important." When it came to the freedoms of others, however, support consistently fell. The gap between supporting "my" religious freedoms and the freedoms of "others" ranged from a high of 30 points in India to a low of 3 points

[52] Beckford (2004:29).
[53] The Pew Forum on Religion and Public Life, 2006, "Spirit and Power: A Ten-Nation Study of Pentecostals," http://www.pewforum.org/Christian/Evangelical-Protestant-Churches/Spirit-and-Power.aspx (accessed 5 August 2010).

in Chile, with the United States falling at 6. Across the ten countries, the average gap is 14 points (see Figure 2.3).

This gap opens the door for denying the religious freedoms of minority religions or any religion without political sway. Grim and Wike recently concluded that "the difference between the number of people who consider freedom for their own religion very important and the number who consider freedom for religions other than their own very important represents a 'religious intolerance gap.'"[54] The gap also provides an indicator for the level to which people consider it acceptable to restrict the religious freedom of others, despite protecting their own freedoms. Consistent with the findings of this survey, we will show that social pressures to deny freedoms persist in the United States (see "A Short Discussion on the United States" later in this chapter) and that such pressures are reaching extremely high levels in India (Chapter 5).

ONLINE MORAL MONITORING

The effective and ubiquitious presence of social monitoring and the ability of this monitoring to increase government restrictions can also be illustrated with examples that include religious motives but go beyond restricting religions. Peter Burrows of *Business Week** reports that China "employs a vast arsenal of technologies and thousands of human censors to maintain its Great Firewall." By contrast, Saudi Arabia employs only twenty-five people and "[s]till, Saudi censorship is considered among the most restrictive in the world." The difference, of course, is the social monitoring conducted by the citizens of Saudi Arabia. Saudi Arabia's Communication and Information Technology Commission (CITC) receives approximately 1,200 requests each day to block specific sites. Religious leaders and students, some with training from elite American universities, lead the charge in locating and reporting the offensive sites. As with the government's restrictions on religion, social pressures and restrictions fuel increases in the government's restrictions.

* Peter Burrows, 2008, "Internet Censorship: A Community Effort," *Business Week*, November 24, p. 68.

---

[54] Grim & Wike (2010).

TABLE 2.3. *Practicing my Religion Freely is "very important" versus Freedom of Religion for Others is "very important"*

	Country	My Freedom (%)	Other's Freedom (%)	Difference (points)
Greatest survey difference	India	73	43	30
	Nigeria	90	69	21
	Philippines	71	52	19
	South Africa	75	62	13
	Kenya	87	75	12
	South Korea	42	34	8
Smallest survey difference	United States	91	85	6
	Brazil	84	79	5
	Guatemala	73	69	4
	Chile	75	72	3

Note: Question wording: How important is it to you to live in a country where (insert item below)? Is it very important, somewhat important, not too important, or not important at all?

   you can practice your religion freely
   there is freedom of religion for religions other than your own

Source: 2006 Pew Forum Pentecostalism Survey

The social pressures for restricting religions are fueled by many sources, but some of the most potent are social, religious, and political movements organized either to advance their own religious agenda or to stop the religious activities of others. As shown in Table 2.3 these movements are commonplace, with 40 percent of the country reports mentioning such groups. The most highly publicized are Islamic movements promoting the adoption of Sharia law or demanding a stricter version of such law, but movements calling for restrictions on religious freedom are common throughout Europe and North America as well. The anticult movements, in particular, have garnered numerous allies in their attempt to limit the freedoms of new religions. Throughout Europe, the media have been some of the most influential partners. Cyrille Duvert, a French law professor, recently described French journalists as working "hand in hand" with anticult movements and noted that some specialized in "battling the cults" and served as "moral entrepreneurs" for the cause.[55] Shterin and Richardson acknowledge the powerful role the media plays in the West but argue that the influence of the media is even stronger in Russia, where the foreign and new religions are presented as dangerous and even

[55] Duvert (2004:43).

horrifying.[56] The anticult movements have also benefited from the support of the state and the established churches. In France, the two main anticult groups receive state subsidies and work closely with state agencies holding similar objectives[57]; in Russia, the first anticult group was formed within the Russian Orthodox Church and was part of a much larger campaign for more restrictive legislation.[58] The end result is that strong social attitudes and discriminatory behavior build against new religions. From broader issues of gaining public acceptance to mundane details of finding landlords willing to rent space for worship, new religious groups face social regulations that go far beyond the formal regulations of the state.[59]

Not only can the informal regulations of social movements and dominant religions receive direct support from the government, they also can benefit from its complacency in protecting minority religions. States can openly deny religious freedoms, or they can simply fail to protect such freedoms. Returning to the Russian example, Pentecostals, Catholics, Baptists, and other groups registered as nontraditional groups bitterly complain that the police fail to protect them.[60] When a Jehovah's Witness Kingdom Hall and its surrounding property were repeatedly vandalized in April 2006, police failed to take any action, stating this wasn't a crime. Even when thirty shots were fired into a Kingdom Hall, police closed the case within two months, stating that they couldn't identify the perpetrators. Catholics, Pentecostals, and others have also complained that police are slow to respond when intruders interrupt their worship services or even attack them.[61] By turning a blind eye to violations of religious freedoms, state agencies allow others to regulate the groups they are seeking to control.

An obvious question, however, is why these religious minorities cause such a stir. The most frequently targeted groups are often numerically insignificant and politically powerless. Yet, both the state and other

---

[56] Shterin & Richardson (1998:337).

[57] Beckford (2004:31).

[58] Shterin & Richardson (2000); Knox (2003).

[59] For examples, see Introvigne (1998) and Geraldine Fagan, 2005, "Russia: Unregistered Religious Groups," *Forum 18 News Service*, April 14, http://www.forum18.org/Archive.php?article_id=543 (accessed 5 August 2010).

[60] The complaints are ongoing and come from many sources. For an example see Geraldine Fagan, 2005, "Russia: Whose Side Are the Police On?" *Forum 18 News Service*, June 7, http://www.forum18.org/Archive.php?article_id=794 (accessed 5 August 2010).

[61] *2006 Report on International Religious Freedom.*

religious and social movements have strong motives for curbing their activities.

Religious freedoms are denied for many of the same reasons other human rights are denied: unbridled practice of such freedoms can threaten the state and other groups in power. Freedom of speech is easy to grant so long as those speaking are supportive or are far removed from public discourse and any attempts to challenge are inept and ineffective. The true test of free speech is when the challenges made effectively sway the opinions and actions of others. So it is with religion. When religious groups are ineffective, hold little sway over the beliefs and behaviors of followers, and are removed from public conversations, they receive little attention. However, as their members increase in number and commitment, and they seek a voice in the public arena, the motives for regulating the groups increase.

Religious and Social Motives

Ignoring for a moment the organizational self-interests of established religions, we should acknowledge that exclusive religious beliefs provide motives for promoting the "one true faith." To the extent that religious beliefs are taken seriously and the dominant religion is held as true, all new religions are heretical at best. Thus, established religions will view the new religions as both dangerous and wrong. Just as the clerics in Afghanistan viewed Rahman's conversion as dangerous as well as illegal, the Catholic Church has expressed strong concern over its flock being misguided by Protestant "sects" in Latin America. At the Fourth General Conference of Latin American Bishops (CELAM) in 1992, Pope John Paul II described Pentecostal and evangelical sects as being like "rapacious wolves ... causing division and discord in our communities."[62] When he toured Latin America in 1996, he championed issues of social justice and true peace, but he warned that many are misled by "sects and new religious groups, who sow confusion and uncertainty among Catholics."[63]

---

[62] Cleary (1992:7).
[63] Stephen R. Sywulda, 1996, "John Paul Woos Straying Flock," *Christianity Today,* April 8, vol. 40, p. 94.

For the faithful, who believe that their faith is the one true faith, other religions pose eternal risks for misguided followers.

Yet, many of the social and religious motives for revoking religious freedoms go beyond religious beliefs and center on a perceived threat to individuals and society.[64] Russian Orthodox Patriarch Aleksii II expressed the views of many when he outlined why freedoms must be limited. Writing to then–Russian president Boris Yeltsin in support of more restrictive laws on religious freedom, he explained that such laws are needed for "protecting the individual from the destructive, pseudo-religious and pseudo-missionary activity that has brought obvious harm to the spiritual and physical health of people, and to stability and civic peace in Russia."[65] Notice that the Patriarch argues that the other religions can be destructive and dangerous both for the individual and for society as a whole. Similar arguments have been developed by those outside of religious institutions to justify denying religious freedoms.

Perhaps the most persistent charge against new religions is that they are guilty of mental manipulation, commonly referred to as brainwashing or sectarian hold.[66] Although some of the earliest versions of the brainwashing arguments were used by religious groups opposing cults in the United States, they continue to be cited around the globe and are now frequently used to justify the actions of secular governments. The specific arguments vary widely, but the underlying fear is that new religions are able to distort the thinking of members and force them to act and believe in ways that are potentially dangerous to themselves and others. This persistent fear of the media and more general population has fueled many government actions to control the groups. For instance, the 2006 report by France's Interministerial Mission of Vigilance and Combat against Sectarian Aberrations (MIVILUDES) to the prime minister explains that the "sects" create a "condition of destabilization, disorientation, and vulnerability" and then use reinforcement techniques to reconstruct the personality.[67] Like the brainwashing arguments of the past, the MIVILUDES report concludes that sects use devious and powerful psychological methods to take advantage of the vulnerable citizens.

---

[64] Wike & Grim (2010).

[65] As quoted in Knox (2003:83).

[66] The 2006 MIVILUDES report to the French prime minister now refers to mental manipulation as "sectarian hold" in Roulet (2006).

[67] Roulet (2006:23). The full report can be downloaded from the MIVILUDES Web site: http://www.miviludes.gouv.fr/English-Report-Miviludes-2006?iddiv=5.

But such conclusions were not the product of careful study; they were a product of social pressures and a more general hysteria.

Despite the ongoing charges of brainwashing and sectarian hold, a long line of research has demonstrated that the groups do not have the powers of mental manipulation attributed to them.[68] Eileen Barker's early studies of the Unification Church (so-called Moonies), a group frequently charged with brainwashing new recruits, were especially instructive. She found that the recruitment techniques not only did not involve brainwashing or coercion, they also weren't very effective. Of those visiting a Unification center to explore the religion, only 0.005 percent of the potential recruits were associated with the group two years later. Barker describes even this small rate as a "generous estimate."[69] Moreover, she reported that the joiners compared favorably with those not joining on measures of emotional and psychological stability. Since Barker's early work, research has consistently refuted the charges of sects mentally manipulating vulnerable and unsuspecting citizens.[70]

But if the notion of brainwashing has lost scientific credibility, it retains a high level of political clout and remains one of the strongest social motives for denying religious freedoms. Reviewing official reports completed by parliamentary and administrative government agencies in Western Europe, Richardson and Introvigne find that "brainwashing" and "mind control" imagery continues to be used and serves as a basis for many policy recommendations.[71] The power of sectarian brainwashing is defined as the problem, whereas restricting the freedoms of these groups is identified as the solution. In the foreword to his 2006 report to the French prime minister, the MIVILUDES chairperson argues that protecting citizens "against sectarian aberrations, is a basic obligation for the state."[72] The irony is that the constitution of the Fifth French Republic strives to free the state from the nonscientific beliefs of religion (*laïcité*), yet the government agency regulating religion retains a belief in sectarian brainwashing despite overwhelming evidence to the contrary.[73]

[68] Shupe & Bromley (1980); Barker (1984); Stark & Bainbridge (1985). The research finds that the vast majority are not a danger to the individual or society and none hold the powers of mental manipulation or brainwashing.

[69] Barker (1984:147).

[70] For a review of the consensus that formed early in this research, see Robbins (1988).

[71] Richardson & Introvigne (2001).

[72] Roulet (2006:7).

[73] The principle of laïcité used in France protects the state from religious institutions and beliefs but is not designed to protect religion from the state. See Beckford (2004:33) and Luca (2004:68).

Yet another social and religious motive for denying religious freedom is to preserve and protect the culture and society as a whole. In December 1994, the Archbishop's Council (Sobor) of the Russian Orthodox Church expanded on why other religions threatened this peace.

These [sectarian] views destroy the traditional organization of life that has been formed under the influence of the Russian Orthodox Church. They destroy the spiritual and moral ideal that is common to all of us; and they threaten the integrity of our national consciousness and our cultural identity.[74]

For countries where ethnicity and religion overlap to form social boundaries or where established religions play an important role in the administration of the state, the relationship between religion and social order becomes even more complex.

Beyond all of the concerns just given, however, established religions hold two powerful motives for restricting the activities of other religions. First, the new religions threaten their favored position with the state and culture. Second, all new religions are an unwelcome source of religious competition.[75] Even small religions provide the population with religious alternatives, and some will show rapid growth. Pentecostalism in Latin America offers one example. The Catholic Church was the established church of colonial powers and retained a favored status with the newly forming nations in the nineteenth century. But as religious freedoms increased in the mid-twentieth century, the Catholic Church could no longer control the presence of new religions. At first, the Pentecostals and other Protestant sects seemed a mere nuisance, appealing only to those on the margins of society.[76] By the 1990s, however, scholars recognized these groups as a powerful social force changing the religious and

---

[74] As quoted in Shterin & Richardson (2000:263). In 1997 Patriarch Aleksii II explained that "we want to preserve our own personality and countenance, the spiritual and cultural heritage which was laid down over the course of the thousand-year history of Russia," as quoted in Knox (2003:584).

[75] Established churches often complain that they have a competitive disadvantage to the well-organized and well-financed sects. In the mid-1990s the highest-ranking Catholic prelate in Guatemala and Russian Orthodox Patriarch Aleksii II charged evangelicals with being instruments of rich foreign governments and organizations. See Stephen R. Sywulda, 1996, "John Paul Woos Straying Flock," *Christianity Today*, April 8, vol. 40, p. 94; Shterin & Richardson (1998:321). The provincial press explained that the "Orthodox only have their faith. But the newcomers-evangelists have their energy and hard currency," as quoted in Shterin & Richardson (1998:321).

[76] When Flora (1976) studied lower-class Colombian Pentecostals in the 1970s, the group was small and the future seemed uncertain. Barrett, Kurian, & Johnson (2001) estimate that the number of Pentecostals jumped from about 565,000 in 1970 to 19.5 million in 2005.

social landscape of Latin America, and their impact continues to grow.[77] Protestants have now been elected into key political positions across Latin America, the favored status of the Catholic Church is increasingly symbolic, and a major recent survey suggests that Latin America may some day be evangelical and Pentecostal.[78] As the political favoritism of the Catholic Church eroded and the religious freedoms of the new sects increased, a handful of groups became the competitive force feared by the Catholic Church.

States' Motives

The state also holds a plethora of motives for denying religious freedoms. As reviewed in Chapter 1, Voltaire, Adam Smith, and David Hume all warned that religious monopolies run the risk of despotism and argued that religious plurality, however, is a source of peace. Yet few governments are willing to answer Adam Smith's plea to "let them [religions] all alone, and to oblige them all to let alone one another."[79] Instead, the state frequently attempts to control religious activity by forming alliances with select religious groups or by restricting the activities of all. The motive for the state is to secure political stability and survival by controlling any potential threats from religion.

Historical examples abound on the role of religious organizations mobilizing support for political action, and this point isn't lost on political leaders. After explaining that "the church played an important role" in the change of power in Eastern Europe, the Chinese state-run press warned, "If China does not want such a scene to be repeated in its land, it must strangle the baby while it is still in the manger."[80] Once confident that religion would soon disappear, representatives of China's Religious Affairs Bureau now acknowledge that religion remains and atheism isn't working.[81] Rather than attempting to wipe out all religions, as was done

---

[77] A few of the many books charting this rapid growth in the 1990s are Martin (1990); Stoll (1990); and Gill (1998).

[78] For a summary of recent survey findings on Pentecostalism in Latin America, see the Pew Forum on Religion and Public Life, 2006, "Spirit and Power: A Ten-Nation Study of Pentecostals," http://www.pewforum.org/Christian/Evangelical-Protestant-Churches/Spirit-and-Power.aspx (accessed 5 August 2010).

[79] Adam Smith ([1776] 1976:315).

[80] Written in 1992, the quote is taken from Marshall (1997:10–11).

[81] Based on multiple conversations with the members of the Religious Affairs Bureau in Beijing and Kunming in July 2005.

during Mao's Cultural Revolution in the 1960s and 1970s, they have now enacted policies that attempt to control the activities of the state-approved religions, tolerate the activities of religions viewed as harmless, and force all others underground.[82] The final goal, of course, is to reduce the threat of religions mobilizing against the state.

Rather than attempting to control all religions, however, many states secure the support of religion by forming alliances with the most powerful religion. This can come in the form of allowing a particular religion's laws to have juridical power, as is the case with Sharia law, where a religion is actively involved in government administration and funding decisions. Or, the support of the dominant religion might be achieved with a more modest alliance, as seen in Russia today, where religious competitors are regulated at the behest of a single religion. In any of the cases, such alliances secure additional support for the state and reduce the risk of the dominant religion serving as an organizational vehicle for challenging the state. As shown by recent research in Eastern Europe and elsewhere, the dominant religions that were able to mobilize support for opposing existing policies or governments were the religions that held autonomy from the state.[83]

The flip side of understanding the state's motives for denying religious freedoms is understanding the motives for granting religious freedoms. Developing and testing a theory on the origins of religious liberty, Anthony Gill[84] finds that politicians will seek alliances with religious institutions to secure political survival. However, as their political tenure becomes secure, their motives for the alliance wanes. He points out that any alliance includes costs to the state. At the minimum, it includes the costs of monitoring and enforcing restrictions on minority religions, and it often includes extensive subsidies to the dominant religion as well. Thus the state's motives for forming an alliance or regulating the activities of other religions will vary with political stability, religious homogeneity and power, and the perceived threats of other religions. When politicians view alliances with established religions as necessary for survival or they perceive religious movements as a potential threat to the state, religious freedoms will be denied.

---

[82] See Yang (2006) for a discussion of the three religious markets in China today.
[83] Froese & Pfaff (2001); Gill (2008). See Gill (2008) for a compelling theory and captivating examples of why and when religious freedoms arise.
[84] Gill (2008).

A SHORT DISCUSSION ON THE UNITED STATES

When explaining America's long-held commitment to religious liberties, it is tempting to attribute this to the larger American culture or the American way of doing things, suggesting a secure stability and certainty. After all, it has been more than two centuries since the First Amendment was ratified, with clauses assuring both the free exercise of religion and the freedom from religious establishment. But the territorial reach of each clause, as well as the boundary between them, is a source of ongoing tension.[85] The remaining chapters of the book will have little to say about religious freedoms in America, but this shouldn't suggest that freedoms are a given or that America is free from pressures to deny freedoms. The motives for denying religious freedoms will always remain, regardless of the heritage, culture, or religion of the nation.

Religious liberties, like all civil liberties, face a struggle between the will of the majority and the "sovereign" rights of all. American religious history is filled with struggles over defining the boundaries of religious freedoms and the rights that should be granted to religious minorities. Indeed, the establishment of religious freedom was surrounded by conflict, and even those supporting religious freedoms varied in their motives. Whereas the rationalists such as Jefferson were seeking to remove religion from the political arena, the evangelical sects such as the Baptists were attempting to remove the state from the religious arena.[86]

Since the passage of the First Amendment, the religious outsiders of each era have tested these boundaries. First it was Catholics, Jews, and a host of Protestant sects. By the late nineteenth and early twentieth centuries Mormons and Jehovah's Witnesses helped to define the borders of religious freedom. The actions of Jehovah's Witnesses, in particular, frequently tested the limits. From 1938 to 1946 alone, they were involved in twenty-three Supreme Court rulings, prompting Justice Harlan Fiske Stone to note that "Jehovah's Witnesses ought to have an endowment in view of the aid which they give in solving the legal problems of civil liberties."[87] Government constraints on religion in America remain low, but "solving the legal problems of civil liberties" mentioned by Justice

---

[85] To the extent that the establishment clause is interpreted more strictly and government outreach continues, the claim is that the voice of religion is excluded from the public arena. A growing body of research would support this claim.

[86] See Mead (1956); Finke (1990).

[87] As quoted in Peters (2000:v).

Fiske remains an ongoing struggle. Returning to the 1990s and early twenty-first century in the United States, we try to illustrate two key points about this struggle. First, we show how even subtle judicial and legislative shifts have powerful consequences on religious freedoms.[88] Second, we document that America is not exempt from efforts to restrict religious freedoms. Many of the motives for denying religious freedoms remain even when freedoms are protected. Like all civil liberties, religious liberties are more fragile than they might first appear.

Religious Freedom and the *Smith* Decision

From 1963 to 1990, the courts frequently relied on the *Sherbert* test (compelling interest) to offer guidelines on how courts accommodated the interest of public welfare without unduly burdening religious freedom. This test required courts to ask if undue burden was being placed on the plaintiff's religious freedom. If the government did not cause an undue burden, the court ruled against the plaintiff. When the court discerned that a burden was present, it asked if there was a compelling interest to carry forth an action that might burden the plaintiff's free exercise of religion. If the court felt that it must rule in the public's interest, it attempted to find an alternative way to satisfy the complaint without infringing on religious freedom.[89]

In 1990, in the case of the *Employment Division of Oregon, Department of Human Resources of Oregon versus Smith*, the Supreme Court severely challenged the *Sherbert* test.[90] In this case the Employment Division of Oregon denied unemployment benefits to Alfred Smith and Galen Black, two rehabilitation counselors who had been fired for ingesting peyote during a Native American religious ceremony. The Court did not dispute the use of peyote as an ancient and genuine sacramental practice, but nevertheless concluded that "the nation cannot afford the luxury of

---

[88] Wybraniec & Finke (2001).

[89] In *Sherbert v. Verner*, 374 U.S. 398 (1963), the defendant, a Seventh-Day Adventist, refused on religious grounds to work Saturdays after her employer shifted her schedule to include this day. Seventh-Day Adventists observe Saturday as the Sabbath and proper day of rest. When Sherbert could not find alternative work and applied for benefits, the state denied them. Claiming a breach of religious freedom, Sherbert sued and the Supreme Court found in her favor. When the Supreme Court overturned a lower court's denial of Sherbert's claim, it established the tripartite (*Sherbert*) test that was used in free exercise cases until 1990.

[90] *Employment Division, Department of Human Resources of Oregon v. Smith*, 494 U.S. 872 (1990).

deeming presumptively invalid, as applied to the religious objector, every regulation of conduct that does not protect an interest of the highest order."[91] Thus, the Supreme Court withdrew the compelling interest test that had been used for the previous three decades.

Many, including Justice Sandra Day O'Connor and Professor Michael W. McConnell, addressed the meaning of the controversial ruling. McConnell stated that the theoretical argument of the *Smith* case left "the court open to the charge of abandoning its traditional role as protector of minority rights against majoritarian oppression."[92] At the 1991 Bicentennial Conference on the Religion Clauses, Justice O'Connor summed up the concerns of many when she explained, "The Free Exercise Clause does not mean very much if all a state has to do is make a law generally applicable in order to severely burden a very central aspect of our citizens' lives."[93] After *Smith*, Congress passed the Religious Freedom Restoration Act (RFRA) in March 1993, which was a legislative attempt to restore the *Sherbert* test. But in June 1997, in *City of Boerne v. Flores* the Supreme Court struck it down as unconstitutional, at least insofar as it applied to the states.[94]

What are the consequences of the *Smith* decision and RFRA? Did this decision reduce the court's role as a protectorate of minority faiths? Initially, bold claims were made, but evidence was anecdotal. More recently, John Wybraniec and Roger Finke eliminated speculation by systematically analyzing court cases making First Amendment claims from 1981 to 1997 (all levels of the judiciary).[95] The more-than-two-thousand religion cases were divided into three distinct legal time periods: before *Smith* when the *Sherbert* or compelling interest test was the standard (January 1981–April 1990); after *Smith* (but before RFRA) when the compelling interest test was challenged (April 1990–March 1993); and during the RFRA period when a legislative attempt was made to restore a version of the compelling interest test (March 1993–June 1997). Dividing the cases into these three time periods allows us to evaluate the impact of seemingly minor changes to the protection of religious freedoms.

---

[91] *Employment Division, Department of Human Resources of Oregon v. Smith*, 494 U.S. 872 (1990) at 888.

[92] McConnell (1990:1109).

[93] Quoted in Wood (1991:677).

[94] *Boerne v. Flores*, 521 U.S. 507 (1997).

[95] Wybraniec & Finke (2001); see also Adamczyk, Wybraniec, & Finke (2004).

The Consequences of *Smith* and RFRA

When reviewing the results of all seventeen years, many of our findings support previous expectations: religious outsiders turn to the courts for protection. Whereas 21 percent of all church members are in mainline Protestant denominations, they are involved in only 4 percent of all religion cases. In sharp contrast, minority religious groups make up only about 18 percent of congregational membership in the United States, but they account for nearly 62 percent of the free exercise cases coming to the courts, and nearly half of all court cases on religion. Finally, despite frequently initiating court cases, minority religions receive less favorable rulings. From 1981 to 1997 they received favorable rulings in 37 percent of their cases, compared to 70 percent for mainline Protestants. Thus, as expected, religious minorities more frequently turn to the courts for protection, despite receiving a lower rate of favorable rulings.

But what was the impact of *Smith* and RFRA? Contrary to the claims of Justice Anthony M. Kennedy and others, our results reveal that the consequences of the *Smith* decision were swift and immediate.[96] The courts' use of the compelling interest test plummeted after *Smith*, dropping from 24 to 12 percent, and quickly returned to 25 percent following the passage of RFRA. The percentage of favorable decisions followed a similar pattern. For free exercise cases, the percentage dropped from 40 percent prior to *Smith* to 28 percent following *Smith*, and rebounded to more than 45 percent after RFRA was passed (see Figure 2.4). Thus, the consequences of the *Smith* decision resulted in an immediate reduction in the use of the compelling interest test and a far lower rate of favorable free exercise decisions.

But even this drop in favorable rulings underestimates the impact of *Smith*. Following *Smith* and prior to RFRA, we also found that religious groups were less likely to initiate free exercise claims, dropping from 7.1 free exercise cases initiated per month prior to *Smith* (from 1981 to 1990) to only 3.2 cases following the *Smith* case and prior to RFRA.[97] When religious groups did not have recourse to the courts for free exercise exemptions, they very quickly limited its use.

---

[96] While speaking for the majority in *City of Boerne v. Flores*, Justice Kennedy asserted that laws of general applicability very rarely burden the free exercise of religion in America. *City of Boerne v. Flores*, 117 S. Ct. 2157 1997. Also see Lupu (1998:589) and Ryan (1992:1417).

[97] Following RFRA, the number of cases increased to 5.9 per month.

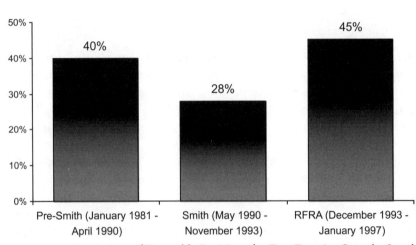

FIGURE 2.4. Percentage of Favorable Decisions for Free Exercise Cases by Legal Period (N = 469); RFRA = Religious Freedom Restoration Act

This last result suggests that if religions were burdened by laws of general applicability, the courts would not know about it because so few religious groups would come requesting an exemption.[98] This concern echoes those raised by colonial Baptists in the late seventeenth and early eighteenth centuries. Historians tell us that Baptists chose not to appeal their cases to the courts because they had no representation "on the bench, none at the bar, and seldom any on the juries."[99] The religious minorities of the late 1990s had far more protections than the colonial Baptists, but the principle remains the same: when religious minorities receive fewer favorable rulings and appear to receive less protection from the courts, they initiate fewer court actions.

Following the *Smith* decision, the reduction in free exercise claims, the increase in unfavorable rulings, and the reduced use of the compelling interest test all weighed most heavily on religious minorities relying on the courts for protection. Justice O'Connor explains:

[T]he First Amendment was enacted precisely to protect the rights of those whose religious practices are not shared by the majority and may be viewed with hostility.

---

[98] Professor Drinan makes the similar point that we will not know what happens to religious individuals and persons if RFRA is not reinstated in some form. As he explains, "At the local level, zoning commissions will quietly deny access to Jewish temples, controversial denominations or Catholic schools. Appeals will not be taken nor will there be any public outcry. The number of individuals who will seek to vindicate their rights under the *Smith* decision will be small." See Drinan (1997:101, 115–116).

[99] See McLoughlin (1971).

The history of our free exercise doctrine amply demonstrates the harsh impact majoritarian rule has had on unpopular or emerging religious groups such as the Jehovah's Witnesses and the Amish.[100]

Using multivariate models with this same data we found that Justice O'Connor is right: minority religions are especially burdened by the removal of free exercise claims. When controlling for region, level of court, legal period, citing the compelling interest test, and whether an individual or group brought the case forward, we found that minority religious groups were significantly less likely to receive favorable decisions when compared to mainline Protestant churches. With the exception of Native American religions, the odds that sects, cults, and Muslims will receive a favorable ruling are about one-third of the odds for mainline Protestants. General Christians, members of the Jewish faith, and Catholics were also *less* likely to receive a favorable decision when compared to mainline Protestant groups.[101]

These results do not suggest that the *Smith* decision abolished the religious freedoms promised in the First Amendment. But evidence taken from this brief window of time does illustrate how seemingly minor changes can have significant impact on implementing religious freedoms. This evidence has stressed the influence of the *Smith* decision on the courts' actions, but evidence could also be produced on how the *Smith* decision influenced the legislative actions of local governments (e.g., zoning and other building codes). Legislative actions might support the will of the majority but can impose heavy burdens on the new and novel religions.

The Capricious Will of the Majority

Religious freedom is often presented as arising from the earliest heritage of America, with the Puritans immigrating to the colonies for religious freedom serving as the most prominent example. On closer inspection, however, we find that the Puritans were seeking religious freedoms and an escape from religious persecution, but they had no intentions of granting religious freedoms to all. Their attempts to regulate religion and restrict

---

[100] *Employment Division, Department of Human Resources of Oregon v. Smith*, 494 U.S. 872 (1990) at 902.

[101] Aside from religious affiliation, legal period, and citing of the compelling interest test, the only other significant variable was level of court. See Wybraniec & Finke (2001:427).

the freedoms of many have been clearly documented and displayed.[102] The Puritans and many other religious immigrants demonstrated the important principle shown by the religious intolerance gap Grim and Wike found in the Pew Forum poll discussed earlier in this chapter: wanting religious freedom doesn't mean that you want religious freedom for all.

So what is the will of the American majority today? Many will argue that religious freedom is now so infused into American institutions and culture that a majority will support religious freedoms and judicial protections are seldom needed. But the actions of local governments and private businesses suggest otherwise. In the *2006 Report on Enforcement of Laws Protecting Religious Freedoms*, the Department of Justice described "religious discrimination" as a growing problem. It noted that from 1992 to 2005 there was a 69 percent increase in the number of complaints filed with the Equal Employment Opportunity Commission on religious discrimination. In contrast, complaints concerning discrimination based on sex, nation of origin, and race arose only 6, 8, and 9.5 percent, respectively, over the same period. A portion of the increase no doubt can be attributed to reactions following 9/11, but the trends have continued, and the problems didn't begin on September 11, 2001. A congressional report completed in 1999 found "massive evidence" that state and local officials were guilty of discriminating against religious organizations.[103] Replicating the findings of our research on judicial decisions reported earlier in this chapter, the congressional report found that minority religions faced the brunt of the blow: "[f]aith groups constituting 9% of the population made up 50% of reported court cases involving zoning disputes."[104]

Furthermore, according to a report by Human Rights First,[105] there were attacks in the United States in 2007–2008 "on people of diverse confessions, on homes and property, and on places of worship, including Catholic, Protestant, and Mormon churches, mosques and prayer rooms

---

[102] McLoughlin (1971).
[103] After RFRA was struck down as unconstitutional by the Supreme Court in 1997, pressures mounted to secure legislation that would protect congregations from local zoning and administrative actions against them. The 1999 congressional report and other evidence were used to justify the 2000 Religious Land Use and Institutionalized Persons Act.
[104] As reported in the Department of Justice's 2006 "Report on Enforcement of Laws Protecting Religious Freedoms," http://www.usdoj.gov/crt/religdisc/ff_report.htm (accessed 5 August 2010).
[105] http://www.humanrightsfirst.org/discrimination/reports.aspx?s=usa&p=index (accessed 5 August 2010).

of Islamic community centers, and synagogues." Among the most highly publicized of these crimes were arson attacks on churches in Alabama and Utah. Also, according to the Federal Bureau of Investigation (FBI), hate crimes motivated by a religious bias have been reported in nearly all fifty states for every year in the twenty-first century. Hate crimes motivated by a religious bias made up 18.9 percent of all hate crimes reported to the FBI in 2006, which is typical across the years. In 2006, there were documented reports of one person being killed, 178 people being physically assaulted, and 718 properties being damaged or destroyed due to religious bias. Of these crimes, 64.3 percent were anti-Jewish, 12 percent were anti-Muslim, 3.9 percent were anti-Protestant, 8.8 percent were anti–other religion, 5.5 percent were anti–multiple religions, 5.1 percent were anti-Catholic, and 0.5 percent were anti-atheism/agnosticism. In 2004 and 2005 combined, there were documented reports of 206 people being physically assaulted and 1,713 properties being damaged or destroyed due to religious bias.

Although challenges to religious freedoms and the level of religiously biased hate crimes reported in the United States every year are matters for concern, the response of the U.S. government to these crimes and complaints is of note. In 2002, the Department of Justice created the Special Counsel for Religious Discrimination within its Civil Rights Division to coordinate enforcement of civil rights laws related to religious freedom and religious discrimination and to file suits and court briefs throughout the country on behalf of religious groups and believers whose religious rights are violated. Actions were also taken against religiously biased hate crimes. Because these crimes are prosecuted by local law enforcement officials and then reported to the FBI, government at both the local and national levels pays attention to this issue. Also, rather than stigmatizing religion, perpetrators of crimes against religious believers are prosecuted, punished, and left with the stigma of having committed a religious hate crime.[106]

If the actions of Americans have demonstrated the need for continued protections of religious freedoms, so too have their attitudes and beliefs. The annual survey of the First Amendment Center has shown that support for basic religious freedoms can and do change in a short period of time. The 2000 national survey found that nearly 73 percent of Americans agreed: "[T]he freedom to worship as one chooses . . . applies

---

[106] The "2009 Global Restrictions on Religion" study by the Pew Forum notes that social hostilities involving religion are higher in the United States than in Canada or Brazil on the Western Hemisphere; http://www.pewforum.org (accessed 5 August 2010).

to all religious groups regardless of how extreme their beliefs are."[107] Only seven years later, however, the number agreeing dropped to 56 percent.[108] Whether it is America or any other nation around the globe, the will of the majority is far too capricious to provide a safe haven for liberties.

SUMMARY

Because civil liberties are inconvenient, they are often conveniently overlooked. Liberties are inconvenient for those in power, who must acknowledge the rights of those opposing their authority, and inconvenient for sizable majorities who see little merit in the minority's position. In his glowing assessment of the young American democracy, Alexis de Tocqueville cautioned that the "main evil" he found in this new system was not the "excessive liberty" that most Europeans feared, but the "inadequate securities...against tyranny." The tyranny of which he spoke was the "tyranny of the majority."[109] His concern was the ability of the majority to impose its will without regard to the sovereignty of all people.

Religious liberties, like other civil liberties, are often inconvenient. As shown in this chapter, constitutions and legislative actions are quick to promise religious freedoms, but the price of granting these freedoms is often more than they are willing to pay. Despite strong international support and frequent constitutional guarantees, religious freedoms frequently fall prey to the interests of the state as well as other social and religious movements. We found that government regulations combine with powerful social and political forces to deny religious freedom.

All civil liberties come with a price, but as we will show in future chapters, the *absence* of religious liberties comes with a price too. Even when the stated intent is to secure social order and protect individuals, the unintended consequences of denying religious freedoms are often the opposite.

---

[107] The results are based on the First Amendment Center's annual "State of the First Amendment" survey conducted by the Center for Survey Research and Analysis at the University of Connecticut. Results from the survey were downloaded from the Association of Religion Data Archives, http://www.theARDA.com (accessed 5 August 2010).

[108] Both surveys were conducted by the Center for Survey Research and Analysis at the University of Connecticut. Results from the survey were downloaded from the Association of Religion Data Archives, http://www.theARDA.com (accessed 5 August 2010).

[109] Tocqueville ([1835] 1945:270–271).

3

Persecution

The Price of Freedom Denied

Following the end of the Cold War, there was a remarkable silence about religious persecution. The atrocities of the Jewish Holocaust during World War II were well known, and Stalin's vicious attack on religion in the Soviet Union was common knowledge, but this all seemed safely distant from a world moving away from Communism. As the 1990s progressed, however, the silence was broken. The Bosnian war quickly revealed the savagery of which humans were still capable as the world witnessed thousands of Bosnian Muslims facing brutal persecution and being driven from their homes. Religion was only one of many elements in this "ethnic cleansing," but in a growing number of instances, religion was at the core of physical persecution. As reviewed in Chapter 1, Michael Horowitz led an unlikely alliance in revealing religious persecution around the globe. But as the awareness of persecution became greater, explanations for the occurrence of violent religious persecution and conflict remained scarce.

Many of the most compelling and highly regarded explanations for conflict around the globe give scant attention to the role of religion. Moreover, religion is seldom included as a force in large cross-national studies of social conflict. Economic and political interests are typically treated as the powerful forces fueling the flames of dissent, with religion merely marking the boundaries for political alliances and economic concerns. Despite a mounting number of credible studies highlighting its significance, religion is seldom at the center of mainstream academic discussions on conflict.[1] One of the few exceptions, which we will discuss

---

[1] For a discussion of why religion is "an (at best) marginal topic" in political science, see Wald & Wilcox (2006:523).

shortly, is Samuel P. Huntington's *Clash of Civilizations* (1993, 1996). But his explanations hold assumptions that many find untenable and face research challenges on multiple fronts.[2]

Chapter 2 had much to say about how and why religious freedoms were denied, but said little about the consequences. Based on the proclamations of established religions and many governments, the regulation of religious freedom was deemed necessary for protecting individuals from dangerous religions and for securing social order. This chapter moves beyond the seemingly benign attempts to restrict religions through such means as legislation, registration, and religious bureaus. It explores the consequences of these restrictions. More specifically, we try to understand how denying religious freedoms contributes to increased levels of violent religious persecution and conflict. We contrast Huntington's clash-of-civilizations argument, in which social conflict is the result of cultural clashes across boundaries between civilizations, with our alternative theory in which we propose that it is the *attempt to restrict religious activity* – regardless of whether it is *across* civilizations or *within a* civilization – that leads to higher levels of social conflict and, specifically, higher levels of violent religious persecution. We propose that diverse religions can coexist in the same geographic space without conflict. But when the restrictions on religion become heavy and deny the religious freedoms of some or all, violent religious persecution and broader social conflict are likely.

In other words, multiculturalism with religious puralities does not lead to violence as Huntington suggests – the attempt to prevent multiculturalism and religious pluralities does. We do not deny that conflict occurs across divisions between civilizations, and we will even suggest that these divides help explain calls for greater restriction of religious freedoms, but we propose that the *mechanism* explaining violent religious persecution within countries is the social and government restriction of religion, not the civilization divide itself. In this chapter we will first review the clash-of-civilizations arguments and then examine evidence that can test whether our counterthesis is supported by realities on the ground.

THE CLASH OF CIVILIZATIONS

The clash-of-civilizations perspective is wide ranging and, at times, general to the point of being untestable. Huntington specifically states that

---

[2] See Fearon & Laitin (2003); Henderson (2004); Jenkins (2002); Midlarsky (1998); Russett, Oneal, & Cox (2000); Tipson (1997); Weede (1998).

his work is "not intended to be a work of social science" but rather a new "paradigm" for the *understanding* of the post–Cold War evolution of global politics.[3] He explains that the world was kept in equilibrium by the alliances that squared off during the Cold War, but the collapse of the Soviet bloc threw this balance out of kilter. Now, instead of geopolitical alliances, "culture and cultural identities . . . are shaping the patterns of cohesion, disintegration, and conflict in the post–Cold War world."[4] Huntington claims that these cultural identities are, at their broadest level, best conceived of as "civilizations," which have been primarily "identified with the world's great religions."[5] The way to avoid conflict (and we would add persecution) from this perspective is to keep the civilizations from clashing.

Although Huntington devotes the bulk of his arguments and examples to conflicts between countries, he explains that the "clash of civilizations . . . occurs at two levels." One level points to the civilization divides across countries and regions; the other refers to the "fault lines between civilizations" within countries or territories.[6] Huntington also describes civilizations as "culture writ large."[7] By including the values, norms, and institutions that provide a way of life for its members, his category of civilizations stresses the cultural components that hold groups together. For Huntington, the fault lines between civilizations are a source of conflict, whereas civilization homogeneity is a source of unity and peace. The centerpiece of this perspective is the thesis that "countries with similar cultures are coming together" while "countries with different cultures are coming apart."[8]

Although civilizations are sometimes associated with political units, Huntington stresses that they typically encompass multiple countries, and seldom is a country limited to representatives from only one civilization. And the presence of multiple civilizations within a single country is his point of concern. Just as civilization divides increase tensions between nations, they can also foster cultural fault lines within nations. Because they transcend political boundaries, he argues, civilization divides lead to tensions within countries that often result in conflict. Reflecting on these two levels for the West, Huntington concludes that "multiculturalism

---

[3] Huntington (1996:12).
[4] Huntington (1996:20).
[5] Huntington (1996:42).
[6] Huntington (1993:29).
[7] Huntington (1996:41).
[8] Huntington (1996:125).

at home threatens the United States and the West; universalism abroad threatens the West and the world."[9]

At the core of these civilizations is religion. Building on the work of others, Huntington notes that scholars typically identify six major contemporary civilizations: Western, Confucian-Sinic, Japanese, Hindu, Islamic, and Orthodox-Slavic. To this list he adds the Latin American and "possibly" African civilizations. Notice that his first list of six includes four of the five major world religions identified by Max Weber. The split in Christianity between Western (or Catholic and Protestant Christianity) and Orthodox-Slavic (Eastern and Russian Orthodox Christianity) accounts for the other two civilizations. He also acknowledges that Buddhism remains important in many cultures but contends that it does not comprise a distinct civilization. Thus, for civilization divides, Huntington argues that religion often provides the cultural core that distinguishes one from another, although, of course, he includes more factors than just religion.

A cursory glance at world events would offer some support for the argument. First, it points to the obvious: culture makes a difference. As mentioned earlier, religion and cultural explanations are often ignored despite overwhelming evidence to the contrary. Huntington recognizes that culture and religion can guide and organize the lives of individuals, regardless of geographic or political residency. Second, the argument has an intuitive appeal that seems to receive substantial support from several prominent global examples. Focusing only on the cultural divides within nations, the argument seems to offer plausible explanations for violent religious persecution or conflict in general. For example, over the past few decades many of the regions facing the highest levels of internal conflict centered on religious conflict (e.g., Sudan, former Yugoslavia, Israel, and India) hold civilization fault lines within their borders.

Even when we move beyond the most prominent examples, the relationship still draws support. We find that countries bordering on one of Huntington's civilization divides, or that have a civilization divide running through the country, exhibit far higher rates of violent religious persecution. As shown in Figure 3.1, all of the ten countries (100 percent) with a civilization divide within their borders had at least one case of violent religious persecution, and 60 percent had more than two hundred cases. When countries didn't have a civilization divide within their country, but bordered on at least one of the major divides, 32 percent had more than two hundred cases, and another 32 percent had at least one

9 Huntington (1996:318).

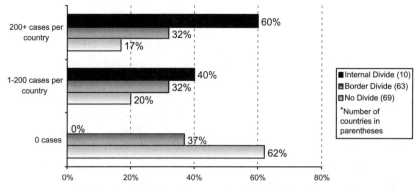

FIGURE 3.1. Civilization Divides *Compared with* Religious Persecution

case of violent religious persecution. But for countries neither bordering a civilization fault line nor harboring one within its borders, none had more than two hundred cases, and 62 percent were found to have no cases. Although this initial glance at the data suggests that civilization divides are important, and that the fault lines are often related to violent religious persecution and related forms of social conflict, when we review the more extended arguments and implications of the clash-of-civilizations perspective, the empirical support soon fades.

LIMITATIONS AND IMPLICATIONS

When the clash-of-civilizations perspective is applied to religion, it faces a number of immediate challenges. First, the clash-of-civilizations perspective fails to account for the great plurality *within* civilizations. It presumes that religions are intrinsically tied to specific societies and cultures, leading an analyst to proceed as if Arabs are Muslims, Indians are Hindu, Europeans are Christians, and so on. In his seminal work, *The Next Christendom*, Philip Jenkins notes that Huntington "refers to 'Western Christendom' as if there could be no other species."[10] However, the center of Christianity, as Jenkins demonstrates, has shifted south and east. The largest single Christian congregation today is the Yoido Full Gospel Church in Seoul, South Korea, with more than 800,000 members; and there are more Christians today in eastern Africa than in Western Europe.[11] Likewise, Vali Nasr, in his book *The Shia Revival*, documents

[10] Jenkins (2002:6).
[11] Johnson & Grim (2008).

that Islam is much more than a monolithic force, but has two very distinct divisions within. Moreover, religious hegemonies can and do change: Spain was once a Muslim land and Algeria a Christian land; India was once a Buddhist land; the United States was once a land of native beliefs; and Latin America was once indigenous, later Catholic, but may eventually be more evangelical and Pentecostal.[12] We acknowledge that religion has served as an integrative force and is interwoven into regional cultures, but history fails to reflect Huntington's simplified image of religious uniformity or stability.

Second, the clash-of-civilizations perspective must overcome the "religious explanation" problem, that is, the difficulty of explaining social behavior based on *general* religious tradition. The classic example of such a general religious explanation is Weber's *Protestant Ethic and the Spirit of Capitalism*. The Protestant ethic is intellectually captivating but empirically elusive.[13] Huntington's work is similarly captivating and has triggered a variety of responses, some of which seek to operationalize his perspective,[14] and others that critique his perspective.[15] When social conflict is attributed to cultural differences, however, explanations for social behavior quickly become obscure, vague, and unsatisfying. For instance, if the lines of conflict in China are assumed to be between Islam and Confucian-Sinic culture, then this would seem to explain the high level of persecution and violence toward Uygur Muslims in China's western province of Xinjiang. It would not, however, explain how the majority of China's Muslims (the Hui) live side by side with non-Muslim neighbors throughout China, largely without incident.[16] Aside from the government's concern over the sensitive geopolitical location of Xinjiang, which borders Russia and Central Asia, the major difference between the government's treatment of the Muslim Uygur and Hui populations is that the Chinese government places more restrictions on the religious activities of Muslim Uygurs.

The most serious challenge to the clash-of-civilizations perspective, however, is that many of its more extended arguments are not supported

[12] The Pew Forum on Religion and Public Life, 2006, "Spirit and Power: A Ten-Nation Study of Pentecostals," http://www.pewforum.org/Christian/Evangelical-Protestant-Churches/Spirit-and-Power.aspx (accessed 6 August 2010).

[13] Stark (2004).

[14] See, for example, Beckfield (2003); Henderson (2004).

[15] See, for example, Russett, Oneal, & Cox (2000); Tipson (1997); Weede (1998).

[16] Some violence has recently occurred between Hui and the Han majority, primarily over economic disparities; *Stratfor China Security Memo*, 2009, http://www.stratfor.com. Also see Gladney (1996).

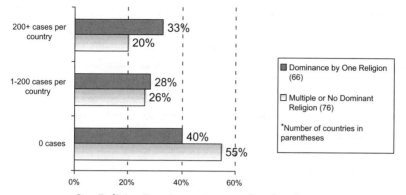

FIGURE 3.2. One Religion Dominant *Compared with* Religious Persecution

by the evidence. As quoted earlier, Huntington predicts that "countries with similar cultures are coming together" and "countries with different cultures are coming apart." The argument is clear: peace and social unity rely on religious and cultural homogeneity. When we explore this more extended argument, however, support erodes.

Prominent examples of religious conflict "within" civilizations certainly challenge the clash-of-civilizations perspective. The sectarian conflict in Iraq pits Sunni Muslims against Shia Muslims. The civil conflict in Palestine pits supporters of Hamas against those of Fatah, and members of both parties are overwhelmingly Muslim. The spring 2008 conflicts in China between the government and Tibetan Buddhists – who are part of the same Confucian-Sinic civilization as China's majority Han population – have until recently been much hotter than between the government and Uygur Muslims, who claim similar political grievances as the Tibetans. And the long-running violence between Protestants and Catholics in Northern Ireland occurred within one of Huntington's proposed civilizations as well.

Returning to our data for all nations, we find that religious homogeneity does not ensure freedom from conflict. In fact, when applied to violent religious persecution, we find the opposite to be true. Figure 3.2 shows that 33 percent of the countries dominated by only one religion have high levels of persecution compared to 20 percent where no religion dominates. Supportive of the predictions of Voltaire, Adam Smith, and David Hume, the "danger of despotism" is real when a single religion dominates, but a plurality of faiths is associated with "public tranquility."[17]

---

[17] Smith ([1776] 1976:314). See "The Pacifying Consequence of Freedoms" in chapter 1 for a more complete discussion.

Rather than pointing to the cultural diversity or specific religious cultures as the source of social conflict, we try to identify the more general mechanism that leads to conflict. That is, what are the mechanisms driving violent religious persecution, regardless of the religions, regions, or civilizations involved? We draw attention to the state's attempt to deny religious freedoms. We propose that this provides a more coherent and useful explanation for social conflict than does attributing conflict to clashes between general and irreconcilable religious traditions or civilizations. In the following sections we develop this thesis more fully and illustrate through analysis of empirical data how denying religious freedoms leads to persecution.

THE RELIGIOUS ECONOMIES PERSPECTIVE

Although the clash-of-civilizations perspective does not address if or when religion should be regulated or how a consensus should be attained, the implications are clear: religious homogeneity and consensus, like other forms of culture, should be promoted to avoid conflicts. The overall thrust of Huntington's work is that civilization clashes should be avoided to prevent conflict.[18] We acknowledge that general religious traditions help to mold and distinguish one culture from another, but viewing social conflict from a religious economies perspective allows us to identify and test whether a common mechanism operates across religious traditions. Is religious plurality the source of the conflict, or is conflict fostered by regulations that aim to ensure religious uniformity?

Whereas the clash-of-civilizations perspective highlights the merits of religious homogeneity, the religious economies perspective points to the inevitability of religious plurality and the potential dangers of attempting to regulate and control such plurality. Previous work has shown that when religious freedoms are granted, the plurality of religions will reflect the diversity of the people being served.[19] In part, this plurality not only reflects variations in ethnicity, social class, and education, but it also

---

[18] Huntington discusses religious persecution and religious liberty in a short article in Elliott Abrams's book *The Influence of Faith*. He concludes that of four possibilities he sees for reducing religious persecution and promoting religious liberty "none... is likely to be very successful" (2001:62). The last possibility is to "develop procedures for extending at least a minimum degree of toleration to non-national religions" (2001:63). Implicit within that point is the recognition of religious hegemonies over nations.

[19] See, for example, Stark & Finke (2000); Scheitle & Finke (2008, 2009).

reflects variations in religious preferences, including preferences within more experiential traditions such as Sufism within Islam and Pentecostalism within Christianity. To the extent that people seek religion, and not all do, preferences will vary. When restrictions are lifted, the diversity of religious organizations will mirror the variation in preferences. Moreover, Peter Berger and Anton Zijderveld cogently argue that a globalized world makes religious plurality inevitable and therefore religious freedom critical.[20]

As we introduced in Chapter 1, the religious economies perspective draws attention to how denying religious freedoms curtails the diversity of religious options available. Because state restrictions stifle the innovations of any religion and sharply increase the start-up costs for new faiths, religious outsiders are seldom welcome when religious freedoms are curtailed. As shown in Chapter 2, new religions are often the first targets for repression when religious freedoms are denied. Registering with the state, securing a meeting space, and a host of other start-up costs can become so burdensome as to prevent new organizations from arising. But even after religious groups are established, they can face ongoing restrictions and increased costs. For local congregations, restrictions on public worship or on the open profession of beliefs translate into increased costs of covert activities, possible litigation, and the loss of state subsidy. For potential and current members, these restrictions increase the costs of joining or remaining in the religion. Not only can they increase the financial costs of members who do not join the state's subsidized religion, but the restrictions can lead to increased social costs as well. Chapter 2 is filled with examples of the costs imposed on religions when religious freedoms are denied and the decline in the supply of religious options that results, meaning less religious plurality and choice.

But here we step beyond regulatory effects on the supply of religious options and look at the potential dangers of religious freedoms denied. Rather than pointing to the risks involved with allowing religious plurality to arise, as Huntington does, we point to the risks of attempting to curtail or eliminate such plurality.[21] Although N. J. Demerath III does not speak from the religious economies perspective, he succinctly reviews

---

[20] Berger & Zijderveld (2009).
[21] We acknowledge that most religious plurality within societies happens within broad religious traditions, i.e., within Huntington's civilizations. Indeed, the plurality that Voltaire (1980), Adam Smith (1976), and David Hume referenced was all within Western Christianity. Yet we argue that the same social science principles hold.

the relationship among religious freedom, religious plurality, and national politics:

> Some contend that a national government can only be successful when it mirrors the surrounding culture instead of countering it, although others concur . . . that the state must set the rules for cultural conflict and assure an equitable framework for religious diversity.[22]

Rather than attributing persecution to irreconcilable differences between religious traditions or more general civilizations, the religious economies perspective proposes that ensuring religious freedoms for all serves to defuse the potential volatility of religious plurality.

FROM RESTRICTIONS TO PERSECUTION

As introduced earlier, our argument focuses on two sources of restrictions on religion: government and social. We propose that to the extent that these restrictions increase, and religious freedoms are denied, violent religious persecution will also rise. But what are the motives and mechanisms that explain this relationship?

Understanding how government restrictions lead to persecution relies on two insights. First, *to the extent that a religious group achieves a monopoly and holds access to the temporal power and privileges of the state, the ever-present temptation is to persecute religious competitors openly.* It often follows that the stronger the alliance between religion and state, the more likely state powers will be used to persecute religious competitors. As we will show in Chapter 6, this is currently most evident with some nations implementing Sharia law where the state actively assists in suppressing religious competitors or other worldviews. But the examples go far beyond Sharia law. Regardless of the world religion involved or the time frame viewed, when a dominant religion forms an alliance with the state, the state's authority can be used to suppress potential religious competitors.[23] Ensuring religious freedoms reduces this form of persecution by offering privileges to all religions and power to none. No single religion can claim the authority of the state.

Second, *to the extent that religious freedoms are granted to all religions, the state will have less authority and incentive to persecute religion.* As shown in Chapter 2, even when states are not aligned with a single

[22] Demerath (2002:124).
[23] See, for example, Finke & Stark (1988); Gill (2008).

religion, they often deny religious freedoms for all or many religions, especially the freedoms of minority religions. When religious freedoms are denied and restrictions remain, the state retains *authority* over how religion is practiced and professed and religions have fewer avenues for protection from the state's authority. This is most evident in states that officially adopt scientific atheism, such as the former Soviet Union or Mao's China, but we will find it in many countries in the chapters that follow.

Religious freedoms also result in fewer *incentives* for the state to persecute religion. Because many states persecute religions to address perceived threats to the nation's traditions, culture, or security, the plurality of religions resulting from increased freedoms reduces this threat. As existing groups splinter into multiple groups and new religious groups proliferate, each religion holds a smaller percentage of the religious allegiance and is less of a threat to the state.[24] This is the same idea proposed by Adam Smith when he noted that the religions would become "sufficiently numerous" if the state would "let them all alone, and to oblige them all to let alone one another."[25] And, as we mentioned in Chapter 1, letting "alone one another" does not mean they cannot propagate their message with the intent of winning new adherents, but rather that one religion does not seek to control the other.

So far, we have highlighted two very different motives for the government's persecution of religion. The first motive points to a close religion–state alliance that attempts to curtail religious competitors, and the second points to a secular state that attempts to retain social control. Yet, regardless of the motive, they each point to our first thesis: *to the extent that governments deny religious freedoms, physical religious persecution and conflict will increase.*

But our attention is not confined to the freedoms denied by the state. Along with formal regulations, we also propose that social pressures can contribute to increased violent religious persecution and that religious freedoms can help to neutralize these pressures. Although religious cartels, anti-religious groups, and other social movements often arise in opposition to minority religions, ensuring religious freedoms can prevent their actions from leading to violent religious persecution. Recall Jefferson's conclusion: "[T]he way to silence religious disputes is to take no

---

[24] For examples on how reducing restrictions on religion results in this plurality of faiths, see Iannaccone, Finke, & Stark (1997, 2005); Lu (2008).

[25] Smith ([1776] 1976:315).

notice of them."[26] We extend this argument to suggest that when religious freedoms are protected by the government, these disputes are neutralized and the result is less violent religious persecution and conflict.

Religious freedoms serve to defuse the religious and social disputes for several reasons. First, the vigilante "policing actions" of religious and social movements are less well tolerated when religious freedoms are protected. Just as state officials often turned a blind eye to the vigilante groups persecuting African Americans in early-twentieth-century America, groups persecuting religious minorities often face little intervention from the state when religious freedoms go unprotected. For instance, as we will show in Chapter 5, religious and social groups can persecute the Baha'i in Iran with impunity. Thus, social pressures can lead to persecution either by increasing government actions against the minority religions or through the direct actions of the religious and social groups mobilized by religious prejudices.

A second reason that religious freedoms help to neutralize the social pressures leading to religious persecution is that protecting religious freedoms helps tame what de Tocqueville called the "tyranny of the majority."[27] Because harsh administrative and legislative actions often arise from social and cultural pressures, freedoms ensure a source of protection for religious groups and individuals lacking cultural and social support. When religious freedoms are protected, social and religious movements lose an avenue for swaying the state's actions against the religious minorities. Groups still mobilize in support of a dominant religion or against selected sects and cults, but they lose the ability to sway the state or to take vigilante actions against the targeted religions. Each of these leads to the second main thesis tested in this book: *to the extent that social forces deny religious freedoms, physical persecution will increase.*

Finally, religious freedoms also reduce the grievances of minority religions. When the social *and* government restrictions on the practice, profession, and selection of religion are removed, minority religions hold fewer grievances and are less likely to protest the actions of the state. Given that protests by the minority religion often result in a response from the state and the larger society, the reduction in grievances also results in a reduction of persecution. Chapter 5 will vividly illustrate how the grievances and modest protests of Falun Gong and other religions

---

[26] Jefferson ([1787] 1954:160–161).
[27] Tocqueville ([1835] 1945:270–271).

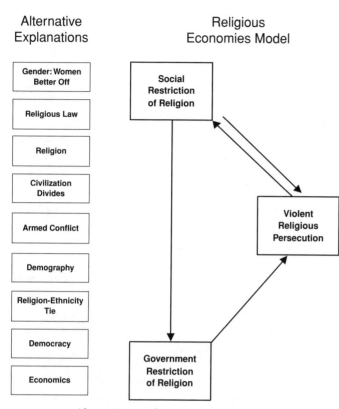

FIGURE 3.3. Alternative Explanations *Compared with* the Religious Economies Model

in China have resulted in violent religious persecution by the government. The same chapter also shows how the vigilante efforts of Hindu movements have resulted in increased grievances, protests, and ongoing conflict with a Muslim minority. Social pressures such as these naturally tend to increase the level of government restrictions on religious freedom unless safeguards protecting religious freedoms are implemented in law and in practice. When these safeguards are missing, then violent persecution of disfavored religious groups by the government and members of society is more likely to occur. Furthermore, once the government begins to persecute a particular religious group, it can reinforce social prejudices and generate social support for more restrictions as well as further vigilante persecution of minority religious groups by individuals and groups in society. Figure 3.3 offers a graphic presentation of the thesis we have proposed. We have empirical measures for each of the arguments and counterarguments pictured.

Our core thesis is that religious restrictions – composed of *social* and *government* restrictions – help explain violent *religious persecution*, which is a specific form of *social and civil conflict*. We expect that when governments ensure religious freedom and equitable treatment for all religions, less persecution will result. But powerful religions and social movements often place strong pressures on states to deny the freedoms of other groups. Governments are especially prone to these pressures when a single religious group is strong and the government is weak.[28] But when government restrictions result in increased persecution (that can often be interwoven with other social conflicts), this fuels even more calls for restrictions to control minority religions. Thus, government clashes with religion often justify a call for reduced religious freedoms, leading to more clashes, and so the cycle continues.

A sampling of the main alternative explanations for violent religious persecution and conflict are also listed in the left-hand column of Figure 3.3, including socioeconomic and political factors in addition to clashes between civilizations. The religious economies perspective acknowledges that conflict does occur across civilization divides, and we suggest that the divides help explain calls for greater restriction. But we propose that the *mechanism* explaining violent religious persecution within countries is the social and governmental restriction of religion. We also acknowledge that restrictions are not always targeted at denying religious freedoms or controlling religious minorities. Yet, even when the intent of a law or action is to increase a nation's security or preserve a religious or cultural heritage, we suggest that it can have the "unintended consequence" of violent persecution and often broader conflict. Our perspective also suggests that violent religious persecution can in turn generate more social restrictions on religion, either by enhancing preexisting prejudices or by serving to mobilize religious groups favoring or opposing the existing restrictions. As we will see in later chapters, this mobilized support will often lead to victims and violence that go beyond the religion being persecuted and draw others into the conflict.

Along with our theory and Huntington's civilization divides as possible explanations of religious persecution, perhaps the most frequently offered explanation is armed conflict. Historians and social scientists have long suggested that violent religious persecution is often "collateral damage"

---

[28] See Gill (2008) for a more complete discussion.

from a larger armed conflict.[29] Many of the remaining explanations listed in Figure 3.3 – demographics, the economy, and (the longevity of) democracy along with gender rights (women being better off) – were included in past social science work that attempted to explain social conflict in general. Finally, we consider a few additional factors related to religion that are also possible explanations for violent religious persecution and conflict: The first is the tie that frequently exists between religion and ethnicity, as was evident in the Bosnian war. A second is the use of religious law (often Sharia law) and its harsh penalties on a person who converts out of a religion. A third is the world religion that is dominant in the country, especially whether the size of the Christian, Muslim, or other population[30] is related to the level of violent religious persecution and conflict.

Before we report on our findings, we should offer two additional comments about the religious economies perspective. Not only does the religious economies theory offer sharply contrasting implications on the outcome of restricting religious freedoms, but the theory also addresses the two challenges to the civilizations perspective described earlier. First, we propose that the religious economies perspective better accounts for the great *plurality* within civilizations and religious traditions than does the civilization approach. The religious economies perspective presupposes a wide variety of religious preferences within any given society and within any given religion.[31] This presupposition also acknowledges that the various residents of the Arab world may be Sunni, Shia, or even loosely Muslim as well as Assyrian, Chaldean, Coptic, and Maronite Christians, not to mention Druze, who draw on elements of Greek philosophy and Christian Gnosticism as part of their Islamic identity. It recognizes that Chinese may be Buddhist as well as Protestant, Muslim, Catholic, Confucian, atheist, and so on.[32] Indians may be Hindu as well as Sikh, Muslim, Catholic, and Baptist. Europeans and Westerners may be one of many denominations of Christianity as well as many other religions, they may believe without belonging,[33] or they may simply lack belief.[34] Indeed,

---

[29] See Stark (2001).

[30] Relatively few countries have majority populations of religions other than Christians and Muslims (see Table 1.1).

[31] Stark & Finke (2000:193–217).

[32] Brian J. Grim, 2008, "Religion in China on the Eve of the 2008 Olympics," Pew Forum on Religion & Public Life, http://pewforum.org/Importance-of-Religion/Religion-in-China-on-the-Eve-of-the-2008-Beijing-Olympics.aspx (accessed 6 August 2010).

[33] Davie (1990).

[34] Voas & Crockett (2005).

none of the three most populous countries in Asia – China, India, and Indonesia, representing well over a third of the world's population – falls neatly into religiously oriented civilizations. They are crossroads at which all the major faiths are significantly represented.[35] Indeed, India is home to the third-largest Muslim population in the world.[36] Plurality within civilizations, what Huntington refers to as the "divisive siren calls of multiculturalism,"[37] is a social fact in much of the world today.

Second, the religious economies perspective addresses the *religious explanation problem* of the civilization perspective by analyzing specific actions and behaviors rather than general religious traditions. Whereas a civilization approach tends to reify religion and culture as constants from a bygone era, the religious economies explanation emphasizes the dynamic nature of religion within culture and analyzes the specific actions of a state and a nation's population. It also recognizes that religious loyalties can change on a large scale, as when the Christian Byzantine Empire gave way to the Muslim Ottoman Empire, or on a small scale, as when the American boxer Cassius Clay became Muhammad Ali. This does not dismiss the importance of religious beliefs or religious groups, but it draws attention to the actions of the people involved in these traditions.

Unlike Huntington's proposed "paradigm" that wasn't offered as a work of social science, our thesis can be statistically tested using cross-national data. The true test of our theory is that it must match the real world. Is it supported by the data? In future chapters we offer detailed examples for individual countries. Here we summarize our findings for all nations.

Testing the Arguments with Data

While much of this book offers theoretical arguments and case studies, one of the central contributions of our study is that we can use data from the International Religious Freedom reports reviewed in Chapters 1 and 2[38] to empirically test whether civilization clashes (as Huntington argues)

---

[35] Cf. Hefner (2000).

[36] *Mapping the Global Muslim Population*, Pew Forum, 2009, http://pewforum.org/Mapping-the-Global-Muslim-Population.aspx.

[37] Huntington (1996:307).

[38] As noted earlier, the United States is not included in the reports because the State Department does not report on regions under U.S. control. See Grim & Finke (2006, 2007).

TABLE 3.1. *Government Restriction of Religion and Violent Religious Persecution*

	Level of Violent Religious Persecution (%)		
	None	1–200	200+
Government interferes with individual's right to worship			
Yes (73)	26	30	44
No (69)	68	23	9
Restrictions on missionaries			
Prohibited or restricted (56)	29	21	50
None (86)	58	30	12
Restrictions on proselytizing, public preaching, or conversion			
Yes (56)	21	30	48
No (86)	63	24	13
The government's treatment of religious freedom is described as			
Limited or does not exist (93)	29	31	40
Legally supported and respected (49)	80	18	2
The government is described as generally respecting religious freedom			
NOT stated or exceptions mentioned (79)	23	33	44
Stated in introduction (63)	76	19	5
Government policy is described as			
Hindering free practice of religion (88)	25	34	41
Contributing to free practice (54)	82	15	4

Note: Number of countries in parentheses.

or restrictions of religious freedoms (as we propose) are at the root of violent religious persecution. In other words, does a statistical analysis of the data support the thesis we make and examples we provide? Also, it may be helpful to mention that because this section will include some discussion of statistical analysis, it will be less narrative than the rest of the book. However, we feel that explaining the analysis in easily understood terms is important because the results show whether we are justified in generalizing the theory and examples to the world at large.

Defining *violent religious persecution* as "physical displacement or physical abuse due to religion," our empirical measure of persecution includes forced relocations and imprisonments due to a person's religion as well as any form of bodily harm, ranging from physical injury to death. We begin our test of the competing arguments by looking at the relationships between persecution and our multiple measures of government and social restrictions on religion (Tables 3.1 and 3.2).

TABLE 3.2. *Social Restriction of Religion by Violent Religious Persecution and Government Restrictions*

	Level of Violent Religious Persecution (%)			Government Interferes with Individual's Right to Worship (%)	
	None	1–200	200+	Yes	No
Societal attitudes toward other religions are reported as					
Negative (81)	33	30	37	68	32
Mostly tolerant (61)	64	23	13	30	71
Societal attitudes toward conversions to other religions are reported as					
Tense (60)	20	45	79	77	23
Limited or no tension (82)	80	55	21	33	67
Attitudes and/or clerical edicts discourage proselytizing					
Yes (41)	22	34	44	90	10
No (101)	56	24	20	36	64
Established or existing religions try to shut out other religions					
Yes (74)	28	31	41	74	26
No (68)	66	22	12	27	74
There are religious social movements seeking power over other religions					
Yes (73)	26	27	47	70	30
No (69)	68	26	6	32	68

Without exception, our data provide support for the first thesis: *to the extent that governments restrict religious freedoms, physical persecution increases.* Table 3.1 reviews the relationships between violent religious persecution and a series of measures on the government's efforts to support or restrict religious freedoms. As previewed in Chapter 1, 44 percent of the governments interfering with the individual's right to worship had more than two hundred cases of violent religious persecution compared to 9 percent for those not interfering. But this relationship is neither exceptional nor even the strongest of those presented in Table 3.1. Each of the restrictions reviewed in the table holds a positive and robust relationship with violent religious persecution; that is, the presence of each type of government restriction is associated with higher levels of violent religious persecution. From the government's restrictions on specific religious behaviors (e.g., worship, preaching, or proselytizing) to the more general policies, treatment, and respect for religious liberties, the relationship remains.

We also find that violent religious persecution holds a similar relationship with the social and cultural restrictions on religion: *to the extent that social restrictions increase, physical persecution increases.* Table 3.2 reveals that there is both an attitudinal and an organizational component. The first two measures in the table (social attitudes toward other religions and attitudes toward conversions) reveal that as the public's attitude toward religious conversions or other religions becomes negative or hostile, persecution sharply rises. This relationship is especially strong for our measure of attitudes toward conversions. The final three measures (attitudes toward proseltyzing, attempts to shut out other religions, and social movements seeking to dominate public life with their perspective on religion) display the strong relationship that violent religious persecution holds with the activities of organized religious and social movements. When religious organizations or other social movements attempt to curtail the public activities and influence of other religions, violent religious persecution rises.

Table 3.2 also shows a strong relationship between social and government restrictions of religious freedoms. When the social attitudes toward other religions become more negative and social and religious movements are organized against alternative religions, the government's interference with an individual's right to worship rises sharply. As expected, the social and cultural restrictions often go hand in hand with government restrictions.

Tables 3.1 and 3.2 confirm that government and social restrictions of religion are strongly associated with violent religious persecution and with each other. Yet we still don't know how they fare with competing arguments. Are the restrictions reviewed in these tables fueling a rise in violent religious persecution or are restrictions and persecution a reflection of the cultural divides described by Huntington? And, finally, do such restrictions lead to persecution or is violent persecution leading to more restrictions on religion? Using structural equation models and our new source of data, we have addressed these questions. To keep this discussion nontechnical, we briefly describe the tests in the Appendix and recommend our previous journal articles for those interested in the details of how the competing arguments were tested.[39] Here we summarize the results.

The dominant finding is that government restriction of religious freedom holds a powerful and robust relationship with violent religious persecution. Regardless of the competing arguments considered, the government's restriction of religious freedom has a strong and highly

---

[39] See Grim & Finke (2007) for a more complete review and test of the competing models.

significant relationship with violent religious persecution. As the restrictions increase, so does violent persecution. We tested for the possibility of persecution leading to government restrictions, but this didn't hold. The best statistical models were attained when government restrictions were predicting persecution, rather than vice versa.[40] Our models consistently found that government restriction of religious freedom was a powerful predictor of violent religious persecution.

Our results on social restrictions also supported the model presented in Figure 3.3. Social restrictions were the most powerful predictor of government restrictions, and religious persecution was a strong predictor of social restrictions. Although we found evidence of social restrictions directly predicting violent religious persecution,[41] the most robust finding was that social restrictions increased persecution by increasing government restrictions. In short, we found that the cycle of persecution illustrated in Figure 3.3 is strongly supported: social restrictions lead to higher levels of government restrictions, which lead to more violent persecution, which increases the level of social restrictions. And so the cycle continues.

Support for the clash-of-civilizations thesis is far more tenuous. Once we controlled for other competing arguments, the clash-of-civilizations measures had no direct relationship with violent religious persecution. Instead, the civilization divides helped to predict the level of social restrictions. As we proposed earlier, it is not the existence of a civilization divide that predicts violent religious persecution; rather, it is the response to that divide. Our models show that civilization divides help to explain the call for social restrictions on religion, but it is enactment of government restrictions that remains the most powerful predictor of violent religious persecution.

Only two of the many other competing measures tested had a direct relationship with violent religious persecution: armed conflict and population size. The finding on population size is not particularly surprising, because we would expect the size of the population to help explain the number of persecution cases. But the finding on armed conflict does lend support to earlier work suggesting that persecution is often a by-product of larger conflicts. As will be evident in later chapters, the victims of persecution are sometimes the intended and final targets; at other times, they

---

[40] The Appendix offers additional discussion, including evidence that the impact of social restrictions may be increasing.

[41] The coefficients were highly significant, although the fit of the model dropped slightly.

are convenient targets for abuse during larger conflicts often involving religion.

For the remaining measures, their relationships with persecution are weaker, indirect (traveling through religious restrictions), and largely expected. Nations with older democracies and stronger economies have fewer government restrictions on religious freedoms, and those with higher levels of gender inequity have increased social restrictions. The one surprising result is that population growth is negatively associated with government restrictions. Rather than offer a post hoc explanation, we will simply note that the effect of population growth may be different depending on the type of growth involved.[42]

The measures of religion point to some key findings that will be explored more fully in later chapters. They each hold an indirect relationship with persecution through their close association with social and government restrictions. For example, the adoption of religious law (mostly Sharia law) and the higher the percentage of Muslims is in a country are *positively* associated with higher social restrictions, whereas higher percentages of Christians in a country are associated with lower levels of government restrictions on religion. The results also show that when religion and ethnicity are tightly interwoven, a government's restrictions of religious freedoms tend to increase. The recurring finding is that many of the religious, demographic, and political measures have indirect relationships with violent religious persecution. Rather than holding a direct relationship, they work through government and social restrictions on religious freedoms. The restrictions placed on religious freedoms remain the Rosetta stone for understanding violent religious persecution and conflict.

Finally, to verify that our findings are not being driven by regions of the world where persecution is highest, we ran the same model excluding the twenty-four countries from South Asia, the Near East, and North Africa – the countries with some of the highest levels of government and social restrictions as well as high levels of violent religious persecution. This second analysis shows *no change* in the substantive findings. The paths from social restriction to government restriction, from government restriction to violent religious persecution, and from violent religious persecution to social restriction show little change. The measure for government restrictions actually increases in strength and continues to have the strongest total effect on violent religious persecution.

---

[42] See Crenshaw, Ameen, & Christenson (1997).

In addition, we conducted a statistical test using measures from 2001, 2003, 2005, and 2007 to see if the same statistical relationship is present over time. In social science, such "panel" or "time lag" data are important for testing whether the measures from one year actually statistically predict the outcomes in later years. The results, shown in the Appendix, are strong and support our thesis that restrictions precede persecution in time. The statistical support for our thesis is robust.

Beyond the Statistical Models

The findings just reviewed used data from 143 countries to test general arguments explaining violent religious persecution, with each of the statistical findings pointing to the importance of government and social restrictions of religion. What the models don't allow, however, is a review of individual nations or a closer look at how restrictions lead to persecution. Chapters 4 and 5 will offer this more detailed review, but we close this chapter by "plotting" countries based on their levels of government and social restrictions in each country. This exercise will place the nations into meaningful categories, highlight the location of the most populous countries, and help us to select a representative sample of countries for review in later chapters.

Figure 3.4 diagrams where the countries with populations of two million or more fall on the two measures of restricting religious freedoms. The scores for each country, based on the six measures shown in Table 3.1, are added together to give each country a score showing their overall level of *government restrictions on religion*. Their government restriction score is shown by how far a country is placed toward the right side of the chart (horizontal axis).[43] The *social restriction on religion* score is based on the five items reported in Table 3.2 and is shown by how high a country is placed toward the top of the chart (vertical axis). Both the government and social restriction indexes are standardized to be on a zero-to-ten scale, with ten being high. As expected from our previous discussion, there generally is a linear relationship between the two scores, with one score tending to rise as the other rises.[44] Rather than focus on the relationship between the scores, however, we want to identify the main commonality among groups of countries that share similar levels of government and social restrictions on religion.

---

[43] For more information on how the items were selected and the scores were computed, see Grim & Finke (2006).

[44] The Pearson's *r* (or correlation) is strong and statistically significant at 0.74.

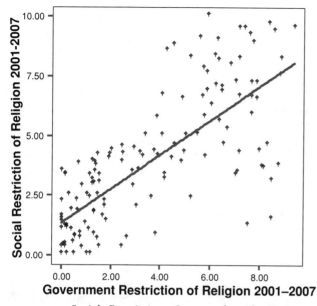

FIGURE 3.4. Social Restriction *Compared with* Government Restriction of Religion

Figure 3.5 takes the scatter plot in Figure 3.4 and identifies six main "squares" where countries tend to group, ranging from fourteen to forty-five countries. Each of the groups is composed of countries with similar social and government restriction scores, and in many cases they also hold similar scores on violent religious persecution (measured 0–10, with 10 being high). As expected, the groups of countries that score high on restricting religion also hold a high score on violent religious persecution. We will look briefly at each group and the nations composing them. The countries named in Figure 3.5 are the fourteen most populous countries, accounting for more than two-thirds (67%) of the world's population in 2009.

Sociopolitical Monopoly: For this group of thirteen countries, a single religion either holds a political and social monopoly or is battling to do so. Driven by high levels of *both* social and government restriction of religion, violent religious persecution is consistently high. This group includes some of the most frequently cited violators of religious freedoms, such as Iran, Iraq, and Sudan. Of note is that countries such as Saudi Arabia and Kuwait, which face far less scrutiny from the U.S. government, hold equally high rates, according to our coding of the State Department reports themselves.

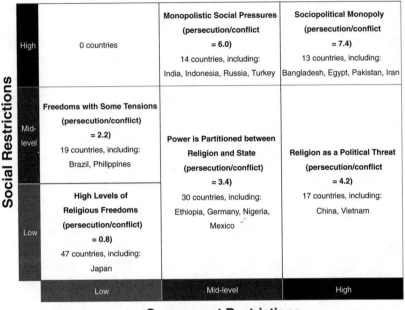

		Monopolistic Social Pressures (persecution/conflict = 6.0) 14 countries, including: India, Indonesia, Russia, Turkey	Sociopolitical Monopoly (persecution/conflict = 7.4) 13 countries, including: Bangladesh, Egypt, Pakistan, Iran
High	0 countries		
Mid-level	**Freedoms with Some Tensions** (persecution/conflict = 2.2) 19 countries, including: Brazil, Philippines	**Power is Partitioned between Religion and State** (persecution/conflict = 3.4) 30 countries, including: Ethiopia, Germany, Nigeria, Mexico	**Religion as a Political Threat** (persecution/conflict = 4.2) 17 countries, including: China, Vietnam
Low	**High Levels of Religious Freedoms** (persecution/conflict = 0.8) 47 countries, including: Japan		
	Low	**Mid-level**	**High**

Social Restrictions (vertical axis label)

Government Restrictions

* The 17 countries used as examples in Figure 3.5 are among the most populous countries and account for nearly two-in-three (62%) of the world's population in 2009.

FIGURE 3.5. Typology of Social and Government Restriction of Religion *Compared with* the Level of Violent Religious Persecution and Conflict (in parentheses), Ranging from 0 = none to 10 = high)

Religion as a Political Threat: Despite the governments of these countries scoring high on restricting religion, the countries fall in the mid- or even low range on social restrictions. For this group, religion is viewed as a political threat or, at the very least, as an undesirable nuisance, but there are fewer social pressures from other religions or the culture at large to deny religious freedoms. Including seventeen countries, many of the members are current or past Communist governments that hold an anti-religious ideology or view religion as a threat to government rule. China and Vietnam serve as two prominent members in this group. Despite the reduced social pressures, violent religious persecution remains high in this group. We should also note that lower levels of social pressure may result from the heavy hand of the government squashing civil society rather than these societies having intrinsically lower levels of social restrictions, as became evident in numerous situations following the collapse of the Soviet Union and its satellites. Certainly, this is the case in North Korea, where any social restrictions that may naturally occur are overwhelmed by the totalitarian nature of the regime.

Monopolistic Social Pressures: For many countries within this group, the government attempts to hold a neutral or at least less antagonistic view toward religion when compared to the first two groups; that is, their government restriction scores do not fall in the far right-hand column. This attempt at neutrality, however, is often challenged by religious or social groups calling for more restrictions on select groups. India and Indonesia are two obvious examples, but Russia and Turkey also fall into this group. In each of these eleven countries, governments are facing strong pressures to increase restrictions on selected groups. Not surprisingly, the level of violent religious persecution is nearly as high for this group as it is for the sociopolitical monopoly.

Power Is Partitioned between Religion and State: This group of thirty countries represents the middle of the scatter plot. Government and social restrictions consistently fall in the middle range for this group. The pressures for maintaining at least some restrictions on religion in these countries vary widely, from current secular and religious concerns to the preservation of a past religious culture. Religious freedoms granted in these nations are often graduated, with religions that support the state and the local culture receiving more freedoms.[45] France is one of the most prominent countries in this group, but Nigeria and Mexico are also members.

Freedoms with Some Tensions: Scoring low on government restrictions and in the middle range of social restrictions on religion, these countries occupy a transitional territory. Religious freedoms are granted by the government but, at the same time, there is an elevated level of social restrictions. Restrictions may be rising or falling. Although these countries generally have few government restrictions that inhibit the practice, profession, or selection of religion, the level of social restrictions is elevated. This elevation may be the result of some extraordinary influence, such as an incident of religion-related terrorism, or even just the natural tensions between religious groups or their members as they vie for influence in society. At the same time, several of these countries appear to be moving steadily toward greater religious freedoms. Brazil and Italy are two examples where many of the formal state restrictions have been lifted and social pressures are increasingly modest. The level of violent

---

[45] See Ferrari (2003:11) for a discussion of the "selective cooperation" that the state shows toward religion in many European countries.

religious persecution in this group of countries remains slightly higher than the countries with uniformly high levels of religious freedoms, but it is on average far lower than any of the other groups in Figure 3.5.[46]

High Levels of Religious Freedoms: The countries with a high level of religious freedoms represent an opposite extreme from the sociopolitical monopolies, scoring low on both the government and social restrictions on religion. For these countries, the restrictions that frequently inhibit the practice, profession, or selection of religion are largely removed. Of the six groups shown in Figure 3.5, this group holds the most members (forty-seven countries) and by far the lowest level of violent religious persecution.

One striking feature of looking at countries in these categories is that it becomes obvious that the groups in each category represent a variety of countries – rich and poor, northern and southern, allies and adversaries, Muslim-majority and Christian-majority, and so on. And when we organize the countries into these crude categories, the same relationships we found in the more advanced structural equation models still hold. Government and social restrictions are tightly interwoven, and both are associated with higher levels of violent religious persecution and conflict.

CONCLUSIONS

So, what have we learned? The key finding is that *government and social restrictions of religion are the mechanisms through which social, political, economic, and religious differences make a difference.* Civilization divides, the dominant religion, and other social and political forces are influential to the extent that they shape the restrictions placed on religion. But the restrictions placed on religion – both government and social restrictions – are the driving force behind higher levels of violent religious persecution and conflict. Supportive of the religious economies model,

---

[46] Although the State Department reports do not cover the United States, coding managed by Brian Grim that looked at sources beyond the State Department places the United States in the "Freedoms with Some Tensions" category: see the Pew Forum's "Global Restrictions on Religion," 2009, http://pewforum.org/Government/Global-Restrictions-on-Religion.aspx. As discussed at the end of the previous chapter, there is a fair degree of religion-related social pressure in the United States. This has been demonstrated by the number of religiously biased hate crimes reported by the FBI as well as by changes in attitudes toward basic religious freedoms measured in the annual survey of the First Amendment Center.

violent religious persecution and conflict increase to the extent that governments place restrictions on religion.

What the models and measures we have presented don't show us, however, is how the restrictions contribute to violent religious persecution and conflict or how the government and social restrictions on religion combine to fuel such persecution and conflict. To better understand the interactions between government and social restrictions and how these interactions contribute to increased violent religious persecution and conflict, we take another step closer and explore these interactions within countries through a series of case studies.

4

Case Studies

Japan (High Levels of Religious Freedoms), Brazil (Freedoms with Some Tensions), and Nigeria (Partitioned Religion–State Power)

Previous chapters have shown that violent religious persecution rises as religious liberties fall. Or, stated more positively: when governments ensure religious freedoms for all, there is less violent persecution. Reviewing the empirical data,[1] we have shown that when religious freedom is routinely denied, violent religious persecution and conflict are common. We also found that when a single religious group is dominant and holds access to the temporal power and privileges of the state, the ever-present temptation is to persecute religious competitors openly. Conversely, when religious freedoms are granted to all religions, and power to none, the state (and the culture as a whole) has less *authority* and *incentive* to persecute religion; consequently, violent religious persecution and conflict are less likely.

OVERVIEW OF CASE STUDIES

What the summary statistics of previous chapters fail to do, however, is to tell the stories of individual countries. In this chapter and the one that follows, we tell the stories of six countries. The case studies will look at how violent persecution is decreased by granting all individuals and religious groups the freedom to believe or not believe, to speak and worship openly (including proselytizing and converting), and to administer their religious affairs without government and social restrictions. This small sample of countries represents more than 45 percent of the world's population and includes countries that vary widely in their level of

[1] As described in previous chapters.

religious freedom (see Table 4.1).[2] Some have extensive freedoms; others have relatively few. For some countries, the restrictions on religion are initiated by the government; for others, the restrictions are initiated by social pressures – often other religions. Each of the stories will help to explain how and why religious freedoms are denied and how and why violent religious persecution results.

We begin this chapter by offering an extended historical discussion of one of the most dramatic cases of a country going from nearly no religious freedom to extensive religious freedom in the twentieth century – Japan. As we will show, the religious freedoms in Japan have resulted in dramatically lower levels of violent religious persecution. We will then look at the case of Brazil – the second-most populous country in the Western Hemisphere after the United States. Brazil's process of granting religious freedoms has been more gradual, with some religious and social tensions still lingering, but the outcomes have been the same: lower levels of violent religious persecution. We conclude by looking at Nigeria, the most populous country in Africa. Power in Nigeria is partitioned between religious structures and the state, resulting in higher levels of violent religious persecution, particularly at the hands of non-state actors, than in the first two case studies.

In the next chapter we review three countries where religious freedoms are routinely denied and violent religious persecution is at a high level: China, India, and Iran. But the countries vary in how and why religious restrictions are enacted. For China, as we do for Japan, we offer an extended historical backdrop to explain why religion is viewed as a potential political threat and is strictly regulated by the state, despite relatively few social pressures to do so. We then discuss China's huge neighbor to the southwest, India, where there has been significant social support to establish a religious monopoly. Although the Hindu monopolization of public life has been rejected by the national government, it has found support from local governments, which has increased the level of violent persecution. We then turn to Iran, a country where social pressures and government restrictions are both high and where one religious group monopolizes both social and political life. These social and government restrictions result in religious competitors being strictly controlled and violently persecuted. This brief discussion of Iran leads into Chapter 6, where we offer an extended discussion of how and why restrictions on

---

[2] The total population of these six countries was more than 3 billion in 2009. Each of the countries falls into one of the six "types" of countries reviewed at the end of Chapter 3.

TABLE 4.1. *Religious Freedom Typology with Countries Profiled in Chapters 4 and 5 Highlighted (17 Most Populous Countries Shown; see pages 52–60 for U.S.)*

Country	Typology	Government Restriction of Religion, 2001–2007 (0–10, 10 = high)	Social Restriction of Religion, 2001–2007 (0–10, 10 = high)	Level of Violent Religious Persecution (0–10, 10 = high)	Population in Millions, 2009
Japan[a]	High levels of religious freedoms	1.8	2.0	2.6	127.2
Brazil[a]	Freedoms with tensions	0.8	2.8	1.0	193.7
Philippines	Freedoms with tensions	1.5	4.2	5.0	92.0
Nigeria[a]	Power partition	5.8	6.7	8.0	154.7
Mexico	Power partition	3.8	5.8	7.6	109.6
Ethiopia	Power partition	4.1	6.7	5.6	82.8
Germany	Power partition	3.0	4.4	2.6	82.2
China[b]	Religion as threat	8.3	4.6	10.0	1345.8
Vietnam	Religion as threat	8.1	3.6	6.0	88.1
India[b]	Monopolistic social pressures	5.9	10.0	9.6	1198.0
Indonesia	Monopolistic social pressures	6.3	9.0	8.6	230.0
Russia	Monopolistic social pressures	6.2	7.1	5.6	140.9
Turkey	Monopolistic social pressures	5.2	8.3	3.0	74.8
Iran[b]	Sociopolitical monopoly	8.6	9.4	7.6	74.2
Pakistan	Sociopolitical monopoly	8.3	9.7	6.6	180.8
Bangladesh	Sociopolitical monopoly	6.8	8.0	7.0	162.2
Egypt	Sociopolitical monopoly	7.7	8.9	8.0	83.0

[a] Country profiled in Chapter 4.
[b] Country profiled in Chapter 5.

religious freedom lead to higher violent religious persecution in many (but not all) Muslim-majority countries.

JAPAN: CASE STUDY OF EMBRACING RELIGIOUS FREEDOMS

Japan is one of forty-five countries or autonomous territories with a population of two million or more[3] that hold high levels of religious freedoms. This means that roughly one-quarter of the world's countries are religiously deregulated, including nearly 700 million people, or accounting for approximately one in ten of the world's total population. These countries are generally characterized by having few government and social restrictions that inhibit the practice, profession, or selection of religion. As discussed in the previous chapter, these countries by far have the lowest level of violent religious persecution. Deregulated countries are present in almost every region in the world, including Asia (Australia, Hong Kong, South Korea, and Taiwan), Africa (Angola, Madagascar, and Mozambique), Europe (Denmark, Finland, Portugal, and Sweden), and the Western Hemisphere (Canada, Chile, and Costa Rica). Countries in this group can be rich (New Zealand), poor (Haiti), predominantly Muslim (Albania, Mali, and Senegal), predominantly Catholic (Ireland), former Communist (Czech Republic), and even plagued by conflict (Sierra Leone). The common feature of these very diverse countries is that they have governments and societies that generally respect religious freedom. Table 4.2 shows each of the forty-five countries in this category with their average government restriction scores, social restriction scores, and violent religious persecution for July 2000 through June 2007, along with their total populations.

Although each of these country's paths to religious freedom is unique, the example of Japan, the world's tenth-most populous country, is particularly interesting for several reasons. First, Japan evolved from being a country with severely violent religious persecution to one having virtually no persecution. The example of Japan shows clearly how the level of regulation directly affects the level of violent religious persecution and conflict. Second, Japan illustrates how the direct intervention of the United States (following World War II) played a positive role in developing a legal, social, and political framework for religious freedom. This is a useful juxtaposition to the deterioration of religious freedom that followed the

---

[3] Countries with populations of 2 million or more represent 99.6% of the world's total population.

TABLE 4.2. *High Levels of Religious Freedoms*

Countries	Average Government Restriction of Religion Level (July 2000– June 2007) (0–10, 10 = high)	Average Social Restriction of Religion Level (July 2000– June 2007) (0–10, 10 = high)	Average Persecution Level (July 2000– June 2007) (0–10, 10 = high)	Population in Millions (2009)
All countries	0.7	1.1	0.8	688.6
Albania	0.6	0.8	1.6	3.2
Angola	1.1	2.4	1.0	18.5
Australia	0.6	1.8	2.0	21.3
Benin	0.0	0.0	0.0	8.9
Bolivia	0.1	0.4	0.0	9.9
Burkina Faso	0.2	1.1	0.6	15.8
Burundi	0.6	0.7	2.6	8.3
Canada	0.4	1.8	2.0	33.6
Chile	1.8	1.4	0.6	17.0
Congo, Republic of the	0.0	1.5	0.0	66.0
Costa Rica	0.8	0.7	0.6	4.6
Czech Republic	0.3	2.5	0.0	10.4
Denmark	1.7	1.6	1.0	5.5
Dominican Republic	1.3	0.8	0.0	10.1
Ecuador	0.1	0.4	0.6	13.6
El Salvador	0.8	0.3	0.6	6.2
Finland	1.3	1.7	0.6	5.3
Haiti	0.6	2.3	0.6	10.0
Honduras	1.5	0.3	0.0	7.5
Hong Kong	0.8	0.9	1.6	7.0
Hungary	1.0	2.5	1.0	10.0
Ireland	0.0	0.3	0.0	4.5
Jamaica	1.3	1.8	0.6	2.7
Japan	1.8	2.0	2.6	127.2
Korea, South	0.5	0.5	3.6	48.3
Lesotho	0.0	0.0	0.0	2.1
Madagascar	1.5	0.6	1.6	19.6
Malawi	0.0	2.2	0.6	15.3
Mali	0.0	1.3	2.0	13.0
Mozambique	1.0	1.3	0.0	22.9
Namibia	0.0	0.0	0.0	2.2
New Zealand	0.1	0.3	0.0	4.3
Norway	1.5	2.5	0.6	4.8

Countries	Average Government Restriction of Religion Level (July 2000– June 2007) (0–10, 10 = high)	Average Social Restriction of Religion Level (July 2000– June 2007) (0–10, 10 = high)	Average Persecution Level (July 2000– June 2007) (0–10, 10 = high)	Population in Millions (2009)
Panama	1.1	1.0	0.0	3.5
Papua New Guinea	0.0	1.6	0.0	6.7
Paraguay	0.1	1.2	0.0	6.3
Portugal	1.2	0.0	0.0	10.7
Senegal	0.0	0.0	0.6	12.5
Sierra Leone	0.2	1.2	1.6	5.7
Sweden	0.4	1.0	2.0	9.2
Taiwan	0.2	0.0	1.0	23.1
Togo	1.0	0.0	0.0	6.6
Uruguay	0.0	1.0	0.0	3.4
Venezuela	1.7	2.2	1.0	28.6
Zambia	0.5	0.0	2.0	12.9

Note: Government restriction of religion ≤2.13; social restriction of religion ≤2.52.

U.S. invasion and occupation of Iraq[4] in 2003, which will be discussed in Chapter 6. One main difference is that the legal provisions for religious freedom in Iraq are contradictory as in Afghanistan, but in Japan they are clear. And third, the Japanese government's and the public's measured response to a severe case of Buddhist-related violence in 1995, which sorely tested the public commitment to religious freedom, seems to have consolidated religious freedom in the country, despite some indications to the contrary.

Table 4.3 and Figure 4.1 offer a brief general profile of Japan.

Japan's Historical Record of Restrictions

Since the end of World War II, Japan has had one of the lowest levels of violent religious persecution among the world's most populous countries. However, this has not always been the case. Japan is a remarkable example of a country turning from a long history of social and government

---

[4] Brian J. Grim, 2008, "The Plight of Iraq's Religious Minorities," Pew Forum on Religion & Public Life, May 15, http://pewforum.org/The-Plight-of-Iraqs-Religious-Minorities.aspx (accessed 6 August 2010).

TABLE 4.3. *A Profile of Japan*

1.8/10 – low	Government restriction of religion score (average July 2000–June 2007)
2.0/10 – low	Social restriction of religion score (average July 2000–June 2007)
2.6/10 – low	Violent religious persecution and conflict (average July 2000–June 2007)
Democracy	2010 political typology (1950 Protectorate, 1900 Constitutional Monarchy) (Freedom House, 2000)
127.2 million	Population (United Nations, 2009)
$34,200	Per capita GDP adjusted for purchasing power parity ($PPP, CIA, 2008)
82.1 years	Life expectancy at birth (CIA, 2009 est.)
Religious Adherence (World Religion Database, 2010 est.)	

FIGURE 4.1. Religious Adherence in Japan

Japanese Constitutional Provisions for Religious Freedom (adopted May 3, 1947)	**Article 14.** All of the people are equal under the law and there shall be no discrimination in political, economic or social relations because of race, creed, sex, social status or family origin.
	Article 20. Freedom of religion is guaranteed to all. No religious organization shall receive any privileges from the State, nor exercise any political authority. No person shall be compelled to take part in any religious act, celebration, rite or practice. The State and its organs shall refrain from religious education or any other religious activity.
	Article 21. Freedom of assembly and association as well as speech, press and all other forms of expression are guaranteed. No censorship shall be maintained, nor shall the secrecy of any means of communication be violated.

Article 89. No public money or other property shall be expended or appropriated for the use, benefit or maintenance of any religious institution or association, or for any charitable, educational or benevolent enterprises not under the control of public authority.
(Located using Constitution Finder, University of Richmond: http://confinder.richmond.edu/; taken from: http://www.kantei.go.jp/foreign/constitution_ and_ government_of_japan/constitution_e.html)

---

restrictions on religion to religious freedom. This deregulation of religion and granting of religious freedoms has resulted in dramatically low levels of violent religious persecution.

Historically, the motivation for restricting religion in Japan has been to establish political control by ensuring social uniformity. Religions that presented an alternative international "organic unity"[5] were viewed as threats to social and national cohesion, providing Japanese governments of old an incentive to regulate such religions. The Japanese historical response to one particular religion that offered an "alternative international organic unity" – Christianity – shows how social and government regulation of religion interacted to promote violent religious persecution in previous centuries.

Christianity initially entered Japan at a time when central government control of Japan was weak and Japanese society was looking for relief from a long sequence of wars. From the mid-1400s through the end of the 1500s, Japan was beset by a series of social, political, and military conflicts known as the Warring States' period (or *sengoju jidai*). But this chaotic period was also a time of receptivity to new ideas and social expressions. The centralized Japanese state was weakened to the point that the social conformity that often characterizes Japanese culture gave way to more localized socioeconomic collectives. An example of the social receptivity during this period was the spontaneous eruption of *fūryū* dancing ("drifting on the wind") in the streets among the general population.[6] It was a time when the "stability of the preceding era had faded and the demand for a new order had not yet coalesced."[7] During those years, government and social restrictions on religion were lax.

---

[5] Norihisa (1996:65).
[6] Berry (1994).
[7] Norihisa (1996:64).

Jesuit missionary Francis Xavier introduced Christianity to Japan in 1549, which led to a variety of European Catholic orders competing to establish followings in Japan. Within sixty-five years, the number grew to between 300,000 and 500,000 Christians,[8] reaching a percentage (nearly 2.5 percent) that exceeds current levels. Some even estimate that the number of Christians in Japan was as high as 760,000 by the 1630s.[9]

However, the demand for a unified cultural identity returned. In 1587, Toyotomi Hideyoshi (1536–1598) unified Japan and brought an end to the Warring States' period.[10] One strategy for unity was that the government linked what it called "subversive creeds," such as Christianity, to possible Western attempts to invade and colonize Japan, stoking societal fears toward this religious newcomer.[11] Strict religious restrictions were promulgated in 1587; Hideyoshi issued an edict expelling all Christian missionaries. Despite this, Franciscan missionaries were able to enter the country in 1593, and the Jesuits remained active in western Japan. In 1597, supported by the power of the edict, Hideyoshi had twenty-six Christians crucified in Nagasaki (twenty Japanese and six foreign missionaries). The initial regulation justified the persecution, which in turn led to even harsher government restrictions. Hideyoshi ordered *all* Christians to renounce their faith or face exile or death.

Although Hideyoshi died in 1598, the restrictions against Christianity continued to have force and were legitimized through nearly two centuries of reiteration of edicts and active enforcement. That the government pronounced a religion evil made it easier for social enforcement of the edicts. An official government notification in 1711 (reproduced in the box) indicates how social cooperation was enlisted, leading to ongoing violent persecution and the virtual eradication of Christianity from Japan for many years.

---

[8] Boxer (1951).

[9] Moffett (1998:95) – 1595–1596: "137 Jesuit missionaries (only 10 legally); 660 seminarians and catechists, and 300,000 Christians; 10 Christian daimyos. 1609: Jesuits reported 220,000 Christians under their care in Japan; 1614: 300,000 to 500,000 Christians in Japan; population of Japan was about 20 million. Other estimates include Ebisawa & Ouchi (1970:54). Around 1580, the numbers of believers was 350,000; around 1600, there were more than 600,000 believers. In Miyazaki (2003:7), in 1559 the number of Kirishitan converts stood at around 6,000; in 1569 they numbered about 20,000; and in 1579...they had increased to 130,000; by 1601...the number had increased approximately 300,000. Finally...the number of converts in the early 1630s totaled 760,000."

[10] Berry (1982).

[11] Norihisa (1996).

OFFICIAL NOTIFICATION, FEBRUARY 1711, OFFICE OF
THE GOVERNOR

The Christian faith, as heretofore, is strictly prohibited. Anyone
knowing of a suspect shall report to the authorities without fail.
The following shall be given in reward:

> To an informer on a Father [i.e., Priest]: 300 pieces of silver
> To an informer on a Brother: 200 pieces of silver
> To an informer on a Retrovert: 200 pieces of silver
> To an informer on a Catechist or lay Christian: 100 pieces of silver

Even if the informer himself is a member of a Christian household,
he shall be rewarded with goods in the value of 100 pieces of silver.
If anybody sheltering such persons is found out by information by
others, severe punishment will be inflicted on him, on his family,
on the four other households with which his household is legally
bound, and even on the representative of the district.

Source: Tamaru & Reid (1996: center plate 30).

Japan was not only closed to Christians, but to most foreigners as
well. That was, however, until U.S. Navy commodore Matthew Perry
forced Japan's Meiji government to open to the West with the Treaty of
Kanagawa in 1854. The ability of the United States to force this concession was in part made possible by Japan's having entered into another
period of weakened central power.[12] But the concession to open ports to
foreigners did not radically change the government's disposition toward
religion. By the late 1860s, the Meiji government established State Shinto
as a religious practice that would unite the population in the shared belief
of the divinity and authority of the emperor, and the ban on Christianity
and persecution of known adherents continued.

However, a challenge came to the consolidation of State Shinto with
the discovery of more than three thousand secret Christians near Nagasaki
who had survived the many years of bans and violent persecutions.[13]
Drawing on the existing ban on Christianity, along with the new regulations making Shinto the Meiji state religion, officials in Nagasaki ordered

---

[12] Treat (1918).
[13] Norihisa (1996).

the persecution (physical exile) of the Nagasaki Christians. Western diplomats, now present in the country, raised loud cries of protest. Joining their protest in 1872 was Mori Arinori, one of the first Japanese to study abroad and one of the first Japanese diplomats to the United States, who wrote a booklet in response, *Religious Freedom in Japan*.[14] Mori Arinori's specific arguments for religious freedom are also embodied in a separate document he wrote called "The Religious Charter of the Empire of Dai Nippon." He argued that one clear incentive for loosening the restrictions was the desire by the Japanese government to be an accepted member of countries deemed "civilized." The Meiji government did respond to the external pressure and removed the public signs and markers that proscribed Christianity, and in 1873, it ended official prohibitions against Christianity and its propagation.[15] The Meiji constitution of February 11, 1889, went so far as to provide a qualified statement of religious freedom: "Japanese subjects shall, within limits not prejudicial to peace and order, and not antagonistic to their duties as subjects, enjoy freedom of religious belief."[16] This qualified yet stated freedom, which was supported by voices such as Mori Arinori, seems to have coincided with less regulation and a concomitant reduction of violent persecution of Christians. A report by the World Missionary Conference of 1910 concluded that "Japanese Christians have secured for themselves a firm position in society, and are not persecuted. They are able to protest if there should be injustice of any kind: and it would be unwise for foreigners to interfere on their behalf."[17]

This breath of freedom was short lived. The promised freedoms were soon denied, State Shinto was co-opted, and dissenting voices were silenced. The constitution not only qualified the promised freedom, it contradicted the very concept of religious freedom by recognizing the emperor as a "sacred and inviolable" head of state, the chief military authority as well as the religious leader of the country.[18] Despite a brief period of freedom, the groundwork for further violent persecution was being laid, and not just of Christianity. Ordinances passed in 1900 and 1908 gave police surveillance power over religion and the authority to suspend "undesirable" religious activities. Leaders of such religious groups were arrested. One incident in 1935 involved 550 police attacking the

---

[14] Arinori ([1872] 2004).
[15] Van Sant (2004:152).
[16] World Missionary Conference (1910:5).
[17] World Missionary Conference (1910:6).
[18] Tsuyoshi (1996).

headquarters and temple of the Omotokyo Shinto sect, reducing "its buildings to pieces no larger than one Japanese foot, lest larger pieces be used to rebuild these edifices."[19]

The increased restriction of religion also included laws, such as the 1939 Religious Organizations Law, which provided a legal structure for regulating not only religion in Japan but also religion in the countries it occupied during World War II. This ensured that religious groups would not raise their voices against the designs of the empire, which, as the history of World War II tragically demonstrates, included conflict resulting in the subjugation and violent persecution of many throughout East Asia and the Pacific. A fact few have commented on is the clear connection between the lack of religious freedom in Japan and its restrictions on religious groups abroad. This religious regulation that extended beyond Japan is discussed later in the section on China in Chapter 5.

The revised Public Security Preservation Law of 1941 gave the state authority to destroy any religious group that propagated beliefs in contradiction to emperor worship. Some were jailed, but the vast majority of religious groups, including Buddhists and Christians, adjusted and kept under the radar to escape violent persecution.[20] In doing so, they could offer no voice of protest against Japan's imperial and violent conquests.

Embracing Religious Freedom

Japan's unconditional surrender on August 15, 1945, ending World War II, placed Japan under the direct administration of the Allied powers. Japan's postwar legal system was established during the Allied occupation. On December 15, 1945, the occupation administration issued an order known as the Shinto Directive, which laid out three principles on religion for postwar Japan: "religious freedom, strict separation of religion and state, and eradication of militaristic and ultranationalistic thought."[21] On December 28, 1945, the restrictive Religious Organizations Law was abrogated and the Religious Corporation Ordinance was promulgated in order to provide a nonrestrictive legal basis for religious organizations to operate, with the sole restriction being that a religious organization notifies the government of its formation.[22]

---

[19] Hardacre (1989:127).
[20] Sumimoto (2000).
[21] Tsuyoshi (1996:118).
[22] Tsuyoshi (1996:119).

The basic laws promising religious freedom in Japan today are contained in the 1946 constitution, which went into effect on May 3, 1947 (see Table 4.3). Unlike the Meiji constitution of 1889, the promise of religious freedom is clear and unqualified. Although article 28 of the Meiji constitution (1889) claimed a right to "freedom of religious belief," no such freedom existed in practice. In her study *Shinto and the State, 1868–1988*, Helen Hardacre concludes that prior to World War II "Japanese subjects were free to believe in a religion but not necessarily to practice it publicly."[23] Moreover, she reports that participation in Shinto shrine observances, the religious observances condoned by the state, "had an obligatory character." The new constitution, however, explicitly promises that "freedom of assembly and association as well as speech, press and all other forms of expression are guaranteed," and that "[n]o religious organization shall receive any privileges from the State, nor exercise any political authority."[24]

This understanding of religious freedom in Japan goes well beyond the legal revisions. Following World War II, religion was not only deregulated in the *laws* of the country, but among the *populace* as well in that they accepted that the emperor relinquished holding temporal and religious power simultaneously. In other words, the populace accepted both the disestablishment of religion and the principle of religious freedoms for all. The importance of public acceptance was presaged in Mori Arinori's 1872 brochure on religious freedom: "While the laws are the best protection for our liberty, its greatest security depends wholly upon the character and potency of our popular education."[25]

These freedoms opened the floodgates for new religions to arise. The period immediately following 1945 is called *kamigami no rasshu awa*, the "rush hour of the gods." It was said that "new Religions rose like mushrooms after a rainfall."[26] By 1949, 403 new religious groups were founded, and 1,546 other groups established independence through secession from the shrines, temples, or churches to which they had previously belonged. In contrast, only 31 religious groups had received official recognition in the decades before 1945 – thirteen Shinto sects, twenty-eight Buddhist denominations, and two Christian groups.[27]

---

[23] Hardacre (1989:131).
[24] Hardacre (1989:131).
[25] Arinori ([1872] 2004:147).
[26] McFarland (1967:4).
[27] Tsuyoshi (1987). Also see Finke (1997).

Despite all of these new religions arising, however, violent religious persecution has been extremely rare in Japan since 1945. Whereas the Soka Gakkai association was suppressed in 1930 for refusing to worship talismans from the Ise Shrines and its leader, Makiguchi Tsunesaburo, was arrested and later died in prison, it now claims 8 million members in Japan and is highly visible in the public arena.[28]

But the public response to and acceptance of religious freedom was put to the ultimate test in the late 1990s, as the following section shows.

Pacific Consequences of Maintaining Religious Freedoms

In Tokyo's early morning rush hour on March 20, 1995, five members of the Aum Shinrikyo (Aum) religious group boarded different subway lines that headed into the center of the city. Shortly after 7:45 A.M., each person cut open plastic bags of the deadly nerve agent sarin and then fled the subway. At approximately 8:00 A.M. the five trains approached the downtown Kasumegaseki and Nagatachō subway stations, which serve the government district of the city. The sarin acted quickly, causing twelve deaths and hundreds of illnesses. Fortunately, the sarin used in the attack was not pure, resulting in many fewer deaths than might have occurred had the sarin been more effectively weaponized.[29]

At the time of the attack, Aum had tens of thousands of members in several countries and assets estimated at $1 billion (U.S.). It was not just an organized social group; it was also a religious one, propagating supernatural explanations of existence and meaning. The Aum's doctrines draw on a Japanese Buddhist perspective of cosmic history, which divides time into three millennial periods.[30] The first millennium since the death of the Buddha was an ideal age of peace and harmony when people followed the "perfect law" (*shoho*) of the Buddha. The second millennium was a step removed from the ideal. Faith was weaker and perfunctory, and the perfect law turned into "imitated law" (*zoho*). The third millennium is a time of apostasy, of the "degenerated law" (*mappo*), the age we are in today. For Aum, the Japanese government was an impediment to the realization of the religious destiny of Asia and the world, which involved

a massive war between the West, led by the United States, and the "Buddhist world" led by Asia. The combatants would use nuclear, chemical, and

---

[28] See Soka Gakkai's Web site: http://www.sgi.org/ (accessed 6 August 2010).
[29] Pangi (2002).
[30] Metraux (1995). Also see Kitagawa (1966:366).

bacteriological weapons. Japan would be completely destroyed by American air attacks, but those who have achieved enlightenment through Aum would survive.[31]

Thus, the motives for the attack were based on religious teachings and were implemented by the religious group Aum.

The response of the Japanese government was instructive for both what it *did* and what it *did not* do. The actions taken were many. First, immediate action was taken against all individuals involved in or supporting criminal behaviors. Second, based on the Religious Corporation Ordinance, Aum's status as a religious organization was revoked.[32] Third, a new law authorized the surveillance of Aum. The Public Security Investigation Agency could now "enter Aum facilities without notice or warrant."[33] Overall, the government made strong attempts to prevent any future criminal activity, but it stopped short of criminalizing religious behavior.

The actions that the Japanese government *did not* take are perhaps even more instructive than the actions taken. First, they did not outlaw or ban Aum. As noted, members guilty of criminal acts were arrested, and the group as a whole fell under increased surveillance, but the group was not forced to disband. Second, the government did not pass general laws targeting all religious groups. Recall the reaction of France, Germany, and Belgium when the "Order of the Solar Temple" committed mass suicide in 1994 (see Chapter 2). Using vague and ill-defined definitions of "cult-like" activity, 173 religious groups were identified as dangerous and became the targets of local officials who were given discretion in identifying and policing these groups. Third, they avoided much of the public hysteria over the fear of religious groups brainwashing their members.[34] In particular, the courts continued to protect minority religions from the tyranny of the majority. In 2000 the Tottori District Court

---

[31] Metraux (1995:1152).

[32] Aum changed its name to Aleph in 2000, which seemed not only to have religious significance but was the name used by other organizations in Japan as well. The Japanese public was further alarmed in 2001 when an Aum plot was uncovered to set off explosives in Tokyo as part of a plan to free the mastermind of the sarin attacks, Shoko Asahara, who is sentenced to death. See Calvin Sims, 2000, "Japan Sect's Name Change Brings Confusion and Fear," *New York Times*, January 24, http://www. nytimes.com/2000/01/24/world/japan-sect-s-name-change-brings-confusion-and-fear. htm (accessed 6 August 2010).

[33] Richardson & Edelman (2004:366).

[34] As reviewed in Chapter 2, a long line of research has refuted the arguments that "cults" have the powers of mental manipulation or brainwashing. See Shupe & Bromley (1980); Barker (1984); Stark & Bainbridge (1985).

ruled against a mother who had kidnapped her daughter from the Unifi-cation Church (so-called Moonies), hired the services of a deprogrammer, and held the daughter against her will until she renounced her religious beliefs.[35] Brainwashing remains the argument of choice for many in the media and the general public when explaining the growth of minority religions, but this explanation was not used by the Japanese government to justify taking actions against such groups.[36]

Richardson and Edelman make the following comparative observation between the case of Aum in Japan and Falun Gong in China:

In Japan the basic democratic character of the society has been demonstrated, even as great concern developed within the society over certain of the new reli-gions. Whereas Chinese officials reacted quite swiftly to outlaw Falun Gong after the peaceful demonstration that took place on April 25, 1999, Japanese political leaders have had to deal with the problems perceived as a result of new reli-gions in a more deliberative and generally open manner. This was shown when, even after the Aum sarin gas attack in the Tokyo subway, a move to apply the Anti-Subversive Activities Act to Aum was rejected by the Diet. Some restrictive legislation was passed...and there have been recurring problems of citizens in various regions not wanting the remnants of Aum to live in their areas. But the treatment of Aum members differs markedly from that of Falun Gong in China.[37]

Despite initial reactions that would have in essence declared a war on the religious group itself, the Japanese government's focus remained on Aum's criminal activities. In the end, Aum has not successfully conducted further attacks, its current leader has renounced violence, and its mem-bership has drastically decreased.[38] The instrumental role of religious freedom in defusing the violent side of Aum seems to be clear. Grant-ing and respecting religious freedom lowers persecution and, in this case,

---

[35] Also, there are some reports that the Japanese government does take action against those who abduct family members to prevent them from joining the Unification Church. According to the U.S. State Department, "The Unification Church reports that on Febru-ary 10, 2008 an adult member of the Church who had been held against his will by his family members for over 12 years was released and went to Unification Church head-quarters. The Unification Church alleges no one has yet been charged and an investi-gation has not been conducted as of the end of the reporting period," http://www.state.gov/g/drl/rls/irf/2009/127272.htm.

[36] See Richardson & Edelman (2004) for more discussion. Recall that France's Intermin-isterial Mission of Vigilance and Combat against Sectarian Aberrations (MIVILUDES) explained the actions of the sects and cults using a mental manipulation argument that resembled previous brainwashing arguments (see Chapter 2).

[37] Richardson & Edelman (2004:374).

[38] See Terrorist Group Profiles provided by the U.S. State Department, http://www.state.gov/documents/organization/65479.pdf (accessed 6 August 2010).

defused what could have been a cycle of violent conflict. Persecution has been low since Japan disestablished State Shinto and removed restrictions on the free practice of religion, which includes the freedoms to convert and proselytize or have no beliefs at all.

BRAZIL: CASE STUDY OF RELIGIOUS FREEDOM WITH SOME TENSIONS

Brazil is one of twenty countries where religion is deregulated by the government but, at the same time, has a slightly elevated level of social restrictions on religion. These countries represent a combined population of nearly 681 million people, or almost one-tenth of the world's population. As in the first group of countries with high levels of religious freedoms, these countries are generally characterized by having few government restrictions that inhibit the practice, profession, or selection of religion. The restrictions remaining on religion are largely the result of social pressures beyond the government. Although the average level of violent religious persecution in these countries is slightly higher than in the countries with high levels of religious freedoms, it is far lower than in any of the other groups discussed later in this chapter and in Chapter 5. Countries with religious freedoms accompanied by social tensions are present predominantly in Europe (eleven countries, including Austria, Italy, Poland, Spain, Switzerland, and the United Kingdom), the Western Hemisphere (Argentina, Brazil, Guatemala, and Nicaragua), and Africa (Ghana, Guinea, and South Africa), with only one country in Asia (the Philippines) (see Table 4.4).

Brazil, the world's fifth-most populous country, occupies nearly half of the land area of South America and has more Catholics than any other country. Brazil is particularly interesting because it provides a dramatic example of the effects of religious freedoms on both increasing religious participation and decreasing violent persecution. Since Brazil granted full religious freedoms (or deregulated them), a rich religious pluralism has formed there, and new religions have quickly arisen. The result is that violent religious persecution is rare and no single religion can lay claim to the authority or power of the state – nor threaten the state (see Table 4.5). Brazil is a particularly interesting example when compared with Mexico, the next-largest country in Latin America, where religion–state power is partitioned into separate spheres of influence. Mexico established a strict form of separating church and state that imposes strict limits on religion's public role, similar to the anticlerical and extreme secularism of France.

TABLE 4.4. *Religious Freedoms with Tensions*

Countries	Average Government Restriction of Religion Level (July 2000–June 2007) (0–10, 10 = high)	Average Social Restriction of Religion Level (July 2000–June 2007) (0–10, 10 = high)	Average Persecution Level (July 2000–June 2007) (0–10, 10 = high)	Population in Millions (2009)
All countries	1.1	3.3	2.2	680.8
Argentina	1.5	3.3	2.6	40.3
Austria	1.9	4.0	1.0	8.4
Brazil	0.8	2.8	1.0	193.7
Croatia	1.4	3.7	1.6	4.4
Ghana	1.5	3.0	6/0	23.8
Guatemala	1.3	3.9	1.6	14.0
Guinea	2.0	4.2	1.0	10.1
Italy	1.4	3.8	1.0	59.9
Kosovo	2.0	4.3	6.6	2.2
Netherlands	0.1	3.3	1.0	16.6
Nicaragua	1.3	3.1	1.6	5.7
Philippines	1.5	4.2	5.0	92.0
Poland	0.1	3.3	1.6	38.1
Slovakia	1.4	3.5	0.0	5.4
Slovenia	0.7	3.8	0.0	2.0
South Africa	0.0	3.5	3.0	50.1
Spain	1.1	3.3	2.6	44.9
Switzerland	1.3	3.0	1.6	7.6
United Kingdom	1.3	2.9	4.0	61.6

Note: Government restriction of religion ≤2.13; social restriction of religion ≥2.53.

Consequently, Mexico has been plagued with periods of violent religious persecution and conflict, especially in the state of Chiapas.[39]

---

[39] The *2008 Report on International Religious Freedom* for Mexico finds: "As in previous reporting periods, village leaders imposed sanctions on evangelicals for resisting participation in community festivals or refusing to work on Sundays. Common complaints by evangelicals included local leaders cutting off the water, expelling residents from the villages, or denying them benefits from government programs because of their religious affiliation. This was particularly common in Chiapas, where many residents follow a unique and centuries-old syncretistic mix of Catholicism and native custom (Catholic-Mayan). Endemic poverty, land tenure disputes, and lack of educational opportunities also contributed to tensions, which at times resulted in violence." For the full report, see http://www.state.gov/g/drl/rls/irf/2008/108532.htm (accessed 6 August 2010).

TABLE 4.5. *Brazil: Case Study of Freedom with Social Tensions*

0.8 – low	Government restriction of religion score (average July 2000–June 2007)
2.8 – low-moderate	Social restriction of religion score (average July 2000–June 2007)
1.0 – low	Violent religious persecution and conflict (average July 2000–June 2007)
Democracy	2010 political typology (1950 Protectorate, 1900 Constitutional Monarchy) (Freedom House, 2000)
193.7 million	Population (2009)
$10,100	Per capita GDP adjusted for purchasing power parity ($PPP, CIA, 2008)
72	Life expectancy at birth (CIA, 2009 est.)
Religious Adherence (World Religion Database, 2010 est.)	

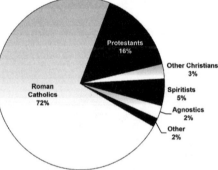

FIGURE 4.2. Religious Adherence in Brazil

Brazilian Constitutional Provisions for Religious Freedom (adopted 1988, revisions 1993)	**Article 5 [Equality]** (0) All persons are equal before the law, without any distinction whatsoever, and Brazilians and foreigners resident in Brazil are assured of inviolability of the right of life, liberty, equality, security, and property, on the following terms: VI. freedom of conscience and of belief is inviolable, ensuring the free exercise of religious cults and guaranteeing, as set forth in the law, the protection of places of worship and their rites; VII. under the terms of the law, the rendering of religious creed or of philosophical or political belief, unless such are claimed for exemption from a legal obligation imposed upon everyone and the person refuses to perform an alternative obligation established by law; **Article 210 [Elementary and Basic Curricula]** (0) Minimum curricula shall be established for elementary school in order to ensure a common basic education and respect for national and regional cultural and artistic values.

(1) Religious education is optional and shall be given during the regular school hours of public elementary schools.

Article 213 [Public Funds]

(o) Public funds are allocated to public schools, and may be channelled to community, religious, or philanthropic schools, as defined in the law, which:

    I. prove that they do not seek a profit and invest their surplus funds in education;

    II. ensure that their equity is assigned to another community, philanthropic, or religious school or to the Government in the event they cease their activities.

Brazil was not always known for religious tolerance. In fact, it was the Brazilian persecution of Jews in the 1600s that sent the first group of Jews to New York in 1654.[40] However, having been under Portuguese rather than Spanish rule provided Brazil several unique developments in the relationship between religion and the state. For one, the Portuguese crown controlled the colony and dominated the political activities of the country much more strongly than did the Catholic Church, which had greater influence elsewhere, such as in Mexico. This made the process of separating church and state less contentious. After three centuries of being ruled by Portugal, Brazil became an independent nation in 1822 and a republic in 1889. The Imperial Constitution, in effect from 1824 to 1889, however, stated that "the Roman Catholic Apostolic religion will continue being the religion of the empire."[41] During this period, when the Catholic Church was officially favored, the government still provided aid to other churches, including subsidizing German Protestant chapels. Even before 1890, it was clear that temporal authority rested with the government, not with the church.[42]

The republican constitution of 1891 accomplished the complete separation of church and state, which included compulsory civil marriage, secularization of cemeteries, and the privatization of religious instruction.[43] Initially, the Roman Catholic Church seemed to embrace many of the

---

[40] See Catharine Cookson, ed. (2003), *Encyclopedia of Religious Freedom*, New York: Routledge, 236. Also, "Chronology of Religious Development in America: 1607–1835," The Library of Congress, http://memory.loc.gov/ammem/collections/petitions/rpchron2.html (accessed 6 August 2010).

[41] Bates (1945:224).

[42] Bates (1945:224).

[43] Bates (1945:224).

changes, welcoming the institutional autonomy it was given from the state and showing few objections to the freedoms given to others.[44] Writing in 1923, University of Texas legal expert Herman G. James noted that "it is safe to say that there is no other country in the world where the Roman Catholic faith is the traditional and prevailing faith of the inhabitants, where there is a more complete separation of Church and State, or where there is greater freedom of conscience and worship."[45]

As the twentieth century progressed, however, the Catholic Church made efforts to regain the lost institutional privileges and to control the ever-growing number of new religious groups – efforts that were apparently supported by the pope. M. Searle Bates points out that when the pope addressed the First Plenary Council of the Church in Brazil in 1939 he supported the "effort to overthrow and extinguish the evils that emanate from 'Protestant errors' and from the practice of spiritualism."[46] The Catholic Church would eventually regain portions of its partnership with the state: clergy were allowed to teach Catholicism in public schools, funding was increased, and laws were passed making proselytizing more difficult for the new sects. In the 1940s, President Vargas stopped the issuing of visas for Protestant missionaries.[47]

But these concessions were short lived. Attempts to control the new sects were increasingly unfeasible and undesirable, and granting special privileges and subsidy to the Catholic Church was increasingly unnecessary. Controlling the new sects was often impractical because they had made such extensive inroads into the nation and the local leadership was now indigenous. It was unfeasible to prevent the growth by merely stopping foreign missionaries, and any attempt to monitor the sects and their indigenous clergy was too costly to the state. Moreover, because Brazil was seeking new immigrants, especially skilled immigrants, it was undesirable to screen out potential immigrants based on religion.[48] Finally, as the government became more stable and the upstart sects became more numerous, the state's alliance with the Catholic Church was unnecessary. When the military regime ceded power in 1985, the state had fewer incentives for granting privilege or subsidy to any one religion, and the politically active minority religions sought even more religious freedoms.

---

[44] Gill (2008).
[45] James (1923:140).
[46] Bates (1945:79).
[47] Gill (2008).
[48] Gill (2008). See also Dawson (2007).

As a result, the government's regulation of religion is virtually absent, and only a few remnants of favoritism remain.

Rather than leading to violent conflict, however, the lack of overt religious favoritism and the defense of religious freedom for all have resulted in a religiously active and diverse society. In Brazil today, a rich mosaic of religious groups is present. According to an analysis[49] of the latest Brazilian census, 73.6 percent of its 2000 population of 170 million is Roman Catholic, and 15.4 percent is Protestant or Evangelical. The next largest category includes those who said they had no religion (7.4 percent). Other groups reported by the census include Spiritists (1.3 percent), Jehovah's Witnesses (0.7 percent), Brazilian Catholics (0.3 percent), Afro-Brazilian religions (0.3 percent), and other Christians (0.2 percent). Mormons, Jews, Buddhists, and other East Asian religions had approximately 0.1 percent each. Christian Orthodox, Muslims, Hindus, Spiritualists, and traditional and indigenous religions each made up less than 0.1 percent of the population. The census also reported 0.4 percent who either did not declare a religion or whose religion could not be determined.

But the Brazilian religious market is highly fluid. Over the past decade alone, the breakdown of religions has shown dramatic change. According to the 2000 Brazilian census, 10.4 percent of the population belonged to Pentecostal denominations, up from 5.4 percent in the 1991 census and 3.3 percent in the 1980 census. Census figures make clear that new Pentecostal groups are growing rapidly. For example, the Universal Church of the Kingdom of God added 1.8 million new members between the 1991 and 2000 censuses. This represents a sixfold increase in that denomination's share of the Brazilian population, from 0.2 percent in 1991 to 1.2 percent in 2000. In a 2006 Pew Forum survey conducted in predominantly urban Brazil,[50] approximately one in seven respondents indicated membership in a Pentecostal denomination, and an additional three in ten identified themselves as charismatic, bringing the total for renewalists to roughly half of the urban population. Approximately eight in ten Protestants interviewed indicated they were either Pentecostal or charismatic, and roughly half of Catholics identified themselves as charismatic.

Brazil's dynamic and growing pluralism is also accompanied by extremely low levels of violent religious persecution, and the rare incidents of persecution that do occur are generally related to social acts, not to acts

---

[49] See Pew Forum on Religion & Public Life, http://pewforum.org/pewforum.org/Christian/Catholic/Pope-to-Visit-Pentecostalized-Brazil.aspx (accessed 6 August 2010).

[50] See http://pewforum.org/Christian/Evangelic-Protestant-Churches/Spirit-and-Power.aspx (accessed 6 August 2010).

by the government. There are, for example, some ongoing social tensions related to indigenous populations who practice their own traditional religions. Tribal wars and commercial development sometimes interfere with their religious practices. Also, anti-Semitism in Brazil is found primarily in southern Brazil where there are large German communities.[51]

Given that religious freedoms are assured and the government has no formal ties with any one religion, there are few incentives for the government to support violent acts against minority religions. In fact, in August 2004, Brazilian president Lula signed a petition drafted by the World Jewish Congress to condemn anti-Semitism and call for the UN General Assembly to adopt a resolution to denounce anti-Jewish acts. This event marked the first time that a Brazilian president signed an official declaration against anti-Semitism.[52] Part of the incentive for the Brazilian government to protect religious minorities is that they make unique cultural, social, and economic contributions to society. Jews, despite their small numbers, are important to the social fabric of Brazil, especially because they have been present in Brazil longer than they have in any other country in the Western Hemisphere.[53] Although social tensions continue to exist, the persecutions that initially expelled Jews in the 1600s no longer occur, because religious freedoms have been granted and protected in Brazil.

NIGERIA: POWER PARTITION CASE STUDY

Nigeria is one of thirty-seven countries where temporal power is partitioned between the government and religion (see Table 4.6). These countries represent a combined population of slightly more than one billion people. Unlike Japan and Brazil, where the governments assure religious freedoms and equal treatment of all religions, these countries divide power between religion and state, depending on the political realm or the geographic region. A single religion often holds special privileges or authority. Power partitions mean that the political and civic power structure of the country typically involves a tenuous balance between favoring certain religions and controlling others, and partitioning religion–state power into separate spheres of influence. This partitioning may be a rigid

---

[51] See http://www.jewishgen.org/infofiles/BrazilianJewry.htm (accessed 6 August 2010). Anti-Semitism in Brazil has never been as active as it has in Argentina.
[52] See http://www.state.gov/g/drl/rls/irf/2005/51629.htm (accessed 6 August 2010).
[53] Marshall (2008).

TABLE 4.6. *Power Partition*

Countries	Average Government Restriction of Religion Level (July 2000– June 2007) (0–10, 10 = high)	Average Social Restriction of C35Religion Level (July 2000– June 2007) (0–10, 10 = high)	Average Persecution Level (July 2000– June 2007) (0–10, 10 = high)	Population in Millions (2009)
All countries	4.1	4.1	3.4	1002.0
Belgium	2.9	3.5	2.6	10.6
Bosnia and Herzegovina	5.5	5.0	7.6	3.8
Cambodia	2.4	0.3	0.6	14.8
Cameroon	2.4	4.5	2.3	19.5
Central African Republic	4.8	3.9	3.0	4.4
Chad	6.3	5.6	4.0	11.2
Colombia	4.1	5.0	5.6	45.7
Congo, Democratic Republic of the	3.1	3.5	4.6	3.7
Cote d'Ivoire	3.7	4.3	4.0	21.1
Ethiopia	4.1	6.7	5.6	82.8
France	3.9	4.1	2.0	62.3
Germany	3.0	4.4	2.6	82.2
Kenya	3.2	4.3	4.0	39.8
Kyrgyzstan	5.7	6.6	4.6	5.5
Latvia	3.7	2.4	0.6	2.2
Lebanon	4.9	6.5	4.6	4.2
Liberia	2.4	3.9	4.0	4.0
Lithuania	3.1	2.0	0.0	3.3
Macedonia	4.9	4.3	2.0	2.0
Mexico	3.8	5.8	7.6	109.6
Moldova	4.5	4.0	2.6	3.6
Mongolia	5.2	2.4	0.0	2.7
Niger	2.5	4.2	1.6	15.3
Nigeria	5.8	6.7	8.0	154.7
Peru	2.7	0.7	0.0	29.2
Rwanda	3.8	0.8	3.6	10.0
Serbia (without Kosovo)	3.4	5.0	4.0	7.6
Syria	5.8	5.8	4.6	21.9

(*continued*)

TABLE 4.6 (continued)

Countries	Average Government Restriction of Religion Level (July 2000– June 2007) (0–10, 10 = high)	Average Social Restriction of C35Religion Level (July 2000– June 2007) (0–10, 10 = high)	Average Persecution Level (July 2000– June 2007) (0–10, 10 = high)	Population in Millions (2009)
Tajikistan	5.0	5.0	3.6	7.0
Tanzania	4.2	3.3	4.6	43.7
Thailand	4.2	3.2	2.6	67.8
Tunisia	6.0	6.3	5.6	10.3
Uganda	3.3	4.1	7.0	32.7
Ukraine	4.6	4.6	1.6	45.7
United Arab Emirates	5.8	4.1	0.6	4.6
Zimbabwe	2.9	2.8	4.0	12.5

Note: Government restriction of religion ≥2.14 and ≤6.47; social restriction of religion ≤6.68.

separation of church and state that imposes strict limits on religion's public role and thus restricts religion disproportionate to protections for free practice – as in the case of France, discussed in Chapter 2, and Mexico. Or it may be the government's empowerment of a select group of religions in order to offer separate spheres of influence to a certain religion or religions in the country – as in the case of Germany, where the government system supports approved religions, and in the case of Nigeria, where Islam is officially favored in some parts of the country but not in others. Usually this results in elevated restrictions on religious freedoms. As mentioned in the previous chapter, the average level of violent religious persecution in these countries is more than four times higher than it is in countries with high levels of religious freedom. Once again we propose that persecution is a consequence of these elevated levels of government and social restrictions on religious freedom.

The pressures and incentives for imposing these restrictions vary, but generally countries that partition power between the government and religion are striving to preserve a balance between current secular and religious conditions or to preserve a traditional religious culture. Religious freedoms are granted in these nations but are often graduated, with religions supporting the state and local culture receiving more freedoms. Sometimes power is partitioned between the government and religion because a single religion was historically dominant and remains closely tied to the political life of the country (such as Orthodox Christianity in Serbia, Buddhism in Mongolia, Alawi Islam in Syria, Buddhism in Thailand, and Sunni Islam in the United Arab Emirates). In other instances, power is partitioned and the population is roughly split between two main religious allegiances, such as Orthodox and Catholic or Protestant Christianity (Latvia and Ukraine); Christianity and Islam (Bosnia and Herzegovina, Lebanon, Macedonia, and Nigeria); Catholicism and secularism (Mexico and France); or where certain sections of a country are predominantly one religion or another (Kenya and Tanzania). For these countries, partitioning often varies among regions of the country. Several of these countries also face insurgencies or situations with religion-related conflict (Colombia and the Democratic Republic of Congo).

Nigeria is also a country facing these challenging situations, so much so that its social restriction score is the highest among the countries in this category and on the cusp of being in an even higher category. Its government restriction score is third highest, after Chad and Tunisia, and is comparable with the UAE and Syria. One particularly important factor that embeds religious regulation into the fabric of Nigerian social and political life is the formalization of Sharia law in the twelve northern provinces. There is a long tradition of Sharia law based on the Maliki school of jurisprudence in the north, one that operated long before and even while the British were the colonial rulers. That tradition was greatly expanded in the modern state as civilian rule emerged in the fall of 1998.[54] Understanding this situation also requires understanding not only Nigeria's overall religious freedom situation (Table 4.7) but its religious demography (Figure 4.3).

The two most recent Nigerian Demographic and Health Surveys in 2003 and 2008 find that the population of Nigeria is roughly split between Muslims and Christians. Less than two percent are associated with other religions.[55] Because religion is a politically sensitive issue in that country, the 2006 Nigerian census did not ask questions about religion,[56] but the

---

[54] See Paden (2005).
[55] See Nigeria's "Religious Demographic Profile" by the Pew Forum on Religion & Public Life, http://pewforum.org/africa/country.php.org (accessed 6 August 2010). The Nigerian Demographic and Health Survey is a nationally representative sample of women between the ages of 15 and 49 and men between 15 and 59.
[56] See "The Nigerian Census," 2006 report from the Population Reference Bureau by Robert Lalasz, http://www.prb.org/ (accessed 6 August 2010).

TABLE 4.7. *Nigeria: Power Partition Case Study*

5.8 – moderately high	Government restriction of religion score (average July 2000–June 2007)
6.7 – moderately high	Social restriction of religion score (average July 2000–June 2007)
8 – high	Violent religious persecution and conflict (average July 2000–June 2007)
Democracy	2010 political typology (1950 Protectorate, 1900 Constitutional Monarchy) (Freedom House, 2000)
154.7 million	Population (United Nations, 2009)
$2,300	Per capita GDP adjusted for purchasing power parity ($PPP, CIA, 2008)
46.9	Life expectancy at birth (CIA, 2009 est.)
Religious Adherence (World Religion Database, 2010 est.)	

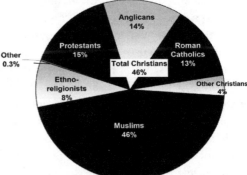

FIGURE 4.3. Religious Adherence in Nigeria

Nigerian Constitutional Provisions for Religious Freedom (adopted 1999)	10. The Government of the Federation or of a State shall not adopt any religion as State Religion.
	38. (1) Every person shall be entitled to freedom of thought, conscience and religion, including freedom to change his religion or belief, and freedom (either alone or in community with others, and in public or in private) to manifest and propagate his religion or belief in worship, teaching, practice and observance.
	(2) No person attending any place of education shall be required to receive religious instruction or to take part in or attend any religious ceremony or observance if such instruction ceremony or observance relates to a religion other than his own, or religion not approved by his parent or guardian.
	(3) No religious community or denomination shall be prevented from providing religious instruction for pupils of that community or denomination in any place of education maintained wholly by that community or denomination.

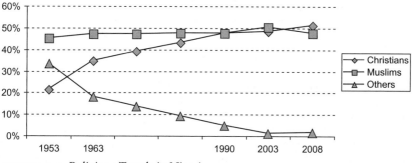

FIGURE 4.4. Religious Trends in Nigeria

1953 and 1963 censuses did.[57] In 1953, 45.3 percent of the population was Muslim, 21.4 percent was Christian, and 33.3 percent belonged to other religions (see Figure 4.4). By 1963, the percentage of the population that belonged to other religions had declined by 15 percentage points, nearly matching the 13.1-point increase for Christians; during this same time period, the percentage of Muslims increased by less than 2 points. The number of Christians increased another 13.1 percentage points from 1963 to 1990. This growth trend flattened out by 1990, with the Christian share of the Nigerian population growing by less than 1 percentage point from 1990 to 2003. The Muslim population, however, increased by 3 percentage points during the same time period.

This neck-and-neck demographic "competition" contributes not only to the desire for the respective religious communities to regulate religion within their own communities, such as through Sharia law, but also to a desire to have God fulfill his purpose through politics.

A 2006 Pew Forum survey, based on a national probability sample of Nigeria's population of adults age 18 and older, found some important differences and similarities between Muslim and Christian religious and political attitudes shown in Table 4.8.[58]

As Table 4.8 demonstrates, sizable percentages of Muslims and Christians consider that religious groups should express their views on politics and that God fulfills his purposes through politics. Muslims and Christians both consider, however, that their own religious freedom is more

---

[57] Archived at the U.S. Census International Data Base (IDB). The 2006 report from the Population Reference Bureau by Robert Lalasz, http://www.prb.org/ (accessed 6 August 2010), indicates that the 1991 census figures are considered unreliable because of a possible undercount of the population. Some irregularities are also alleged for the 1963 census.

[58] See http://pewforum.org/Christian/Evangelical-Protestant-Churches/Spirit-and-Power. aspx (accessed 6 August 2010).

TABLE 4.8. *Nigerian Religious and Political Attitudes: Religion and Politics*

Percentage in 2006 Forum survey who...	Christians	Muslims	All
...believe religious groups should express views on politics	76	73	75
...agree that God fulfills his purpose through politics	43	61	52
...completely agree: guidelines on good and evil are clear	59	72	64
...see religious freedom for others as very important	68	69	69
...see their own religious freedom as important	85	94	90
...trust people from other religions a lot	3	5	4
...see religious group conflict as a very big problem	82	79	81
...favor the U.S.-led efforts to fight terrorism	68	18	44

important than is religious freedom for others. Neither group trusts people from other religions, and both groups overwhelmingly consider religious group conflict a very big problem. Predictably, Christians expressed overwhelming support for the U.S.-led war on terror, whereas very few Muslims expressed such support.

These social attitudes are reflected in the wording of the Nigerian constitution, adopted in 1999. The constitution includes statements that seem like pleas for, rather than guarantees of, a religiously tolerant and religiously integrated society. For example, article 15 states that the motto of the Federal Republic of Nigeria shall be "Unity and Faith, Peace and Progress" and article 23 states that the national ethics shall be "Discipline, Integrity, Dignity of Labour, Social Justice, Religious Tolerance, Self-reliance and Patriotism." Article 15 goes on to state, "For the purpose of promoting national integration, it shall be the duty of the State to... encourage inter-marriage among persons from different places of origin, or of different religious, ethnic or linguistic association or ties." The incentive for the government to include this unusual constitutional provision is the widespread distrust of people from other religions, as evidenced in the 2006 Pew poll.

The 1999 constitution also laid the groundwork for the northern states to expand the role of Sharia law from civil to criminal matters (see box) by permitting states to address areas not prohibited in the constitution, so long as the rulings didn't violate rights promised in the constitution. But as the domain of Sharia law expanded, the contradictions between constitutional assurances and local practices have been many. Until 2003 many states still treated apostasy from Islam as a punishable offense.[59] Even in the area of civil matters, contradictions with the constitution continue.

[59] Paden (2005).

For example, the encouragement of intermarriage in the Nigerian constitution is openly in contradiction with traditional Sharia interpretations. Specifically, Sharia law, which is based on the Quran, allows Muslim men to marry Jews, Sabians, and Christians; however, this is usually interpreted to mean that Muslim women may not marry non-Muslims, in large part because the religious identity of children is the father's, not the mother's. These contradictory constitutional messages have opened the door for local religious and social groups to influence government policies.

Compounding these tensions over local interpretations is the lack of an effective local police force, with the 1999 constitution recognizing the federal police as the only "legitimate police force." John Paden reports in 2005 that "[t]his vacuum at the state and local level was being filled throughout the federation by state-sanctioned vigilante groups, often youth groups with only a modicum of oversight."[60] When these vigilante groups are combined with dual legal systems, the pressures of the dominant religious group can be felt in full force.

NIGERIAN CONSTITUTIONAL PROVISIONS FOR ISLAMIC SHARIA LAW (ADOPTED 1999)

260. (1) There shall be a Sharia Court of Appeal of the Federal Capital Territory, Abuja.

(2) The Sharia Court of Appeal of the Federal Capital Territory, Abuja shall consist of

(a) a Grand Kadi of the Sharia Court of Appeal and

(b) such number of Kadis of the Sharia Court of Appeal as may be prescribed by an Act of the National Assembly.

261. (1) The appointment of a person to the office of the Grand Kadi of the Sharia Court of Appeal of the Federal Capital Territory, Abuja shall be made by the President on the recommendation of the National Judicial Council, subject to confirmation of such appointment by the Senate.

(continued)

---

[60] Paden (2005:153).

(2) The appointment of a person to the office of a Kadi of the
Sharia Court of Appeal shall be made by the President on
the recommendation of the National Judicial Council.

(3) A person shall not be qualified to hold office as Grand
Kadi or Kadi of the Sharia Court of Appeal of the Federal
Capital Territory, Abuja unless

(a) he is a legal practitioner in Nigeria and has so qualified
for a period of not less than ten years and has obtained
a recognised qualification in Islamic law from an institution acceptable to the National Judicial Council; or

(b) he has attended and has obtained a recognised qualification in Islamic law from an institution approved by
the National Judicial Council and has held the qualification for a period of not less than twelve years;
and

(i) he either has considerable experience in the Practice of Islamic law, or

(ii) he is a distinguished scholar of Islamic law.

Source: Constitution Finder, University of Richmond: http://confinder.richmond
.edu. (accessed 6 August 2010); Taken from: http://www.nigeria-law.org/
ConstitutionOfTheFederalRepublicOfNigeria.htm (accessed 6 August 2010).

One of the main incentives for the government to support selected
religious activities of Christians and Muslims and to allow a separate
legal system for Muslims is to lessen religious tensions and ameliorate
religious violence. Has it worked? No. The introduction of Sharia aroused
the suspicions of Christians in the country, further heightening tensions
that were already high. In 2000, the so-called Sharia 1 and Sharia 2 riots in
Kaduna city left at least 2,000 dead. In November 2002, 250 more were
killed and "tens of thousands of persons were relocated in what may
be termed ethnoreligious cleansing."[61] In 2004, thousands fled Plateau
State in central Nigeria following weeks of violence between Muslims
and Christians that left 62 dead and more injured, according to the Red
Cross. Then, between July 2005 and June 2006 another outbreak of
violence between Muslims and Christians occurred in south and central
Nigeria. At least 150 persons were killed and, according to the Red Cross,

[61] Paden (2005:171).

50,000 displaced from Onitsha in 2006. In 2009 and 2010, social violence continued, prompting the U.S. Commission on International Religious Freedom (USCIRF) to issue a public letter to Secretary of State Hillary Clinton, which highlights the intransigency of the problem:

USCIRF concluded that the government of Nigeria has done little to prevent sectarian violence and that there have been no serious efforts to investigate or prosecute the perpetrators of the numerous sectarian killings and crimes that have occurred over the past ten years, most recently in Bauchi (February 2009) and Jos (November 2008). Well over 12,000 people have been killed in communal violence in Nigeria since 1999 and sectarian tensions, exacerbated by inadequate government prevention and response, threaten to further destabilize the country.[62]

Although some might argue that allowing the religious majority in Nigeria's north to have greater powers to regulate society would contribute to less tension, the results on the ground do not support such an argument. Accommodating the dominant religions and allowing them to restrict religious freedoms did not result in more security and less violence, but in *reduced* security and *more* violent religious persecution. Expanding the role of Sharia law, in particular, has heightened the tensions between Muslims and Christians by creating a playing field that greatly favored Muslims in parts of the country without equal favors for Christians. The ideals of religious toleration are better served by protecting the religious freedoms of all.

But if Nigeria's restrictions on religions seem high when compared to Japan and Brazil, they remain far lower than the three countries we will review in the next chapter.

---

[62] "7/30/09: USCIRF Sends Letter to Secretary of State Hillary Clinton on Africa Visit," http://www.uscirf.gov/index.php?option=com_content&task=view&id=2648& Itemid=1. In March 2010, Nigerian officials say more than 500 could have died in clashes between Islamist pastoralists and Christian villagers, http://www. uscirf.gov/index.php?option=com_content&task=view&id=2648&Item=1 (accessed 6 August 2010).

5

A Closer Look

China (Religion Viewed as a Threat), India (Social Monopoly), and Iran (Social and Political Monopoly)

Religious freedoms are routinely denied by the three countries reviewed in this chapter: China, India, and Iran. However, the motivation and even the avenues used for denying the freedoms vary from one country to the next. In China, religion is perceived as a threat to the state and is closely monitored by multiple state agencies, most extensively by the Religious Affairs Bureau. By contrast, the central government of India offers some assurances of religious freedoms, but such freedoms are often perceived as a threat to social and cultural unity at the local level, resulting in strong social pressures to restrict the activities of select religions. Finally, in Iran, religious freedoms are viewed as both a political and a social threat, and both the central government and social and religious groups become involved in restricting the activities of minority religions.

As with the previous chapter, we begin with an extended case study – this time of China. Similar to Japan, China has a long track record of denying religious freedoms. Unlike Japan, however, China continues to deny these freedoms. We discuss the motivations for and outcomes of China's intense regulation of religion. We then review the social pressures for religious restrictions in India and close the chapter by describing how one religious group monopolizes the religious, social, and political life in Iran. As noted earlier, controls are often imposed on religion in an attempt to maintain social order and curb religious violence, but the outcome is typically just the opposite. In each case we show how removing religious freedoms opens the door for physical abuse and displacement.

CHINA: WHEN RELIGION IS VIEWED AS A THREAT TO THE STATE

China is a prominent member of a group of countries in which religion is viewed as a political threat to the state and religious freedoms are denied (see Table 5.1).[1] Despite the view of the state, however, there are relatively few social pressures among religions or in the culture at large to deny religious freedoms. This group of seventeen countries represents nearly 1.6 billion people. Many of these countries are current or past Communist governments that espoused an anti-religious ideology or continue to view religion as a potential threat to government rule (e.g., Vietnam, Cuba, Laos, North Korea, and Turkmenistan). Other countries in this category attempt to keep certain religious groups or religious dynamics in the country under control through the actions of the state (Armenia, Belarus, Bulgaria, Eritrea, Jordan, Kazakhstan, Libya, Malaysia, Mauritania, Oman, and Singapore). The common ground is that the government takes strong actions to restrict religious freedoms, but there are relatively few attempts by local social groups or a single religion to control the religious freedoms of others. In some cases, the government's actions are powerful enough to squelch any social demands for religious restrictions that might be there otherwise.

The Chinese government's heavy regulation of religion has led to three distinct religious markets: the state religions *"officially permitted"* by the government, the underground religious groups *"officially banned"* by the government, and a large group of religious organizations and practices with an *"ambiguous legal status."*[2] The extensive regulations on the permitted religious groups and the ambiguous or officially banned legal status of the remaining groups have opened the door for the physical abuse of the groups' members. Yet, despite heavy government regulation and ongoing violent religious persecution, religion is quite alive in China, in part due to uneven enforcement of restrictions throughout the country as well as the lack of a single religion endorsed by the state.

A recent survey reported by researchers at Shanghai's East China Normal University found that "31.4% of Chinese aged 16 and above, or about 300 million adults, are religious." Although the actual survey data

---

[1] This section on China was originally presented by the lead author as "The Yin and Yang of Religious Freedom in China: Current Dynamics in Historical Perspective," Purdue University Symposium on Religion and Spirituality in China Today, West Lafayette, IN, April 30, 2009, http://www.news.uns.purdue.edu/x/2009a/090415YangChina.html (accessed 6 August 2010).

[2] Yang (2006:97).

TABLE 5.1. *Religion as Threat*

Countries	Average Government Restriction of Religion Level (July 2000–June 2007) (0–10, 10 = high)	Average Social Restriction of Religion Level (July 2000–June 2007) (0–10, 10 = high)	Average Persecution Level (July 2000–June 2007) (0–10, 10 = high)	Population in Millions (2009)
All countries	7.7	4.3	4.3	1572.4
Armenia	7.2	6.6	3.0	3.1
Belarus	7.6	6.6	3.6	9.6
Bulgaria	7.2	4.3	2.6	7.5
China	8.3	4.6	10.0	1345.8
Cuba	7.1	3.5	4.0	11.2
Eritrea	8.1	3.7	5.6	5.1
Jordan	7.9	6.5	3.6	6.3
Kazakhstan	6.7	5.3	3.0	15.6
Korea, North	8.5	1.5	7.0	23.9
Laos	8.5	3.1	5.0	6.3
Libya	7.0	3.3	5.0	6.4
Malaysia	7.6	5.9	4.6	27.5
Mauritania	8.0	4.3	2.0	3.3
Oman	6.5	4.6	1.0	2.8
Singapore	7.5	1.3	3.0	4.7
Turkmenistan	8.7	3.8	5.0	5.1
Vietnam	8.1	3.6	6.0	88.1

Note: Government restriction of religion ≥6.47; social restriction of religion ≤6.68.

are not available, the fact that the number was reported by the state-run *China Daily*[3] is an indication of the large number of people the government believes may be religious. Other recent surveys report similar findings. A 2006 survey by the Pew Global Attitudes Project found that 31 percent of the Chinese public considers religion to be very or somewhat important in their lives, compared with only 11 percent who say religion is not at all important. When asked a somewhat different question in a 2005 Pew poll, an even greater percentage of the Chinese public (56 percent) considered religion to be very or somewhat important in their lives.[4]

[3] See Wu Jiao, "Religious Believers Thrice the Estimate," *China Daily*, February 7, 2007, http://www.chinadaily.com.cn/china/2007-02/07/content_802994.htm (accessed 6 August 2010).

[4] Grim (2008).

These survey results do not suggest that all who find religion important are *affiliated* with a particular religion, but other estimates suggest that a surprising number are involved. The official count, based on a 2005 Chinese government white paper, reports one hundred million religious adherents in China.[5] But this estimate does not include the officially banned religions and probably excludes many or most of the legally ambiguous groups. When describing the three religious markets, Chinese scholar Fenggang Yang estimated that there were approximately one hundred million in the "officially permitted" religions, two hundred million in the "officially banned," and many others involved in the groups holding an "ambiguous legal status."[6] Table 5.2 offers recent estimates from the World Religion Database (WRD).[7] When attention is confined to underground Christian churches, the WRD estimates that among the Han majority there are approximately seventy million Chinese associated with more than three hundred Christian house church networks – virtually all operate with tenuous or no recognition by the government. Regardless of the estimates used, however, it is obvious that a large number of adherents fall outside of the state-approved religions.

Decades of Cold War rhetoric have equated restrictions on religious freedom with Communism, but the Communists were not the first to deny religious freedoms in China. The following section provides some historical bearings that allow us to understand the dynamics of religion in China today.

Historical Religious Regulation in China

The long history of China is filled with struggles and alliances between religion and the state. In his detailed study of *Religion in Chinese Society* C. K. Yang writes that "[h]istory shows ample evidence of the persistent

---

[5] Chinese government figures indicate dramatic growth among Protestants and Catholics, as seen by comparing the numbers reported in the government's 1997 white paper on religion with an updated 2006 "Background Brief" provided to the senior author by the Chinese Embassy in Washington, DC. The officially reported number of Christians increased from 14 million to 21 million, or 50 percent, in less than 10 years. During this time, Protestants increased from 10 million to 16 million – a 60 percent increase – and Catholics from 4 million to 5 million – a 25 percent increase. Although some of this growth may be due to independent Christians registering with the official Protestant and Catholic associations, the new background brief goes so far as to say that Protestantism, in particular, has increased "by more than 20 times" since it "was first brought to China in the early 19th century."

[6] Yang (2006:113).

[7] Johnson & Grim (2008); www.worldreligiondatabase.org (accessed 6 August 2010).

TABLE 5.2. *China: Case Study of Religion Viewed as a Threat*

8.3 – high	Government restriction of religion score (average July 2000–June 2007)
4.6 – moderate	Social restriction of religion score (average July 2000–June 2007)
10 – very high	Violent religious persecution and conflict (average July 2000–June 2007)
Democracy	2010 political typology (1900 and 1950 Colonial Dependency) (Freedom House, 2000)
1.35 billion	Population (United Nations, 2009)
$6,000	Per capita GDP adjusted for purchasing power parity ($PPP, CIA, 2008)
73.5 years	Life expectancy at birth (CIA, 2009 est.)
Religious Adherence (World Religion Database, 2010 est.)	

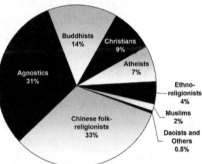

FIGURE 5.1. Religious adherence in China

	Article 36
	Citizens of the People's Republic of China enjoy freedom of religious belief.
Religious Freedom in the Constitution	No state organ, public organization or individual may compel citizens to believe in, or not believe in, any religion; nor may they discriminate against citizens who believe in, or do not believe in, any religion.
	The state protects normal religious activities. No one may make use of religion to engage in activities that disrupt public order, impair the health of citizens or interfere with the educational system of the state.
	Religious bodies and religious affairs are not subject to any foreign domination.

role of religion in political struggles against ruling dynasties."[8] He begins with the Taoist Yellow Turban rebellion in the Han dynasty (A.D. 184) and continues with examples from the many dynasties that would follow, including the White Lotus society that helped to topple Mongolian rule (1368).[9] As early as the Tang dynasty (A.D. 618–907), Chinese law had the power to recognize or deny "a person's membership in a Buddhist religious community."[10] Yang notes that the time frame comprising the fifth to tenth centuries was a "period of sharp conflict between Buddhism and the state" and goes on to explain that it was "consistently a one-sided persecution by the state and not a struggle between two equal forces."[11]

The state also formed alliances with select religions. China scholar Mayfair Yang points out that political and religious authorities often worked in tandem in many Chinese societies. In the sixteenth and seventeenth centuries of the Ming dynasty, for example, the Chinese government was a quasi-religious entity, in which the emperor presided over state rituals, sacrifices, and religious rites. Only the emperor could directly access *Tian*, or the supreme deity. During that time, one of the six imperial ministries was the Ministry of Rites, which oversaw sacrifices throughout the empire. This government function later coincided with a Confucian system that was instituted through strict laws that regulated the empire.[12] When the Ming dynasty came to an end in 1644 and the Manchurian leaders of the new Qing dynasty (sometimes referred to as the Manchu dynasty) established policies for governing a large and predominantly Han Chinese Empire, they largely adopted the existing systems of law and administration. The Manchu Qing rulers thus inherited a body of well-established law regulating religion, which they apparently adopted wholesale.[13]

The laws of particular interest are the laws "Against Heresies of Religious Leaders or Instructors, and of Priests." The heresy laws had specific provisions for how religious leaders, the army, the people, and village chiefs would be punished (reprinted in the accompanying box), but they were often vague on what constituted "heretical gods" or unacceptable

---

[8] Yang (1961:218).
[9] The White Lotus society, an ardently Buddhist and vegetarian group, refused to pay taxes or provide labor for the Mongols. See Morton (1995).
[10] Storch (2000).
[11] Yang (1961:211).
[12] Mayfair Yang (2008). See also Yang (1961:187).
[13] Yang (1961:187).

AGAINST HERESIES OF RELIGIOUS LEADERS OR
INSTRUCTORS, AND OF PRIESTS

Article I.

Religious leaders or instructors, and priests, who, pretending
thereby to call down heretical gods, write charms or pronounce
them over water, or carry round palanquins (with idols), or in-
voke saints, calling themselves orthodox leaders, chief patrons, or
female leaders; further, all societies calling themselves at random
White Lotus communities of the Buddha Maitreya or the Ming-
tsun religion, or the school of the White Cloud, etc., together with
all that answers the practices of *tso tao* or *i twan*; finally, they who
in secret places have prints and images, and offer incense to them,
or hold meetings which take place at night and break up by day,
whereby people are stirred up and misled under the pretext of cul-
tivating virtue, – shall be sentenced, the principal perpetrators to
strangulation, and their accomplices each to a hundred blows with
the long stick, followed by a lifelong banishment to the distance of
three thousand miles.

Article II.

If any one in the army or among the people dress or ornament the
image of a god, and receive that god with the clang of cymbals and
the beating of drums, and hold sacrificial meetings in his honor,
one hundred blows with the long stick shall be administered, but
only to the principals.

Article III.

If village-chiefs, when privy to such things (as detailed in art. I and
II), do not inform the authorities, they shall receive each forty blows
with the short bamboo lath. Services of prayer and thanksgiving
(for the harvest) in honor of the common local gods of the Soil,
performed in spring and autumn respectively, do not fall under
these restrictions.

Source: De Groot (1903).

practices.[14] Like many regulations on religion both past and present, the final interpretation remained open to the discretion of local officials.

So what was the driving motivation behind such laws? Once again, we find that minority religions can threaten both the dominant religion and the state. Commenting on the long history of the association between religion and state in China, M. Searle Bates writes that "China from early times has known large and powerful secret societies, reaching on occasion into the millions of members, able in fact to *make and break dynasties.*" He went on to explain that the Confucianists "both scorned and feared these heterodox, superstitious associations of the masses."[15] Rather than accepting such groups as part of the Chinese religious landscape, Confucianists viewed these societies as potential threats to their favored status and worked with the state to control their activities.

The state also feared these groups. C. K. Yang has argued that, in part, the state feared them because they undermined the "traditional submission and loyalty to the state" and because they produced an "economically nonproductive class of priests."[16] But the greatest fear was that of political rebellion, a fear that resulted in regulations that went far beyond the religious sects with political aspirations. Yang explains that the "gnawing fear of rebellion" brought restrictions and persecution on all of the religions not condoned by the state.[17] In the following sections, we review three episodes in Chinese history to illustrate why these groups were feared and to provide a historical backdrop for understanding the denial of religious freedom in China today. By the standards of Chinese history, they are three very recent episodes: one happened at the time of the American Revolution (1770s), the second at the time of the U.S. Civil War (1860s), and the third primarily during the Japanese occupation in the 1930s and 1940s.

(1) *The Shandong Rebellion*

In the late summer and early autumn of 1774, during the very same weeks as the meeting of the First Continental Congress in Philadelphia, Pennsylvania, an uprising occurred in northeast China that challenged the ruling Manchu Qing dynasty. It was a homegrown Chinese rebellion in Shandong against the Manchurian overlords, who had by that time been ruling for 130 years. The Shandong rebellion, led by martial arts master

---

[14] Yang (1961:139–140). De Groot's original version (1903) also contains the Chinese text.
[15] Bates (1945:274).
[16] Yang (1961:199).
[17] Yang (1961:208).

Wang Lun, sought to establish a new China based on his White Lotus–style religious teachings and practices, which were appealing because "traditional modes of religious expression were not satisfying to everyone and that certain individuals or groups were...shut out from control of popular [rural and urban] religious institutions."[18] The uprising was not epoch-making in itself, but it marked a series of religiously inspired uprisings propelled by "prophets" with millenarian beliefs who believed that heaven chose them to usher in a new golden age.[19]

The Shandong rebellion ended on November 1, 1774, when – surrounded and outnumbered – Wang set fire to the tower that he was defending and perished in its blaze.[20] Such religiously charged uprisings would ultimately claim the lives of many millions of Chinese over the next century, but as De Groot noted, the Chinese policy of "no lenity towards the sects, no religious tolerance, but increase of persecutions" meant that each new movement was like "oil thrown into a smoldering fire,"[21] perpetuating a cycle of increased social and government restrictions leading to more persecutions, and more persecutions leading to more clashes, and the clashes leading to a call for increased restrictions. And so the cycle continues. And the policies were not limited to White Lotus–style sects. The Decree of 1784, for example, addressed Muslims and demanded "the extermination of the new Wahhabi sect."[22] It is worth noting that Wahhabism was familiar to the Chinese centuries before Americans even knew the term.

(2) The Taiping, Heavenly Kingdom, Rebellion

During the next ninety years, the Manchu Qing dynasty continued to face insurrections, and many of these had religious elements. The most pivotal and deadly religious rebellion against the Qing rule was the Taiping Rebellion led by Hong Xiuquan – claiming an estimated thirty million lives. Hong was born near Guangzhou and had some contact with Christianity. Through a series of visions, he came to believe he was the younger brother of Jesus Christ and was called by God to establish a heavenly kingdom on Earth. Blending a form of Christian "socialism" with the call to rid the Chinese of enslavement from their Manchurian masters, Hong established a rival dynasty in the south, with its heavenly

---

[18] Naquin (1981:48).
[19] Gaustad (2000).
[20] Naquin (1981).
[21] De Groot (1903:306).
[22] Bates (1945:275).

capital in Nanjing.[23] Interpreting the biblical book of Revelation, Hong commented that the Apostle John saw

> the celestial hall in heaven above. Heaven above and earth are alike. The new Jerusalem is the present [Nanjing]. . . . God and Christ have descended to make us lords and open the lower celestial hall, so the heavenly hall of God is among man.[24]

The kingdom envisioned by Hong was marked by the equality or brotherhood of all based on the religious conviction that God is the father of all. Hong's liberal mixing of heterodox Christianity with a kingdom-building war plan did not win the sympathies of the foreign powers that, at that time, had strong-armed the Manchu Qing rulers into a series of concessions that were on the verge of dividing up China between them, somewhat as Africa had been divided among the European colonial powers. Nonetheless, Hong did reach out by letter to another Western leader also engaged in a great civil war, Abraham Lincoln. The letter reportedly said the following:

> I have heard that your country emphasizes the importance of the people, that in everything they are considered equal, that freedom is your fundamental principle, and that there are no obstacles in the association of men and women. In these things, I am greatly delighted to find that your principles agree completely with those upon which we have based the establishment of our dynasty.[25]

Some Western scholars saw the Taiping Rebellion as a lost opportunity for "the formation of an empire with freedom of religion."[26] Others have called it "the nineteenth century's most gigantic man-made disaster."[27] Chinese Communists, writing in the early years of the People's Republic, saw the rebellion as the prototype of a peasant revolt against landlords and Western imperialism.

> The Taiping Revolution failed. But its brilliant deeds and its marvelous contribution to history will live forever in people's memories. . . . The great struggles of the Taiping Revolution propelled history forward and inspired those who came later to take the revolutionary course of overthrowing those lackeys of imperialism – the [Qing] rulers. The martyrs of the Taiping Heavenly Kingdom will never be forgotten.[28]

---

[23] For a discussion of Taiping ideology, see Shih (1967).
[24] Shih (1967:91), quoting Forrest (1867: 200).
[25] Shih (1967:47), quoting [from Chinese] Ling Shan ch'ing, ed., *T'ai-p'ing t'ien-kuo yeh-shih*, 20:2, Shanghai.
[26] De Groot (1903:554).
[27] Kuhn (1977).
[28] Compilation Group (1976:178).

The rebellion was put down after a series of defeats with tacit and tactical support from the colonial powers.[29]

The irony, at least on the surface, is that a Christian-related and clearly religiously motivated movement such as the Taiping Rebellion was embraced by Chinese Communists.[30] The irony is understandable because, despite Communism's propagation of atheist materialism, fidelity to the Chinese revolutionary spirit was the most important "virtue." When religion was viewed as working toward the central authority's objectives – in that case, revolting against feudalism – there was retrospective support. However, where religion is perceived to run counter to the central authority's objectives, harsh consequences would have been expected in China then – and now. Also, for our main purposes of demonstrating the connection between religious restrictions and persecution, we note that the Taiping Rebellion was an instance of total regulation of the religious marketplace by the powerful Taiping overlords – resulting in massive religion-related conflict.

(3) Extremity Issues, Imperialism, and the Japanese Occupation of the 1930s and 1940s

In the 1930s and 1940s, some Western observers were not certain that the Communists would become staunchly anti-religious, despite the fact that Communism was inherently atheist. There were even some indications of shared values between Chinese Christians and Communists. For instance, the Communist Party expressed "much appreciation" for the social service provided by Christians.[31] Also, there appeared to be no imminent threat from the religions themselves, because there were generally "good relations between Buddhist, Moslem, Roman Catholic, and Protestant leaders."[32] Such reports surely did not represent or foresee the harsh anti-religious campaigns that were to come. The militantly negative stance Chinese Communists took toward religion was related to several religiously related challenges. There were geographically strategic sections of China where the social pressures from dominant religions were extremely high. Despite the generally amicable relations between religions, Bates, writing in 1945, points out that "Tibet, legally under

---

[29] For chronological perspective, Abraham Lincoln outlived Hong Xiuquan by less than one year.

[30] Since the early years, there have been various reappraisals of the history. See Volkoff & Wickberg (1979).

[31] See Volkoff & Wickberg (1979).

[32] Bates (1945:121).

Chinese sovereignty, tolerates no religion but that of the official (Buddhist) Lamaism [and some] bodies of Moslems in Northwest China [Xinjiang] are traditionally fanatical and intolerant."[33] Thus, to subdue these strategic border regions, the Communists saw that the task directly involved bringing the religions of these regions under strict control.

Another religiously related challenge was that the Chinese directly associated Western missionaries with imperialism. Ironically, the West, having just prevailed in the Opium Wars, opposed the Taiping movement in favor of the weaker Qing dynasty, in large part because it could win territorial and economic concessions. The West, in the Communist point of view, was thus in league with enemies of the revolutionary spirit, the sort of spirit embodied in the Taiping Rebellion.

A third challenge is seldom discussed by Western observers. Following the collapse of the Qing dynasty,[34] which resulted in various interim governments, China ultimately faced Japanese aggression in the 1930s. The Kuomingtong (KMT), or Nationalists, held power but faced a growing Communist insurgency that erupted into all-out civil war once the Japanese were defeated. Although the United States and China both suffered during World War II, there was a special religious element to the Imperial Japanese occupation of China, which was referred to briefly in the previous chapter. During World War II, Japan instituted religious regulation on the lands it occupied in Southeast Asia and East Asia, including Taiwan, Korea, Manchuria, and much of China proper. In Imperial Japan, all religions were subordinated to State Shinto. As Japan expanded its geographic control into China, it utilized a structure called the "League of Religions" that aimed to

combine Shinto, Buddhist, and Christian bodies in order to contribute to the realization of the aims of the "Holy War," to establish a spiritual basis for peace in East Asia, and to combat communism by a united front of East Asian religions.[35]

As long as Chinese religious groups were in conformity with the Japanese imperial design, they were allowed to operate. However, the results of this alliance, which included the *opposition of Communism*, were ominous for religions in China once the Communists came to power.

After their victory in 1949, the Chinese Communist Party "spent the first 17 years attempting to bring all religions under control, followed

---

[33] Bates (1945:121). Also see G. Raquette (1939).
[34] The Manchu Qing dynasty was toppled during the revolution of 1911.
[35] Bates (1945:56).

by 13 years of eradication measures before relenting to a toleration policy."[36] Attempts to bring the religions under control (1949–1965) quickly resulted in the Communist Party limiting religious activity to a small number of groups that were patriotic and committed to the revolution and met the "Three-Self" standards: self-administrating, self-supporting, and self-propagating. By 1957, the government had established five heavily monitored religious groups: the Protestant Three-Self Patriotic Movement, the China Buddhist Association, the China Islamic Association, the China Daoist Association, and the China Catholic Laity Patriotic Committee, which later became the China Catholic Patriotic Committee.[37] All other religions were banned, all foreign missionaries were expelled, and relations with foreign religious organizations, such as the Vatican, were severed.

But even these limited freedoms were removed when the Cultural Revolution (1966–1979) sought to build a new revolutionary culture, throwing off old ideas, values, customs, and traditions. Religions, universities, businesses, and many other institutions became immediate targets of the Red Guards.[38] Seeking a complete annihilation of religion, places of worship were shut down; temples, churches, and mosques were destroyed; artifacts were smashed; sacred texts were burnt; and it was a criminal offence even to possess a religious artifact or sacred text.[39] Many of the regulations were eerily reminiscent of those promulgated in the Ming and Qing dynasties and codified in the law on heresies (see the box).[40] Atheism had long been the official doctrine of the Chinese Communist Party, but this new form of militant atheism made every effort to eradicate religion completely.

Following Mao Zedong's death in 1976, however, many of the former "tolerations" for religion gradually returned. The new party leader Deng Xiaoping, whose own son was paralyzed when Red Guards threw him from a window during the Cultural Revolution, introduced greater economic and social liberties. Like the former policies of religious toleration, however, freedoms were limited and tenuous. Modern China remains a nation where there are few social pressures preventing involvement, but religion is still closely regulated by the state and atheism remains part of the official policy.

---

[36] Yang (2006:100).
[37] Yang (2006:100).
[38] See Zuo (1991) for a review of the "Four Olds": old ideas, old values, old customs, and old traditions.
[39] Goldman (1986).
[40] Lang (1988).

The Yin and Yang of Religious Freedom in China Today

The Chinese philosophical concept of *yin* and *yang* captures the two opposing but complementary regulatory forces of religion in China today. The light yang side grants freedoms in selected circumstances, whereas the dark yin side revokes or denies freedoms to groups the state disfavors.

The Yang, or Light Side

Despite the fact that many in the West doubted the survival of religion in China, religion remains and is growing. By the late 1970s and early 1980s, a growing number of approved places of worship were operating, and by 1982 religious toleration was officially reinstated by a Communist Party policy statement known as "Document 19."[41] Following a period of civil unrest, a 1991 document (Document 6) called for an expansion of the Religious Affairs Bureau and closer monitoring of religion, but a similar level of toleration remained. Similar to article 36 of the Chinese constitution, Document 6 gave assurances "not to interfere with normal religious activities or the internal affairs of religious organizations," but the government retained the right to define what constituted "normal."[42] The leader of religious affairs, Ye Xiaowen, stated that they still "hope to effect a gradual weakening of the influence of religion," but few held out the hope that religion would be eradicated any time soon.[43]

These limited religious freedoms in tandem with relatively few social or cultural pressures against religion have allowed for increased religious practice.[44] Even the official government figures show a dramatic growth among Protestants and Catholics. When comparing the numbers reported in the government's 1997 white paper[45] on religion with an updated 2006 government "Background Brief,"[46] the number of Christians increased from fourteen million to twenty-one million, or 50 percent, in less than ten years. During this time, Protestants increased from ten million to sixteen million – a 60 percent increase – and Catholics from four million to five million – a 25 percent increase. Although some of this growth

---

[41] Document 19 is "The Basic Viewpoint and Policy on the Religious Affairs during the Socialist Period of Our Country." See Yang (2006).

[42] Potter (2003:14).

[43] Yang (2005:36) and based on conversations with representatives from the Religious Affairs Bureau of Yunnan Province.

[44] The following survey report is taken from Grim (2008).

[45] See http://www.china.org.cn/e-white/Freedom/index.htm (accessed 6 August 2010).

[46] The "Background Brief" was provided to the senior author by the Chinese Embassy in Washington, DC.

may be due to independent Christians registering with the official Protestant and Catholic associations, the new background brief goes so far as to say that Protestantism, in particular, has increased "by more than 20 times" since it "was first brought to China in the early 19th century." Likewise, Buddhist numbers are estimated by the government at one hundred million or more, and Muslim ethnic groups continue to grow, although primarily through slightly higher than average fertility rates rather than through conversions.

Because of China's large population, even a small percentage of involvement results in very large numbers. China scholars have pointed out that in China there are now "more Catholics than in Ireland"[47] and "on any given Sunday there are almost certainly more Protestants in church in China than in all of Europe."[48] The presence of more than twenty million Muslims places China among the top twenty countries in Muslim population size – almost equal to that of Saudi Arabia, for instance, and nearly double that of all twenty-seven European Union countries combined.

Possibly the most intriguing finding regarding religion in China today, however, is that 33 percent of Communist Party officials and government employees are very or somewhat interested in having media access to information on the topic of religion. Responses to a 2005 Intermedia survey[49] of ten thousand adults across twenty-one of China's thirty-one mainland provinces, municipal districts, and autonomous regions show that, among the dozen or so occupational groups reported, Communist Party officials and government employees were the most interested in learning more about religion. No doubt, some or even most might be interested in access to information for the purpose of restraining religion, but regardless of their motives, this survey's evidence appears to indicate that Communist Party officials and government employees recognize that religion is a force in China today that cannot be ignored.

There are other signs that the Chinese Communist Party is taking note of the growing interest in religion. Former president Jiang Zemin's 2001 visit to a recently renovated Buddhist temple in the Hebei Province was described by local Buddhist leaders as a "great support" and "helpful for the whole Buddhist community."[50] More recently, Hu Jintao, president

---

[47] Madsen (2003).
[48] Hayes (2003).
[49] Grim (2008).
[50] Some local officials have justified that developing Buddhist temples fosters economic growth, especially tourism. See Yang & Wei (2005:78).

and general secretary of the Communist Party of China, broke with former practice and included a formal discussion of religion at the 2008 National Congress. Addressing the Chinese Politburo, Hu stated, "We must strive to closely unite religious figures and believers ... to build an all-around ... prosperous society while quickening the pace toward the modernization of socialism."[51]

The Yin, or Dark Side

However, the freedoms granted and acknowledgments of religion are begrudging and preferential. The official policy of the Communist Party for its own members has not changed: "[P]arty membership and religious belief [are] incompatible and ... religious believers should resign their party membership."[52] The Chinese government recently took preliminary steps to promote a select group of religions, including promoting World Buddhist Forums in 2006 and March 2009 and an International Taoism Forum in 2007 without similar forums for other religions. Some representatives from these religions see this as "the best time of religious freedom in Chinese history,"[53] but the story is much more nuanced.

Most of the freedoms are tenuous and easily revoked. Even the approved groups must be careful to avoid "infringing on the interests of the state," and they must demonstrate their support to the Communist Party. Indeed, the officially permitted groups are required to hold public meetings for reviewing state policies and laws and must meet a long list of regulatory demands. Included on this list are the regulations known as the "three fixes": worshiping in a fixed place, having a fixed and approved leadership, and conducting ministry in a fixed location. The "fixes" allow for closer monitoring of the groups and are designed to prevent evangelizing across administrative borders. Urban groups, in particular, face closer scrutiny that even extends to the messages given. A Protestant pastor reports that the "Religious Affairs Bureau has given him hints against topics like the doomsday, the final judgment, and the creation of the world."[54] These are the groups with the greatest religious freedoms.

All groups know, however, that freedoms can be quickly revoked by defining a group as an evil or dangerous cult. Both the constitution and

---

[51] Cody (2009).
[52] U.S. State Department, *2007 Country Reports on Human Rights, China*, http://www .state.gov/g/drl/rls/hrrpt/2007/100518.htm (accessed 6 August 2010).
[53] Yang (2009).
[54] Huang & Yang (2005:51).

party documents grant freedoms to "normal" religions, and they grant government officials the authority to define what is normal. Although most routine monitoring and registering of local religious groups are conducted by the Religious Affairs Bureau (also known as the State Administration of Religious Affairs), the Public Security Bureau (Chinese police) is involved when violations have occurred or when the state views a religious group as a potential threat. It is here that the *vague definitions and broad discretionary powers of local authorities open the door for violent religious persecution.*

Whereas the actions of the Religious Affairs Bureau are largely regulatory, the Security Bureau holds a broad range of powers for enforcement. Indeed, the Security Bureau can both deny freedoms and administer sentences without a trial. What begins as a seemingly benign regulation for maintaining social order can quickly transform into physical confinement or abuse. The 2008 *International Religious Freedom* report explains that "[c]itizens may be sentenced by a nonjudicial panel of police and local authorities to up to three years in reeducation-through-labor camps to punish members of unregistered religious groups."[55] Moreover, this is a frequent occurrence. The 2007 *Country Reports on Human Rights Practices* reported that there are "250,000 officially recorded inmates in reeducation-through-labor camps" in China. The report went on to explain that house arrest was yet another nonjudicial means used for detaining underground religious leaders, political dissenters, and others.[56] These nonjudicial enforcement techniques are used most frequently against the banned religions, especially Falun Gong, but the broad discretionary powers and sentencing options of local authorities make all religions more attentive to their presence.

Three religious groups, in particular, have raised the concern of Chinese leadership: the *Muslims in Xinjiang*, with reported ties to the East Turkestan Islamic Movement (ETIM),[57] a militant Islamic separatist group, although the Chinese government has not produced convincing documentation of its actual existence[58]; the more than five million ethnic *Tibetans in China*, most of whom are Buddhist followers of the Dalai Lama; and *Falun Gong* (also known as *Falun Dafa*), a spiritual movement

---

[55] *2008 Report on International Religious Freedom, China*, http://state.gov/g/drl/rls/irf/2008/108404.htm (accessed 6 August 2010).

[56] 2007 Human Rights, http://www.state.gov/g/drl/rls/hrrpt/2007/100518.htm (accessed 6 August 2010).

[57] See http://www.cfr.org/publication/9179/east_turkestan_islamic_movement_etim.html (accessed 6 August 2010).

[58] Richardson (2009).

that draws on Taoism, Buddhism, and Qigong, a traditional Chinese exercise that is much like shadow boxing. Of these three, the government's response to Falun Gong has been especially severe.

On April 25, 1999, more than ten thousand Falun Gong adherents surrounded the Beijing leadership compound in a silent protest. Objecting to recent criticisms of their movement, they sought to be recognized as a legitimate spiritual movement. In less than three months, however, they were officially banned and labeled as an "evil cult." By February 2000, an estimated "35,000 practitioners had been detained, 300 jailed, 5,000 sent to labor camps, and 50 committed to mental hospitals."[59] The numbers detained and arrested have increased sharply over the past ten years, with some now estimating that Falun Gong adherents constitute more than half of the 250,000 inmates in reeducation-through-labor camps.[60] In an official statement, the government justified the crackdown because "Falun Dafa had not been registered according to law and had been engaged in illegal activities, advocating superstition and spreading fallacies, hoodwinking people, inciting and creating disturbances, and jeopardizing social stability."[61] But Chinese scholars have found that more credible explanations acknowledge that the Chinese government is especially wary of well-organized religious groups and was especially alarmed by Falun Gong's demonstration "because they didn't see it coming."[62]

As noted in Chapter 4, the Japanese government's reaction to the severe criminal activities of the Aum stands in sharp contrast to the Chinese government's reaction to the silent protest of Falun Gong. Whereas the Japanese government did take action against all criminal activity of the Aum and placed them under surveillance, they did not pass laws that were targeted at all religious groups and, most significantly, did not outlaw Aum. Both their action and their limited reaction helped to defuse the tension. By contrast, the strong and violent reactions of the Chinese government have resulted in an enduring and escalated controversy and in additional policies and staff for controlling religions.[63] Thousands of Chinese citizens, both within Falun Gong and members of other

---

[59] Richardson & Edelman (2004:368).

[60] *2008 Report on International Religious Freedom, China*, http://state.gov/g/drl/rls/irf/2008/108404.htm (accessed 6 August 2010).

[61] "China Bans Falun Gong," *People's Daily Online*, July 22, 1999, http://english.peopledaily.com.cn/special/fagong/1999072200A101.html (accessed 6 August 2010).

[62] See Bhattacharji (2008).

[63] See Richardson & Edelman (2004) for a review of the government reactions.

religious groups, have faced increased persecution following the silent protest.

Two other religions facing harsh government crackdowns are located on the border regions of China: Xizang (Tibet) and Xinjiang ("New Border"). Recent events in these two regions help to illustrate the model developed in Chapter 3: religious restrictions lead to more persecution (and increased social conflict), leading to a call for even more restrictions, and so the cycle continues.

Government involvement in the internal religious affairs of Tibet, as well as government rhetoric against the exiled Dalai Lama, whom many in Tibet look to for spiritual and temporal leadership, have long been key parts in the bundle of grievances Tibetan Buddhists hold toward Beijing. But on February 1, 2008, the grievances escalated when the Chinese government selected a seventeen-year-old as the "reincarnation of the Panchen Lama, Tibetan Buddhism's second-highest figure."[64] In a rare public appearance, the young man "vowed to support the [Communist Party of China's] leadership and make more contributions to the Tibetan economy and social harmony by guiding more religious work to adapt to China's socialist society."[65] A month later, violence broke out, with Tibetans setting fire to Han Chinese shops in Lhasa, presumably in reaction to the encroachment of Han Chinese into the business sector in the city.[66] The Chinese government responded with a forceful crackdown on Tibetan protests and violence that included the detention (i.e., persecution) of nonviolent Buddhist monks.[67] In putting the Tibetan unrest down forcefully, the Chinese government won wide praise among the Han population throughout the country, transforming the image of Tibetans from a pacifist ethnic group into a security threat.[68] Yet this quick solution resulted in extensive collateral damage: persecution of Tibetan Buddhists monks uninvolved in the violence, calls for more religious restrictions, and an increase in the tensions between Tibetan Buddhists and the Chinese government. Despite the decisive action, the Tibetan "problem" remains. The more the Chinese government attempts to control and restrict Tibetan

---

[64] "China's Panchen Lama Appears Publicly," *Associated Press*, http://pewforum.org/news/display.php?NewsID=14874 (accessed 6 August 2010).

[65] Quoted in *USA Today*, http://www.religionnews.com/index.php?/rnsblog/comments/chinese_lama_says_communism_is_just_dandy/ (accessed 6 August 2010).

[66] Macartney & Page (2008).

[67] "Appeasing China: Restricting the Rights of Tibetans in Tibet," *Human Rights Watch*, 2008, http://www.hrw.org/sites/default/files/reports/tibetnepal0708web.pdf (accessed 6 August 2010).

[68] Shakya (2009).

Buddhism, the more they pave the way for future persecution and more ongoing clashes.

The large and sparsely populated Xinjiang-Uygur Autonomous Region is situated in China's northwest directly north of Tibet. Uygurs make up approximately half of the region's population today, but just a few decades ago the Uygurs were a clear majority of the population.[69] For the Uygurs, there is no single spiritual leader, such as the Dalai Lama, who stands in opposition to Chinese rule. Rather, the opposition comes from the Uygur people's sense that several factors separate them from China proper, specifically their ethnic Turkic identity, centuries of autonomy and isolation, and, to some degree, their Sunni Muslim heritage.[70] Indeed, many Uygurs support separation from China[71] along the lines that their neighbors to the west separated from the Soviet Union in 1991 (e.g., Kazakhstan and Kirghizia).[72] To the Chinese government, this is untenable. Like Tibet, Xinjiang is a strategically important border region that has been in the Chinese sphere of influence for many years. More important is its strategic location, sometimes referred to as the pivot of Asia.[73] Xinjiang has some of the world's largest untapped oil reserves and provides Beijing with installations and resources that support its nuclear program. Controlling these resources and territory means that the Chinese are especially sensitive to any suggestions of separatism.

Although religion is only part of the Uygur motivation for separatism, it is one of the most visible elements of collective identity that the government can control. Controls today range from limiting religious training of children by parents, to restrictions on religious dress, to prohibition of any government employee from attending religious worship services, regardless of whether that employee is a party member. While the restrictions on the religious practices of Muslims in Xinjiang increased following the breakup of the Soviet Union, the most noticeable increase followed the terrorist attacks of September 11, 2001. As expected by our model, the jump in restrictions resulted in an equally high jump in persecution. The government has used the new restrictions and the global war on terror as justification to impose seemingly arbitrary arrests and detentions. When Uygurs protested and attacked a few Xinjiang police

---

[69] See censuses, http://www.stats.gov.cn/english/.

[70] Senior author's own observations, having spent numerous years teaching and doing research in Xinjiang; other recent studies include Gladney (1996, 2009).

[71] Minority Rights Group International (2008).

[72] See Bovingdon (2004); Dwyer (2005).

[73] Lattimore (1950).

stations in the weeks and months before the 2008 Olympics, the government designated groups such as the East Turkestan Islamic Movement (ETIM) as chief security threats to the Olympic Games, justifying even greater restrictions on Muslim practices in Xinjiang. Rather than focusing on other cultural and economic reasons for separatism, the Chinese government continues to increase restrictions on religion: restrictions that have led to violent religious persecution, social unrest, and calls for more government restrictions.[74] And so the cycle continues.[75]

India: Case Study of Monopolistic Social Pressures

In contrast to the government-driven efforts controlling religion in China, India's attempts to restrict religious freedoms are fueled by strong social pressures. Pressures from religious groups, political groups, and the culture as a whole have resulted in a loss of religious freedoms and, as our model would predict, a high level of violent religious persecution.

But India is not alone. Nearly 1.8 billion people live in thirteen countries where there are social pressures for a single religion to monopolize public life. For many countries within this group, the government attempts to hold a less antagonistic view toward religion when compared to China and other countries where minority religions are viewed as a political threat. However, this is often challenged by religious or social groups calling for more restrictions on select groups. India, Indonesia, and Israel are obvious examples, but Russia, Turkey, and Greece also fall into this group. As shown in Table 5.3, others in this group include Georgia, Morocco, Nepal, Palestine, Romania, Sri Lanka, and Yemen. In each of these countries, governments are facing strong pressures to increase restrictions on selected groups while favoring others.

Like its northern neighbor, China, India shares the distinction of having a population greater than one billion and having a growing economy with many citizens still facing poverty. Beyond these similarities, however, there are many sharp differences. Some involve their political histories. Unlike China, which generally maintained a Han- or Manchu-dominated empire and consolidated its far western extremities of Xinjiang and Tibet, India faced incursions from Arabs, Turks, and the British and eventually

---

[74] Radio Free Asia, 2008, "Crackdown on Xinjiang Mosques, Religion," August 14, http://www.rfa.org/english/news/uyghur/directive-08142008114700.html (accessed 6 August 2010).

[75] The tensions are further increased in Xinjiang and Tibet as the Chinese government encourages the immigration of more Han Chinese into those regions. See Ford (2008).

TABLE 5.3. *Monopolistic Social Pressures*

Countries	Average Government Restriction of Religion Level (July 2000–June 2007) (0–10, 10 = high)	Average Social Restriction of Religion Level (July 2000–June 2007) (0–10, 10 = high)	Average Persecution Level (July 2000–June 2007) (0–10, 10 = high)	Population in Millions (2009)
All countries	4.7	6.7	5.0	1951.7
Georgia	5.7	7.8	4.6	4.3
Greece	6.5	6.8	2.6	11.2
India	5.9	10.0	9.6	1198.0
Indonesia	6.3	9.0	8.6	230.0
Israel	4.5	8.8	5.6	7.2
Morocco	6.5	7.0	5.6	32.0
Nepal	6.2	8.3	4.6	29.3
Nigeria	5.8	6.9	8.0	154.7
Palestine	4.2	8.5	8.6	4.3
Romania	6.3	8.1	4.0	21.3
Russia	6.2	7.1	5.6	140.9
Sri Lanka	5.6	9.1	8.6	20.2
Turkey	5.2	8.3	3.0	74.8
Yemen	5.8	7.6	5.6	23.6

Note: Government restriction of religion ≥2.14 and <6.47; social restriction of religion ≥6.68.

lost its extremities. Rather than maintaining strict central and cultural control, India became a cultural crossroads. After India achieved independence from Britain in 1947, social demands for Hindu and Muslim states soon violently split the country into India, Pakistan, and Bangladesh. But the differences between India and China extend beyond politics and history. The religious differences are striking (see Table 5.4).

India is imbued with religion.[76] According to the 2001 World Values Survey, 80 percent of the population identify themselves as a "religious person" compared to 27 percent in Japan and 15 percent in China. When survey respondents were asked about religious practice, the percentages jumped even higher, with 93 percent "belonging to a religious denomination" and 88 percent reporting that they "meditate or pray."[77] But

---

[76] The following religious demographic summary was originally reported by the Pew Forum: http://www.thearda.com/internationalData/countries/coutry_108_1.asp (accessed 6 August 2010).

[77] Taken from the Association of Religion Data Archives (http://www.theARDA.com) (accessed 6 August 2010).

TABLE 5.4. *India: Case Study of Social Monopoly*

5.9 – moderately high	Government restriction of religion score (average July 2000–June 2007)
10 – very high	Social restriction of religion score (average July 2000–June 2007)
9.6 – very high	Violent religious persecution (average July 2000–June 2007)
Democracy	2010 political typology (1900 Colonial Dependency and 1950 Democracy) (Freedom House, 2000)
1.2 billion	Population (United Nations, 2009)
$2,800	Per capita GDP adjusted for purchasing power parity ($PPP, CIA, 2008)
69.9 years	Life expectancy at birth (CIA, 2009 est.)
Religious Adherence (World Religion Database, 2010 est.)	

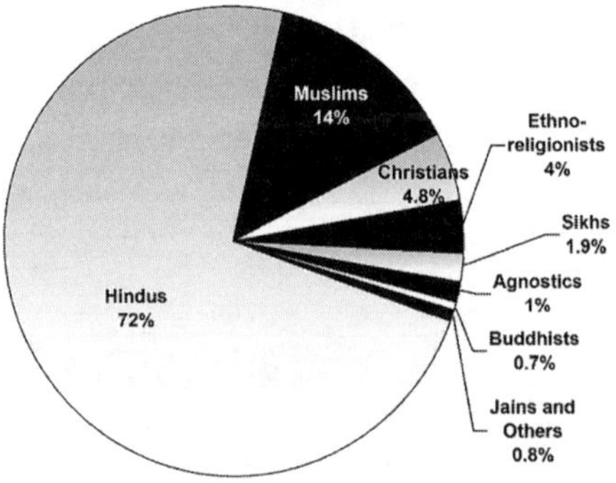

FIGURE 5.2. Religious adherence in India

Religious Freedom in the Constitution	Part III
	Fundamental Rights
	Right to Freedom of Religion
	25. Freedom of conscience and free profession, practice and propagation of religion. – (1) Subject to public order, morality and health and to the other provisions of this Part, all persons are equally entitled to freedom of conscience and the right freely to profess, practise and propagate religion.
	(2) Nothing in this article shall affect the operation of any existing law or prevent the State from making any law –
	  (a) regulating or restricting any economic, financial, political or other secular activity which may be associated with religious practice;
	  (b) providing for social welfare and reform or the throwing open of Hindu religious institutions of a public character to all classes and sections of Hindus.

Explanation I. – The wearing and carrying of kirpans shall be deemed to be included in the profession of the Sikh religion.

Explanation II. – In sub-clause (b) of clause (2), the reference to Hindus shall be construed as including a reference to persons professing the Sikh, Jaina or Buddhist religion, and the reference to Hindu religious institutions shall be construed accordingly.

26. Freedom to manage religious affairs. – Subject to public order, morality and health, every religious denomination or any section thereof shall have the right –

(a) to establish and maintain institutions for religious and charitable purposes;

(b) to manage its own affairs in matters of religion;

(c) to own and acquire movable and immovable property; and

(d) to administer such property in accordance with law.

27. Freedom as to payment of taxes for promotion of any particular religion. – No person shall be compelled to pay any taxes, the proceeds of which are specifically appropriated in payment of expenses for the promotion or maintenance of any particular religion or religious denomination.

28. Freedom as to attendance at religious instruction or religious worship in certain educational institutions. – (1) No religious instruction shall be provided in any educational institution wholly maintained out of State funds.

(2) Nothing in clause (1) shall apply to an educational institution which is administered by the State but has been established under any endowment or trust which requires that religious instruction shall be imparted in such institution.

(3) No person attending any educational institution recognised by the State or receiving aid out of State funds shall be required to take part in any religious instruction that may be imparted in such institution or to attend any religious worship that may be conducted in such institution or in any premises attached thereto unless such person or, if such person is a minor, his guardian has given his consent thereto.

this high level of religious activity is nothing new. India has served as the birthplace for many religions, such as Hinduism, Buddhism, and Sikhism, and the religious fires of India have served to forge many others, including Christianity and Islam.[78] Indeed, one of the most influential writers and leaders of the Islamic revivalism in the twentieth century was India's Sayyid Abul Ala Maududi, who experienced the religious tensions and eventual religious partitioning of India firsthand.[79] Calling for a new Islamic order, he has been both credited and blamed for many of the transnational Islamic movements of today. Virtually all major religions can trace significant influences to India.

Although India's population majority is Hindu, there is considerable variation by state. According to the 2001 census, Muslims make up the majority of the population in Lakshadweep (95.5%) and in Jammu and Kashmir (67.0%), Christians predominate in Nagaland (90.0%) and Mizoram (87%), and Sikhs are the majority in Punjab (59.9%). Buddhists are most prevalent in Sikkim (28.1%) and Jains in Maharashtra (1.3%). Also, there are some trends in and controversies about the religious affiliation data worth noting. First, by census counts, the overall percentage of Hindus in the population has decreased by 3 points since 1961, dropping from 83.5 percent in 1961 to 80.5 percent in 2001. Muslims have increased by nearly 3 percentage points in the same period, going from 10.7 percent in 1961 to 13.4 percent in 2001. During this same 40-year span, other religious groups seem to have shown little change. For example, according to the census, Christians made up 2.3 percent of the population in both 1991 and 2001. But some have pointed to a potential bias against reporting changes in religious identity, for example, from Hinduism to Christianity, among certain groups in India such as the dalits (formerly called "untouchables") and tribal peoples who benefit from government-sponsored affirmative action programs. The 2006 International Religious Freedom report on India notes, "According to a 2004 Indian Government National Commission for Minorities report, 24 percent of government jobs were reserved for members of Scheduled Castes and Scheduled Tribes, including dalits. Benefits accorded dalits were revoked once they converted to Christianity or Islam, but not to Buddhism or Sikhism."[80] Because of the the pragmatic advantages of

---

[78] Demerath (2002:93) stated it succinctly: "Israel and India share the blessing and the curse of religious fecundity."

[79] See Nasr (1996).

[80] http://www.state.gov/g/drl/rls/irf/2006/71440.htm (accessed 6 August 2010).

maintaining a Hindu identity, the World Religion Database estimates that religious minorities are more numerous than indicated in census figures, meaning that Hindus make up less than the 80 percent indicated in the 2001 census.

The religious demography of India and the religiously charged history and politics have infused India with tensions across multiple social and religious groups. Whereas in China the government was the first to revoke religious freedoms, in India, forces in society led the charge. The dominant form of social regulation in India today arises from the nationalist "Hindutva" movement composed of multiple groups. Prema Kurien explains that this movement is "multistranded" and stresses the "greatness of Hinduism and Hindu culture, the importance of Hindu unity, and the need to protect Hinduism and Hindus." Some Hindutva groups are militant, whereas others are moderate; some are political, and others are apolitical. However, all of the strands "are related to the central Hindu nationalist perspective." In short, the Hindutva movement promotes Hinduism above all other cultures and religions.[81]

The origins of the modern nationalist movement are often traced to the 1920s and even earlier, but it wasn't until the 1980s and 1990s that the impact of the movement was openly displayed in the political arena. When it formed in 1980, the Bharatiya Janata Party (BJP) quickly mobilized the Hindu nationalist vote and became a major force in national politics. The number of seats held by the BJP in the Lok Sabha (lower house of the Indian parliament) jumped from two to eighty-eight in 1989 and continued to climb throughout the 1990s. In 1999 the BJP and its allies took over power at the national level and remained there until a surprising defeat in 2004 and another defeat in 2009.[82] Even with a reduced role in national government, however, the influence of the BJP and the larger Hindutva movement remains. The BJP continues to control state governments and the related social movements continue to work outside of the formal government channels to curb the freedoms of religious minorities. As we review the actions of the BJP and the larger Hindutva movement, however, we should note that these groups do not reflect all Hindus in India. Recent surveys by R. Barry Ruback (2009, p. 375) and colleagues found that most Hindu leaders favored their own group but did not devalue Muslims. For members of the BJP, however, they reported a "devaluation of Muslims rather than favoritism of

---

[81] Kurien (2007:138). See also Frykenberg (1989).
[82] Jaffrelot (2007).

Hindus."[83] The desire for a favored position for Hindus and the devaluation of religious minorities by the BJP and other Hindutva groups has opened the door for violent religious persecution and conflict.

One of the most prominent examples of Hindutva groups attacking a minority religion occurred in 1992 in a small town in northern India, Ayodhya. Birthplace of Lord Ram, one of the incarnations of Vishnu, Hindu nationalists charged that the sixteenth-century Babri Masjid mosque was built on the site of a Ram temple and the exact place of his birth. Following clashes between Muslims and Hindus and a lengthy series of judicial proceedings in the 1950s, the mosque was closed as a place of worship. But in the mid-1980s a series of organized efforts, including efforts by the militant Bajrang Dal, began to call for the "liberation" of Ram's birthplace. On December 6, 1992, a group of Hindu nationalists destroyed the Mosque, despite efforts by the central government to prevent the attacks. The BJP, which held power in the local state government, described it as a spontaneous act; other accounts described it as "meticulously planned and orchestrated by Hindu nationalists." The riots that followed resulted in thousands of Muslim deaths.[84]

The presence of Hindu nationalists continues to be felt in many states across the country. In February and March 2002, attacks against Muslims in Gujarat resulted in approximately 2,000 dead and 100,000 displaced into refugee camps. Moreover virtually all religious minorities have faced attacks.[85] In 2007, Christians in the eastern state of Orissa were attacked on Christmas day, with 100 Christian churches and buildings damaged, 700 Christian homes destroyed, and many Christians fleeing to nearby forests for refuge. A Christian nongovernmental organization (NGO) estimated that "excluding the Orissa violence, during 2007 an average of approximately three to four religiously-motivated attacks per week was recorded against the small Christian minority community."[86] But the lengthy reports of violent religious persecution are not limited to human rights groups, religious organizations, or the U.S. State Department. According to the Indian Ministry of Home Affairs, there were 698 instances of religion-related violence, which left 133 persons dead and

---

[83] Ruback, Kohli, & Pandey (2009).

[84] Kurien (2007:134).

[85] We should acknowledge that the Hindutva groups have also faced attacks. Atheistic Maoist guerrillas, seeking a class war, have targeted key Hindutva leaders for persecution and death. See Blakely (2009).

[86] As quoted in the State Department International Religious Freedom report, 2007, India, http://www.state.gov/g/drl/rls/irf/2008/108500.htm (accessed 6 August 2010).

2,170 injured in 2006 alone. The question that arises, however, is whether the government will take stronger action to prevent the persecution.[87]

When reviewing the list of attacks, clear patterns begin to emerge. First, rather than being attacks orchestrated by government agencies, as in China, they often result from groups identified with the nationalist Hindutva movement, or other movements outside of the government. Many accounts refer to them as "communal" activities. Second, the local government often turns a blind eye to the attacks. Knowing that attacks were imminent, a police chief in a district of Orissa announced that Hindus attacking Christians would be prosecuted. After making his announcement, however, he was quickly transferred, and his former district became the "epicenter of massive anti-Christian violence."[88] As might be expected, violent persecution is higher in the states where the BJP is either in power or is part of a ruling coalition (twelve of twenty-eight states in 2008).[89] Third, the response of the federal government is erratic and sometimes weak. According to the State Department, this was the case in the attacks against Muslims in 2002:

It was alleged widely that the police and state government did little to stop the violence promptly, and at times even encouraged or assisted Hindus involved in the riots. Despite substantial evidentiary material, the judicial commission responsible for investigating the riots reported inconclusive findings. No Hindus have been charged for the violence. There were widespread reports of intimidation and harassment of witnesses. Violence and discrimination against Muslims and Christians continued in other parts of the country as well.[90]

But the Hindutva movement seeks more than impunity for members' actions; the group wants more formal regulatory actions favoring Hinduism and fewer freedoms for religious minorities. The group's plea is that without such controls, minority religions will become a threat and violence will result. We propose, however, that the very controls they seek will result in more violent persecution and conflict.

Thus far, we have emphasized the communal or social restrictions on religious freedom, but more formal restrictions have also been placed on religious minorities. Although the Indian constitution provides for freedom of religion, the federal government both regulates religion directly and allows various states and religious communities to design laws that

---

[87] http://www.state.gov/g/drl/rls/irf/2007/90228.htm (accessed 6 August 2010).
[88] Wunderink (2008).
[89] http://www.state.gov/g/drl/rls/irf/2008/108500.htm (accessed 6 August 2010).
[90] http://www.state.gov/g/drl/rls/irf/2003/24470.htm (accessed 6 August 2010).

reinforce the demands of religious and nationalist groups. The Foreigners Act of 1946 serves as one example of a federal regulation. The act bans public speech "against the religious beliefs of others" and prohibits foreign visitors from preaching without first getting permission from the Ministry of Home Affairs. Another example is the Indian Divorce Act of 2001. This act "limits inheritance, alimony payments, and property ownership of persons from interfaith marriages" and doesn't allow Christian churches to hold interfaith weddings, despite allowing other religions to do so. Clergy violating the act "face up to ten years' imprisonment."[91] Other federal regulations curbing religious freedoms include the Unlawful Activities Prevention Act of 1967, the Religious Institutions (Prevention of Misuse) Act of 1988, the Foreign Contribution Regulation Act (FCRA) of 1976, and the Indian Divorce Act of 1969.[92]

But the pressures for restricting minorities are often felt most strongly at the state level, with state-level "anti-conversion" laws serving as a prime example.[93] Himachal Pradesh and several other states restrict proselytism and other activities contributing to religious conversions. "Although these laws do not explicitly ban conversions, many nongovernmental organizations (NGOs) argue that in practice, 'anti-conversion' laws, both by their design and implementation, infringe upon the individual's right to convert, favor Hinduism over minority religions, and represent a significant challenge to Indian secularism."[94] There are also numerous complaints that the police and other local officials are biased in how they respond – or if they respond at all to attacks on religious minorities.

In sum, the Hindutva movement and the many groups it has spawned seek to grant Hinduism a favored position and to reduce the freedoms of religious minorities. The result is that the social pressures exerted by these groups, and the official laws they have promoted, contribute to limiting the freedoms of religious minorities. But even with reduced freedoms, the minority religions are viewed as a threat and open violent

---

[91] Based on information from the State Department IRF report, 2007, India, http://www.state.gov/g/drl/rls/irf/2007/90228.htm (accessed 6 August 2010).

[92] State Department IRF report, 2007, India, http://www.state.gov/g/drl/rls/irf/2007/90228.htm (accessed 6 August 2010).

[93] For a review of the anti-conversion laws, see the congressional testimony of Angela C. Wu, esq., of the Becket Fund for Religious Liberty, July 21, 2006, http://www.becketfund.org/files/581fd.pdf?PHPSESSID=9395e026ffed13e7b427d41c46ae157c (accessed 6 August 2010).

[94] State Department IRF report, 2007, India, http://www.state.gov/g/drl/rls/irf/2007/90228.htm (accessed 6 August 2010).

religious persecution has become a familiar event. Once again, the cycle of persecution often serves to perpetuate itself. The reduced freedoms allow for more violent persecution, and when the minority groups protest the persecution, this leads to calls for fewer freedoms.

USCIRF PLACES INDIA ON WATCH LIST

http://www.uscirf.gov

August 12, 2009

WASHINGTON, D.C. – With the release of its 2009 country report on India, the U.S. Commission on International Religious Freedom (USCIRF) placed India on its "Watch List" today for the government's largely inadequate response in protecting its religious minorities.

USCIRF said India earned the Watch List designation due to the disturbing increase in communal violence against religious minorities – specifically Christians in Orissa in 2008 and Muslims in Gujarat in 2002 – and the largely inadequate response from the Indian government to protect the rights of religious minorities.

"It is extremely disappointing that India, which has a multitude of religious communities, has done so little to protect and bring justice to its religious minorities under siege," said Leonard Leo, USCIRF chair. "USCIRF's India chapter was released this week to mark the one-year anniversary of the start of the anti-Christian violence in Orissa."

Last year in Orissa, the murder of Swami Saraswati by Maoist rebels in Kandhamal sparked a prolonged and destructive campaign targeting Christians in Orissa, resulting in attacks against churches and individuals.

These attacks largely were carried out by individuals associated with Hindu nationalist groups, and resulted in at least 40 deaths and the destruction of hundreds of homes and dozens of churches. Tens of thousands were displaced and today many still remain in refugee camps, afraid to return home. . . .

"India's democratic institutions charged with upholding the rule of law, most notably state and central judiciaries and police, have emerged as unwilling or unable to seek redress for victims of the

(continued)

violence. More must be done to ensure future violence does not occur and that perpetrators are held accountable," said Mr. Leo.

Similarly, during the 2002 communal riots in Gujarat, India's National Human Rights Commission found that the Indian government not only failed to prevent the attacks against religious minorities, but that state and local officials aided and participated in the violence.

In both Orissa and Gujarat, court convictions have been infrequent, perpetrators rarely brought to justice and thousands of people remain displaced.

USCIRF issues its annual report on religious freedom each May. This year's India chapter was delayed because USCIRF had requested to visit India this summer. The Indian government, however, declined to issue USCIRF visas for the trip.

Iran: Country Case Study of Sociopolitical Monopoly

Whereas government agencies are the driving force in restricting religious freedoms in China and religiously charged movements do so in India, both are powerful forces in Iran. Iran is one of fourteen countries representing a total of more than 760 million people where a single religion generally holds both a political and a social monopoly. This group of countries where religious freedom faces severe restrictions from both the government and society includes Afghanistan, Algeria, Azerbaijan, Bangladesh, Burma (Myanmar), Egypt, Iraq, Kuwait, Pakistan, Saudi Arabia, Somalia, Sudan, and Uzbekistan. Violent religious persecution stands at a high level in almost all of these countries, with the exceptions of Azerbaijan and Kuwait (see Table 5.5).

According to estimates,[95] Iran is more than 98 percent Muslim, with 87 to 92 percent being Shia and 8 to 11 percent Sunni, mostly along ethnic lines. Baha'is, Jews, Christians, Sabean Mandeans, and Zoroastrians make up the remaining 2 percent. These small percentages, however, may represent sizable numbers. For instance, according to the World Religion Database,[96] Baha'is may number 212,000, and more than 300,000

---

[95] See World Religion Database (2008) and the U.S. State Department, *2007 Report on International Religious Freedom*, http://www.state.gov/g/drl/rls/irf/2007/90210.htm (accessed 6 August 2010).

[96] Johnson & Grim, 2008.

TABLE 5.5. *Sociopolitical monopoly*

Countries	Average Government Restriction of Religion Level (July 2000–June 2007) (0–10, 10 = high)	Average Social Restriction of Religion Level (July 2000–June 2007) (0–10, 10 = high)	Average Persecution Level (July 2000–June 2007) (0–10, 10 = high)	Population in Millions (2009)
All countries	7.9	8.5	7.4	760.5
Afghanistan	7.4	9.5	7.0	28.2
Algeria	7.0	7.3	9.0	34.9
Azerbaijan	7.6	7.2	5.6	8.8
Bangladesh	6.8	8.0	7.0	162.2
Burma (Myanmar)	8.8	8.2	10.0	50.0
Egypt	7.7	8.9	8.0	83.0
Iran	8.6	9.4	7.6	74.2
Iraq	7.2	9.5	9.6	30.7
Kuwait	7.9	7.2	2.0	3.0
Pakistan	8.3	9.7	6.6	180.8
Saudi Arabia	9.4	9.5	6.0	25.7
Somalia	7.2	8.2	a	9.1
Sudan	7.6	9.2	8.6	42.3
Uzbekistan	8.8	7.5	9.0	27.5

Note: Government restriction of religion ≥6.48; social restriction of religion ≥6.68.
a Somalia's level of persecution is difficult to determine because of its conflation with general anarchy in the country.

indigenous Christians may live in Iran. Up to 17,000 Jews may still live in the country. Other minorities total fewer than 100,000 including Zoroastrians and Sabean Mandeans, who follow the teachings of John the Baptist, with baptism being a central ritual. The government considers the Sabean Mandeans as Christians, even though Sabean Mandeans do not consider themselves as such.[97]

Although some research has shown a recent decline in mosque attendance, there remains strong and steady support for maintaining a religious worldview.[98] When respondents to the World Values Survey were asked to choose favorable qualities for children in 2000 and 2005, support for

[97] U.S. State Department, *2007 Report on International Religious Freedom*, http://www .state.gov/g/drl/rls/irf/2007/90210.htm (accessed 6 August 2010).
[98] Tezcür & Azadarmaki (2008).

TABLE 5.6. *Iran: Case Study of Social and Political Monopoly*

8.6 – very high	Government restriction of religion score (average July 2000–June 2007)
9.4 – very high	Social restriction of religion score (average July 2000–June 2007)
7.6 – high	Violent religious persecution (average July 2000–June 2007)
Authoritarian Regime	2010 political typology (1900 Absolute Monarchy and 1950 Constitutional Monarchy) (Freedom House, 2000)
74.2 million	Population (United Nations, 2009)
$12,800	Per capita GDP adjusted for purchasing power parity ($PPP, CIA, 2008)
71.1	Life expectancy at birth (CIA, 2009 est.)
Religious Adherence (World Religion Database, 2010 est.)	

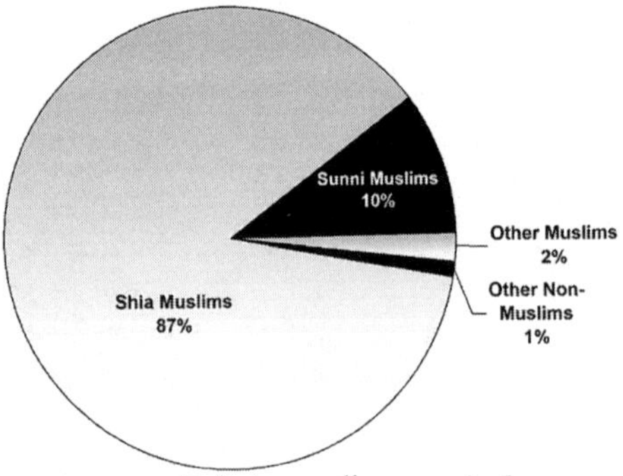

FIGURE 5.3. Religious adherence in Iran

Religious Freedom in the Constitution	Chapter I General Principles Article 4 [Islamic Principle] All civil, penal, financial, economic, administrative, cultural, military, political, and other laws and regulations must be based on Islamic criteria. This principle applies absolutely and generally to all articles of the Constitution as well as to all other laws and regulations, and the wise persons of the Guardian Council are judges in this matter. Article 11 [Unity of Islam Principle] In accordance with the sacred verse of the Koran "This your community is a single community, and I am your Lord, so worship Me" [21:92], all Muslims form a single nation, and the government of the Islamic Republic of Iran [has] the duty of formulating its general policies with a view to cultivating the friendship and unity of all Muslim peoples, and it must constantly strive to bring about the political, economic, and cultural unity of the Islamic world.

Article 12 [Official Religion]
The official religion of Iran is Islam and the Twelver
Ja'fari school, and this principle will remain eternally
immutable. Other Islamic schools are to be accorded
full respect, and their followers are free to act in
accordance with their own jurisprudence in
performing their religious rites. These schools enjoy
official status in matters pertaining to religious
education, affairs of personal status (marriage,
divorce, inheritance, and wills) and related litigation
in courts of law. In regions of the country where
Muslims following any one of these schools constitute
the majority, local regulations, within the bounds of
the jurisdiction of local councils, are to be in
accordance with the respective school, without
infringing upon the rights of the followers of other
schools.
Article 13 [Recognized Religious Minorities]
Zoroastrian, Jewish, and Christian Iranians are the only
recognized religious minorities, who, within the limits
of the law, are free to perform their religious rites and
ceremonies, and to act according to their own canon
in matters of personal affairs and religious education.
Article 14 [Non-Muslims' Rights]
In accordance with the sacred verse "God does not
forbid you to deal kindly and justly with those who
have not fought against you because of your religion
and who have not expelled you from your homes"
[60:8], the government of the Islamic Republic of Iran
and all Muslims are duty-bound to treat non-Muslims
in conformity with ethical norms and the principles of
Islamic justice and equity, and to respect their human
rights. This principle applies to all who refrain from
engaging in conspiracy or activity against Islam and
the Islamic Republic of Iran.

religious faith was strong and unchanged. As shown in Figure 5.4, there
was an increase in the percentage considering independence favorably
(53 versus 64 percent), a decline in those mentioning obedience (41 versus 32 percent), and a consistently positive response for religious faith as
a favorable quality for children (71 percent).[99]

---

[99] Moaddel (2008).

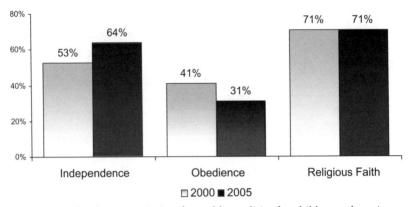

FIGURE 5.4. Iranians mentioning favorable qualities for children to have in 2000 and 2005 (World Values Survey).

Although not all Iranians are Shia, the state religion of Iran is the *Twelver Ja'fari* school of Islam. The Twelvers are one of the three main branches of Shia Islam and, unlike Sunnis, they believe that a lineage of imams have special religious and political authority. Shia Islam not only inherits all the claims of truth inherent in historic Islam in general but also the contemporary claims of truth manifested through the imams. Although Iran's president is the most visible leader to many in the West, the highest-ranking political and religious authority in Iran is the Supreme Leader. A scholar of Islamic studies and an ayatollah, the Supreme Leader is elected by and is accountable to the Assembly of Experts (an assembly of eighty-six Islamic scholars). Thus, Iran feels a special calling to represent true Islam within the broader Muslim world and ensure that Islam in Iran is vouchsafed.

SUNNI AND SHIA (SHIITE) ISLAM

One of the most sensitive issues for many Muslims is discussion of Islam's two main sects: Sunnis and Shias (also called Shiites). Although Sunnis and Shias have many more shared beliefs than differences, the differences that do exist often overlap with ethnic, cultural, and political differences, which sometimes form lines of violent sectarian conflict, such as has been seen in Iraq in recent years.

This sectarian distinction originated with a dispute over the rightful successor to the Prophet Muhammed. Although Sunnis believe that the first four successors of Muhammed were all "rightly guided" (*Rashidun*) caliphs, Shias believe that the only rightful successor was the fourth caliph, Imam Ali, Muhammed's cousin and son-in-law. Imam Ali was killed in a power struggle, and later his son, Imam Husain, and most of his family and companions, were killed by the successor and son of the fifth caliph in Karbala, located in present-day Iraq. Imam Husain's martyrdom is commemorated particularly by Shias with acts of mourning and repentance as well as mass processions each year during Ashoura, the first ten days of the first month of the Islamic calendar (Muharram). Today, most Shias also believe that the twelfth imam of this line went into hiding more than 1,100 years ago and will eventually return as the *Mahdi* to hasten the final judgment.

Another difference between Sunnis and Shias is the role religious leaders have in interpreting Islamic practice as put forth in the Quran and the traditions of the Prophet Muhammed. In general, Sunnis emphasize that proper interpretations emerge largely through the consensus of its learned clerics and the Muslim community. This is reflected in the term *Sunni* ("the traditions"), short for the "people of tradition and consensus" (*ahl al-sunnah wa'l-jama'ah*). Whereas Shias generally agree with this, they also emphasize the interpretations and examples of the imams descending from Imam Ali's bloodline. This belief is reflected in their name, *Shias* ("partisans"), which is the short form of *Shiite Ali* ("partisans of Ali"). Shias also believe that certain clerics, by virtue of their scholarship and abilities, have special authority, such as the ayatollahs in Iran or the Grand Ayatollah Sistani in Iraq.

For a fuller discussion on the distinctiveness of Shia Islam, see Nasr (2006).

Even the top elected position, the president, must promise to support Islam and the Twelver Ja'fari school. The presidential oath requires the president to guard the official religion of the country and to propagate the religion. This is an oath that the current president, Mahmoud Ahmadinejad, takes seriously. In a series of speeches and interviews in 2005 following his first election victory, he spoke of his strong belief in the return of Shia Islam's twelfth Imam: "Our revolution's main mission is to pave the way for a reappearance of the 12th Imam, the Mahdi.... Today, we should define our economic, cultural and political policies based on the policy of Imam Mahdi's return. We should avoid copying the West's policies and system."[100] Yet this effort to preserve the true Islam has not only severely eroded nearly all religious freedoms for minorities, including those officially recognized by the state, but is used to curtail dissent from within as well, as was seen in the forceful suppression of political dissent following the disputed 2009 presidential elections when the Supreme Leader declared Ahmadinejad the victor.[101] When one religious interpretation is protected above all else, violent persecution is inevitable, as was lamented by former president Mohammad Khatami at a meeting of reformist political activists in August 2009: "We can no longer defend our Islamic Republic against rigid-minded, extremist and inhumane groups working under the name of Islam."[102]

The formal restrictions on religious freedoms are many. From practicing and expressing faith to holding public office and gaining employment, the recognized religious minorities face particularly severe restrictions from the state and hold reduced legal privileges. For religious minorities not recognized by the state, such as the Baha'is, virtually all religious freedoms are denied. Government-affiliated media attack all non-Shia religions, with the Baha'is and Jews being the most frequent targets. However, the restrictions and open discrimination against religious minorities go far beyond the formal restrictions of the government. Clerics speak openly against them being granted freedoms, the nongovernment media is filled with attacks on these groups, and virtually all sources agree that the cultural atmosphere is restrictive and often threatening for these groups.[103]

The result has been a mass exodus of religious minorities since the 1970s and persecution for those who remain. The number of Jews has plummeted from 75,000–80,000 in the 1970s to fewer than 20,000

---

[100] "Iran President Paves the Way for Arabs' Imam Return," *Persian Journal*, November 17, 2005. Also see http://www.inplainsite.org/html/imam_mahdi.html (accessed 6 August 2010).

[101] See http://www.cnn.com/2009/WORLD/meast/06/14/iran.election/index.html (accessed 14 June 2009).

[102] Borzou Daragahi, 2009, "Iran's Ahmadinejad Urges Prosecution of Opposition Leaders," *Los Angeles Times*, August 29, http://www.latimes.com/news/nationworld/world/la-fg-iran29-2009aug29,0,4551976.story (accessed 6 August 2010).

[103] For examples, see Sanasarian & Davidi (2007); Sanasarian (2000); Moaddel (1986); and the State Department's International Religious Freedom report, http://www.state.gov/g/drl/rls/irf/2008/108482.htm (accessed 6 August 2010).

today. Christians and most other religious groups have shown a similar decline.[104] Of those who stayed, the Baha'is, Sufi Muslims, evangelical Christians, and Jews have faced the harshest attacks. But the Baha'is have faced the most violent, systematic, and virulent persecution. Eliz Sanasarian explains that the "Baha'is represented everything that was sanctioned (by the state, the ulama, the Shii Muslim community, and the secular, even Western-educated) to hate – namely, apostasy, association with the West and Israel, pro-monarchism, and an elite club bent on self-promotion and propaganda."[105]

The tragic case of Iran's Baha'i community clearly demonstrates the religious persecution cycle and illustrates how government and social restrictions on religion can work in tandem to increase the level of violent persecution, especially of religious minorities that are considered heretical to Islam. The Baha'i faith began in Iran in the nineteenth century. Baha'is believe that God revealed himself to humanity through a series of divine prophets, including Abraham, Krishna, Zoroaster, Moses, Buddha, Jesus, and Muhammed. They believe that the various religions of each of these prophets came from the same source and are successive revelations of one religion from God. For the Baha'is, Bahá'u'lláh (1817–1892) was the latest of many prophets. Of course, this is in sharp opposition to the Islamic teaching that Muhammed is the final prophet. Thus, although Christians and Jews are viewed by Muslims as legitimate religious communities that were in the line of Islam, they reject Baha'is as heretics.

Despite being the largest religious minority in Iran, the Baha'is are in essence "unprotected infidels" with no legal rights.[106] The Islamic regime regards this faith as apostasy, and the elimination of the Baha'i community of Iran is explicit government policy. A secret Iranian government document published by the UN Human Rights Commission in 1993 outlines the official strategy to suppress the Baha'i community. Written by the Supreme Revolutionary Cultural Council and signed by Supreme Leader Ali Khamenei, this document, dated February 25, 1991, set forth specific guidelines for dealing with Baha'is so that "their progress and development are blocked." One of the most ominous signs of the government's current intentions was exposed on March 20, 2006. The UN Special Rapporteur on Freedom of Religion or Belief made public a confidential letter

---

[104] Sanasarian & Davidi (2007).
[105] Sanasarian (2000).
[106] See congressional testimony by Ms. Kit Bigelow, June 30, 2006, http://commdocs .house.gov/committees/intlrel/hfa28430.000/hfa28430_of.htm (accessed 6 August 2010).

from Iran's armed forces calling for Baha'is to be identified and monitored. The Anti-Defamation League called these actions "reminiscent of the steps taken against Jews in Europe."[107]

Not only have the Baha'is lost their freedoms of religious practice, they have also lost nearly all civil liberties and receive few protections from the government,[108] as testimony given to the U.S. Congress graphically depicts:

> By order of the Iranian Government, Bahá'ís are not permitted to elect leaders, and they have been barred from institutions of higher education since 1980. According to Iranian law, Bahá'í blood can be spilled with impunity. They are not allowed to worship collectively. Bahá'ís are also denied jobs and pensions: more than 10,000 have been dismissed from government and university posts since 1979. All cemeteries, holy places and community properties were seized soon after the 1979 Islamic Revolution. Many properties have been destroyed, and none have been returned. The right of Bahá'ís to inherit is denied. Since 1996, Bahá'ís have been strictly forbidden to seek probate. In the years immediately following the Islamic Revolution, more than 200 Bahá'ís were killed or summarily executed, and thousands more were jailed.[109]

Despite recent hopes to the contrary, social support for the government's actions against the Baha'is remains strong, with some social and religious groups calling for even stronger action. The *2008 International Religious Freedom Report* noted the possible "resurgence of the banned Hojjatiyeh Society, a secretive religious-economic group that was founded in 1953 to rid the country of the Baha'i faith in order to hasten the return of the 12th Imam (the Mahdi)."[110] Vandalism was reported at a Baha'i cemetery in Najafabad, and a body was exhumed and desecrated from a Baha'i grave in Abadeh. As noted earlier, anti-Baha'i publications, programs, and broadcasts by the general media are common, and physical attacks also occur, including killings. When reviewing the plight of the Baha'i in his book *Religious Minorities in Iran*, Eliz Sanasarian explained

---

[107] See congressional testimony by Ms. Kit Bigelow, June 30, 2006, http://commdocs .house.gov/committees/intlrel/hfa28430.000/hfa28430_of.htm (accessed 6 August 2010).

[108] The *2008 Report on International Religious Freedom* states, "According to law, Baha'i blood is considered mobah, meaning it can be spilled with impunity," http://www.state .gov/g/drl/rls/irf/2008/108482.htm (accessed 6 August 2010).

[109] Congressional testimony by Ms. Kit Bigelow, June 30, 2006, http://commdocs.house .gov/committees/intlrel/hfa28430.000/hfa28430_of.htm (accessed 6 August 2010).

[110] 2008 IRFR, http://www.state.gov/g/drl/rls/irf/2008/108482.htm (accessed 6 August 2010).

that "[p]ersecution does not only lie in the action of the state or community, but in the mind of every individual."[111]

The open attacks on the Baha'is are the most extreme example of lost freedoms and increased violent persecution, but Jews, evangelical Christians, and Sufi Muslims are facing a similar dilemma. With religious freedoms largely revoked, and neither the government nor the larger culture supportive of religious minorities, the path to persecution is wide open.

CONCLUSION

The case of Iran, and the larger group it represents, brings us to a sensitive issue. Why is the level of religious freedom so low and the level of violent religious persecution so high in many predominantly Muslim nations? Iran is not the only Muslim nation where strong political and social pressures exist for reducing religious freedoms. Indeed, thirteen of the fourteen countries in this group are predominantly Muslim. And, as we illustrated in Chapter 1, the rates of violent religious persecution in Muslim-majority nations are much higher than the world average. Rather than ignoring this obvious but sensitive point, the next chapter offers an extended discussion on why religious freedoms are often denied and how this leads to higher levels of violent religious persecution in Muslim-majority countries.

[111] Sanasarian (2000:53).

6

What about Muslim-Majority Countries?

On April 6, 2007, Jeremy Page of the *Times* of London reported from Pakistan that groups of theological seminary students from Islamabad's Lal Masjid (Red Mosque) policed the capital with bamboo poles as part of a campaign to introduce their version of Sharia law from the bottom up, despite opposition from the government. Maulana Abdul Aziz, prayer leader at the Red Mosque and principal of its seminary for women, gave the government an ultimatum: introduce Sharia; otherwise, "his students would do it themselves."[1] Male and female students approached cars in the city, "telling women to stop driving and asking people playing 'un-Islamic' music to turn it off." Seminarians visited retail shops with the same message, urging shop owners to rid their shops of objectionable material. The seminarians included female squads who brandished bamboo poles and wore full burqas.[2] According to the *Daily Times* of Pakistan, Aziz also "gave the Islamabad administration a week

---

[1] Page (2007). http://www.timesonline.co.uk/tol/news/world/asia/article1620554.ece (accessed 6 August 2010).

[2] Contrary to many popular images, especially in the West, militant Muslim women conducting moral policing are not unprecedented. Dukhtaran-e-Millat ("Daughters of the Faith"), founded by Ms. Asiya Andrabi in Indian-administered Kashmir in 1981, has been in operation longer than has Al Qaeda. There are indications of a growing trend of suicide attacks by Muslim females in Ali (2005). Also see Deborah D. Zedalis, 2004, "Female Suicide Bombers," Strategic Studies Institute, U.S. Army War College, Carlisle, PA, http://www.strategicstudiesinstitute.army.mil/pdffiles/PUB408.pdf. The research of Mohammed Akram Nadwi indicates that the historical role of women in the development, study, and transmission of Sharia is significant. His research, conducted while at Oxford's Center for Islamic Studies, is due to be published in 2010. See http://www.timesonline.co.uk/tol/comment/faith/article1652134.ece (accessed 6 August 2010).

to shut down 'brothels,' otherwise 'seminary students will take action themselves. If we find a woman with loose morals, we will prosecute her...' [Aziz] said."[3] On April 12 the *Economist* reported that more than ten thousand male and female students set fire to mounds of music videos and CDs taken from local retailers and that these seminarians "can be seen practising martial moves with staves... barely a mile from Pakistan's supreme court, parliament building and the headquarters of the Inter-Services Intelligence Agency (ISI)."[4] The Pakistani government was reluctant to intervene and risk violent conflict with the group, especially with female seminarians, so its initial reaction was to look for some sort of accommodation. Within days of these events, however, reporter Fasahat Mohiuddin documented a counterdemonstration in Karachi that attracted tens of thousands chanting slogans against what they termed "Kalashnikov Sharia." The protests were led by Altaf Hussain, chief of the Muttahida Qaumi Movement (MQM). Hussain stated that the party "is not against the *Madrassas* [religious schools; seminaries] which are teaching modern technology as well as Islamic education, but we are against those seminaries which are teaching extremism and terrorism."[5]

In this chapter, we will show that religious social movements challenging the state and restricting religious freedoms in society play a particularly important role in explaining why Muslim-majority countries have higher levels of religious persecution and conflict. We propose that the higher levels of religious restrictions and persecution in Muslim-majority countries are *not* primarily a product of geography or history but are connected to movements within the Muslim world to revive and reclaim the social (and geographic) territory under the "realm of submission" to God, which is known as Dar al-Islam. Central to the concept of Dar al-Islam is that society is regulated by Islamic faith and practice, with the implementation of Sharia law as the means to ensure fidelity to Islam and a well-ordered society. We find that most of these movements are aimed at reviving "true" Islam and restoring the rule of Islamic law. Rather than highlighting the clash of civilizations between Islam and the West, we propose that the clashes within Islam are more important for understanding religious persecution and conflict.

---

[3] "Cleric Gives Govt a Week to Impose Sharia," *Daily Times* (Pakistan), March 31, 2007, http://www.dailytimes.com.pk/default.asp?page=2007/03/31/story_31-3-2007_pg1-2 (accessed 6 August 2010).

[4] "Pakistan's Militant Drift: Taliban All Over," *Economist*, April 12, 2007, http://www.economist.com/world/asia/displayStory.cfm?story_id=9008911&fsrc=nwlbtwfree#top (accessed 6 August 2010).

[5] Mohiuddin (2007).

Building on the general model presented in Chapter 3, we try to explain the origins and consequences of the social regulatory movements that are so prevalent in Muslim-majority nations. In particular, we will explain why this form of social regulation is so influential on the formation of religion–state alliances. As in previous chapters, we will also show that religion–state alliances can lead to a loss in religious freedoms through increased restrictions on religious activities, leading to increased religious persecution. The general model presented in Chapter 3 explained the sources of social and government restrictions on religion and how each is related to religious persecution. This chapter will take a closer look at how the model fits Muslim-majority nations, just as it does other nations.

Before we attempt to understand why persecution occurs in Muslim-majority countries, however, we first provide several historical, social, and geographic background observations about Muslim-majority countries. This allows us to explore the common heritage as well as the wide variation within Muslim-majority countries. The goal, of course, is to provide a contextual backdrop that helps us to understand how variations or common experiences explain levels of religious persecution. Next we describe the level of religious restrictions and persecution for Muslim-majority countries, look at how the levels vary across these countries, and compare their rates to countries dominated by other world religions.

Finally, after explaining why religious restrictions and religious persecution and conflict are so common in Muslim-majority countries, we close the chapter by briefly discussing two additional topics: attitudes of Muslims residing outside of Dar al-Islam and religion-related violence that is defined as terrorism. We provide a brief overview of the more moderate views of Muslims outside of Dar al-Islam, and we show variations and trends in religion-related terrorism. This brief review also allows us to show how terrorism is used in an attempt to alter religion–state alliances: alliances that increase religious restrictions and lead to higher levels of religious persecution.

HISTORICAL, SOCIAL, AND GEOGRAPHIC CONTEXT

We begin by exploring the historical, social, and geographic context of Muslim-majority countries today.[6] Here we try to identify the common

---

[6] Along with cited works throughout the chapter, we also drew on the following works for background information while writing this chapter: Abou El Fadl (2002); Ahmed (1999, 2002); Ali (2002); An-Na'im (1996); Armstrong (2002); Asad (2003);

heritage of today's Muslims as well as acknowledge the rich diversity of Islam. Throughout this discussion we strive to understand how the context has shaped religious restrictions and persecution in Muslim-majority countries.

The Spread of Islam

The Prophet Muhammed is central to the faith of Muslims in ways that are distinct from the founder of Christianity. Muhammed plays a role more akin to the law-giving and military roles played by Moses and Joshua of the Hebrew scriptures than to the preaching and atoning roles of the Apostle Paul and Jesus Christ of the New Testament. Muhammed established a social order that was to be lived in conformity to the will of the one true God as revealed in the holy Quran. Those who have not submitted to the revealed will of God are to be invited to do so, and those who do submit to God (called Muslims) do so with the understanding that they will live by the "revealed" laws of God. Apostasy is therefore a serious offence both to God and to the Muslim community. To God, denying him and his revealed will has eternal consequence. To Muslim society, it is akin to treason. Although the parallel to treason is not exact, it is helpful to understand that when religion and society are one, the dividing line between treason to the state and religious apostasy becomes thin. This correlation between the two is related to the Islamic socioreligious vision of seeing the lands that have not yet submitted to the social and religious will of God (Dar al-Harb) become lands that do submit to that will (Dar al-Islam).

On and off for one thousand years, Islam seemed on the path to global domination. In the twenty years following the death of the Prophet Muhammed in A.D. 632, Muslim conquest and rule quickly spread from Medina and Mecca through what is now Iraq and Iran. By A.D. 750, Muslim influence reached beyond Samarkand (in modern-day Uzbekistan) and the Indus River (South Asia) in the east and all the way across North Africa to Spain, Morocco, and the Atlantic Ocean.

Bearman et al. (1960–2004); Bin Sayeed (1995); Cragg (1971); El Guindi (1999); Esposito (2002a, 2002b); Esposito & Burgat (2003); Esposito & Voll (2001); Hitti (2002); Hunter & Malik (2005); Keddie (1983); Khalidi (1998); Khalidi et al. (1993); Lewis (1992); Mernissi (2002); Moaddel & Talattof (2002); Mortimer (1982); S. H. Nasr (2002); S. V. R. Nasr (2001); Runciman (1951, 1952, 1954); Voll (1994); von Grunebaum (1955); Wright (2001); Zubaida (2003).

Muslim domination grew along the eastern coast of Sub-Saharan Africa, and Islam was established there as a lasting presence by the tenth century.[7] Muslims extended their economic and religious influence along the Silk Road through Central Asia to western China.[8] Long before the Indian Ocean and the South China Sea were navigated by Europeans, Muslim merchants and missionaries navigated these waters with dexterity. Unlike in the Middle East and North Africa where conquest helped propel Islam forward, Muslims traded and proselytized along spice trade routes to the East Indies (modern Indonesia)[9] and beyond, establishing mosques along the eastern coast of China. In fact, when Marco Polo returned from China in 1295, he departed from Quanzhou, where a mosque had already existed for nearly two hundred years.[10]

As Dar al-Islam spread, it encountered customs and social orders different from those of Mecca and Medina. In order to apply the Quran and the teachings of Muhammed to new and changing social situations, Muslims developed a legal science called Sharia law, which interprets the social, legal, and religious aspects of the Quran in light of the collected sayings of Muhammed. As Islam spread, kings as well as paupers were to live in accordance with Sharia. This does not mean that religion and state must be one and the same but that the state is governed by the laws of Sharia just as is an individual. This system also allowed for religious diversity among Sharia interpretations and had provisions for toleration of other scriptural monotheistic religions within Dar al-Islam ("People of the Book," including most Jews and Christians). The major internecine violence within Islam during these years was the dispute over the proper way to follow the Prophet Muhammed. The Party of Ali (Shia) advocated that leadership should pass through those related by blood, whereas the majority felt that it should be through following the ways (Sunna) of Muhammed, not necessarily the bloodline.

---

7 See Foalola (2002).

8 The first Muslim envoy to China came long before that. "Uthman ibn Affan, the third Caliph of Ummah, sent the first official Muslim envoy to China in 650. The envoy, headed by Sa'ad ibn Waqqas, arrived in the Tang capital, Chang'an, in 651 via the overseas route." See http://www.ibiblio.org/chinesehistory/contents/02cul/c05s03.html (accessed 6 August 2010).

9 Islam took root in modern Indonesia by the fifteenth century through trade and missionary work. See Reid (1993). Also see Vlekke ([1959] 1960).

10 The senior author lived in Quanzhou in 1982–1983 and encountered Muslims who were the legacy of the Muslim traders who established the mosque in 1006. The first mosque was built in the first decade of the eleventh century according to Dasheng (1984) (cited in Kumar 1987).

The centuries of Muslim advance were interrupted by a series of Christian Crusades (1095–1291), which temporarily carved out territory from Muslim control; but the Crusader kingdoms endured for less than two hundred years.[11] Ironically, the Fourth Crusade (1201–1209) involved the sack of Byzantine (Christian) Constantinople, creating a weakened eastern Christendom that eventually gave way in 1453 to a Muslim Ottoman Empire that endured from 1299 to 1922. Islam was no longer a Middle Eastern religion. It was directed from Asia (modern-day Turkey) and had the largest populations in South Asia. Indeed, today, sixty percent of Muslims live throughout Asia compared with only twenty percent living in the Arab heartland of the Middle East and North Africa.[12]

Muslim predominance, however, began to be eclipsed with the age of European exploration and commerce. The Indian Ocean and South China Sea were now being navigated by Europeans. In 1521, before dying in a battle, the explorer Ferdinand Magellan introduced Christianity to the Philippines; at the same time, Francis Xavier pushed for a mission into China. As European global conquest and Catholic missionary work expanded, Muslims encountered a series of serious setbacks. The Spanish Inquisition expelled Muslims (and Jews) from Spain by the beginning of the sixteenth century. The Ottoman Turks, who never pushed westward across the Atlantic, suffered a series of defeats in the Mediterranean and Europe at the hands of a newly invigorated and confident Europe. A large Ottoman force was repelled at Malta by the vastly outnumbered Knights of St. John in 1565, and then the Ottomans were decisively defeated at Vienna in 1683.

The Twentieth Century

Much of the current political context surrounding Muslim-majority countries today developed during the nineteenth and twentieth centuries when Western colonial empires were at their apex. Muslims encountered European colonizers during this period who were energized by an Industrial

[11] The legacy lives on. For example, the Crusaders took Jerusalem with merciless slaughter in 1099, but when they lost it less than one hundred years later in 1187 to the famous Kurd from Tikrit, Saladin exercised mercy over the defeated Crusaders that continues to stand in dramatic relief to the Crusader-led slaughter of 1099. See Krey ([1921] 1958). The Crusaders were ultimately expelled from the region in 1291 with the fall of Acre, in present-day Lebanon. Also see Runciman (1951, 1952, 1954).

[12] *Mapping the Global Muslim Population*, Pew Forum, 2009, http://pewforum.org/Mapping-the-Global-Muslim-Population.aspx.

Revolution that emerged from the Reformation and the Enlightenment – a worldview that largely separated religion from politics and law. The separation of religion and law in the West is especially different from the basic approach to law in Islam. As mentioned, Islam's foundation has more similarities with early Judaism than with early Christianity, in which the development of law preceded the development of theology. Islamic law developed along four general schools, but the common element linking the four is the concept that although a political realm can operate separately from religion, political actions should not contradict or do anything forbidden by Islamic law. In the West, and especially in the United States, there is an ongoing, lively debate over the extent to which Judeo-Christian principles, such as those enshrined in the Ten Commandments, can be acknowledged as the source of U.S. law and if the nation is living "under God."[13] For Islam there are strict guidelines on how the nation lives "under God."

By the turn of the twentieth century, Europeans administered almost every Muslim-majority territory. India, including what is now Pakistan and Bangladesh, was administered by the British, as were other Muslim-majority territories ranging from Egypt, Palestine, Sudan, and most of the Arabian Peninsula to southeast Asia including Brunei, the Maldives, and Malaysia. The Dutch colonized Muslim-majority Indonesia, and the French colonized much of North Africa.

As the superior firepower and technology of Western powers dominated much of the world stage, some Muslim-majority societies sought to emulate this powerfully pragmatic model and establish their own "civilized" countries, such as the founding of a "secular" Turkey led by Mustafa Kemal Atatürk from the remnants of the Ottoman Empire. Atatürk rejected a public role for religion and pointed to the scientific and industrial advances of the West for the country's model. Unlike Turkey today, where 51 percent see themselves as Muslims first and Turks second,[14] the spirit of the times was different in 1933 when Atatürk concluded his speech on the tenth anniversary of the republic with the phrase, "Happy is he who says 'I am a Turk.'"[15] Atatürk's speech did not end with or have any mention of God, compared with many Muslim-majority political speeches today that begin, "In the name of God, the

---

[13] For a summary and analysis of church-state issues in the United States, see http://www.pewforum.org (accessed 6 August 2010).

[14] See http://pewglobal.org/reports/pdf/DividedWorld2006.pdf (accessed 6 August 2010).

[15] Atatürk, October 29, 1933, http://www.theturkishtimes.com/archive/02/11_01/f_speech.html (accessed 6 August 2010).

Compassionate." A recent commentary on Atatürk is worth quoting at some length:

Atatürk's posture toward Islam was a function of his personal dislike of the religion, but it was also pragmatic. He wasn't shy about flying the green banner of the Prophet Muhammed when it could lift the spirits of devout Muslims in Turkey's war of liberation against the Italians and Greeks. But almost as soon as he took power he started to clean up the symbols of Turkey's old order. He eliminated the caliphate, and made Sunday the country's official day of rest (instead of Friday, the Muslim day of prayer). He introduced Latin writing instead of Arabic and replaced Sharia with a code composed of Swiss and Italian law. "Progress means taking part in this civilization," Atatürk preached to his people, "the Turks have constantly moved in one direction – we have always gone from East to West."[16]

The secular state established by Atatürk remains in power, owing to the support of the military, but today there is a rekindled interest in bringing Islam back to the Turkish public sphere. The secular government highly regulates religion in Turkey all the way down to controlling the content of sermons in mosques and forbidding university women to wear Muslim headscarves. Despite the authority of the secular state opposing them, the allies of a more traditional view of Islam are gaining support in the general populace as well as the media and civil society at large.[17] In our terms, the mounting social pressures are part of a cycle involving social reaction to pervasive government restrictions on religion, fostering movements seeking for society to be less overtly secular and more in line with Islamic customs and teachings.

Elsewhere, the disorder and dissolution of European colonial empires following the two world wars gave way to a bipolar U.S.–USSR world order that arose from the ashes of the Holocaust and Hiroshima. Parts of the Muslim world came under the orb of Communist USSR, including Central Asia. At least one Muslim-majority country adopted self-styled Communism (Albania). Some became strategically aligned with the Soviet Union (e.g., Syria and Iraq). Other Muslim-majority societies looked to nationalism (e.g., Yasser Arafat's Palestine Liberation Organization) and pan-Arabism (Nasserism in Egypt), all of which tended to exclude religion from the public sphere. One Muslim-majority society, Indonesia, rejected

---

[16] Annette Grossbongardt and Bernhard Zand, 2007, "The Turkish Paradox: A Muslim Steps Aside, and the West Isn't Happy," *Der Speigel*, May 7, http://www.spiegel.de/international/world/0,1518,481404,00.html. Also see Kinross (1965). (accessed 6 August 2010).

[17] See Kuru (2009).

Communism and established a state philosophy, called *Pancasila*, as a way to combat a Communist insurgency. Pancasila requires all citizens to subscribe to monotheism (and thus reject atheist Communism). During this period, the Jewish state of Israel was established and became a staunch anti-Communist ally of the United States. Likewise, Wahhabist Saudi Arabia became a U.S. ally. Note that these two U.S. allies possess the three holiest places of Islam – Mecca, Medina, and Jerusalem. The fact that the United States has had significant influence over these two governments has been noted in the rhetoric of Al Qaeda, which seeks to reclaim these sites from those who allow the influence of non-Muslims within the geographic realm of Dar al-Islam (i.e., the lands ruled by Islam or the house of Islam). Possessing holy sites implicitly requires the need to regulate and protect them, certainly an important factor in the religion-related violence and displacement suffered by many in the holy lands.

Two watershed events in the latter part of the twentieth century gave encouragement to renewing the political and strategic dimensions of Dar al-Islam, where Islam is increasingly viewed as a viable alternative to the secular world order that had come to dominate most Muslim-majority countries. The first was the overthrow of the secular shah of Iran by Ayatollah Khomeini in 1979, which brought into being the Islamic Republic of Iran. Iran is the first major nation-state to see secular rule abruptly ended by a revolutionary Islamic movement. The second watershed is the against-all-odds story of the defeat of the Soviets in Afghanistan, largely by the U.S.-supplied Mujahideen. In Vali Nasr's words,

if the Iranian Revolution was successful in rolling back a regime, Afghanistan pushed the buck further by rolling back a superpower. It made fundamentalism much more of a triumphant phenomenon.[18]

Encouraged by such successes, Islamic political movements are a growing part of the landscape. As mentioned, they are actively resisted by many seculars in Turkey as well as by the current government of Egypt, but they have established holds on power in additional countries including Sudan, Palestine (at least in Gaza), and, in a battle yet to be decided, Somalia.

[18] Interview of Vali Nasr, Conversations with History: Institute of International Studies, UC Berkeley, 2002, http://globetrotter.berkeley.edu/people2/Nasr/nasr-con5.html (accessed 6 August 2010).

AN OVERVIEW: RELIGIOUS RESTRICTIONS AND PERSECUTION

We are aware that commentators on Islam today tend to be either overly critical or timidly uncritical about the situation in Muslim-majority countries. We attempt to avoid either extreme by staying very close to our data. With this opening overview, in particular, we strive to offer a profile of how Muslim-majority countries compare to other countries in the areas of religious freedom and violent religious persecution and conflict. This overview will also explore how the profile varies over time, by ethnicity, and across global regions.

Although violent religious persecution occurs regardless of the majority religion in a country, it is present in every country with a Muslim-majority with a population of two million or more in the first seven years of the twenty-first century compared with 78 percent of Christian-majority countries and 86 percent of other[19] countries. Religious persecution is not only more prevalent among Muslim-majority countries, but it also generally occurs at more severe levels. Sixty-two percent of Muslim-majority countries have a moderate to high level of persecution (where more than two hundred people have been persecuted), compared with only 28 percent of Christian-majority countries and 60 percent of other countries, as shown in Figure 6.1.

As we reviewed briefly in Chapter 1, the contrast between Muslim-majority and Christian-majority countries is even more pronounced at the highest levels of persecution, where more than one thousand persons are reported to have been abused or displaced because of religion. Forty-six percent of Muslim-majority countries are at this level, which is more than four times the percentage of Christian-majority countries (11 percent). The only group that has similarly high levels of persecution (i.e., the "Other Majority" category) is actually a mix of countries, some that

---

[19] Although we did not lump all other majority religions into the "Other Majority" category in Chapter 1, we do so here in order to have groups large enough to compare. The "Other Majority" category includes countries that do not have Christian or Muslim populations making up at least 50 percent of the entire population. *Note:* According to the World Religion Database (2008), there are seven countries with Buddhist majorities: Thailand (87%), Cambodia (85%), Burma/Myanmar (74%), Sri Lanka (68%), Bhutan (67%), Japan (56%), and Laos (53%); Vietnam is 49% Buddhist. Hindu-majority populations are found in India (73%) and Nepal (69%). A Jewish-majority population is found only in Israel (73%). Those falling into the "Other Majority" category where there is no religion making up 50 percent or more of the population include China, Hong Kong, North Korea, Nigeria, Benin, Burkina Faso, Ivory Coast, Eritrea, South Korea, Liberia, Mongolia, Sierra Leone, Singapore, Taiwan, and Togo.

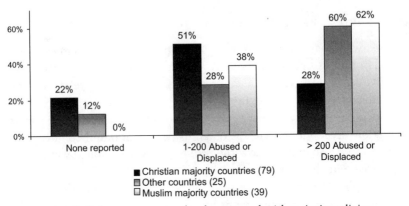

FIGURE 6.1. Religious persecution level *compared with* majority religion

have no religious majority and others that have a religious majority other than Muslim or Christianity. In Chapter 1 we showed that the countries with no single religious majority tend to have low levels of religious persecution and the disparate group of countries with other religious majorities (e.g., atheism, Hinduism, Judaism, and Buddhism) tends to have very high levels of religious persecution. We have discussed many of these cases in previous chapters, including Burma, China, India, and Nigeria, each of which had more than one thousand cases of religious persecution.

In this chapter we propose that the elevated level of religious persecution and conflict in Muslim-majority countries is a consequence of social and government restrictions on religion. Therefore, we expect that higher levels of religious restrictions will follow a pattern similar to the one we saw for religious persecution. The high levels of social and government religious restrictions in Muslim-majority countries, shown in Figures 6.2 and 6.3, support our expectations. Muslim-majority countries have high levels of social and government restrictions, as well as very high levels of religious persecution (shown in Figure 6.1).

Based on these figures and the evidence reviewed earlier, a few results are undeniably clear. First, while religious persecution and conflict can potentially occur in any country, religious persecution is more likely to occur in Muslim-majority countries than in other countries. Second, the levels of religious persecution are far more severe, with the contrast between Christian-majority and Muslim-majority countries being especially striking. Third, government and social restrictions on religion are far higher in Muslim-majority countries, following a pattern similar to religious persecution and conflict. For each of these results the evidence is

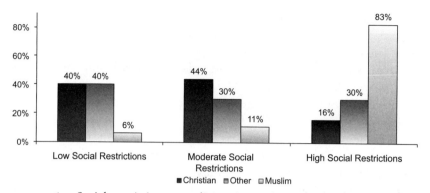

FIGURE 6.2. Social restrictions on religion (countries with populations greater than 2 million)

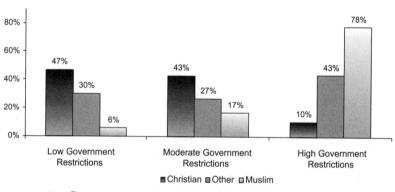

FIGURE 6.3. Government restrictions on religion

convincing. But how do these trends vary over time by region or ethnicity? We will explore these variations.

Changes over Time?

For many, the denial of religious freedom in Muslim-majority countries is associated with a recent surge of Islamic fundamentalism. Volumes have been devoted to explaining this sudden surge and the denial of freedoms that followed. But has there been a sudden shift or simply a shift in awareness?

To explore historical trends in religious restrictions empirically, we draw on a 1945 global investigation of religious liberty. This investigation was carried out under Yale University professor M. Searle Bates, who at the time was a professor of history at the University of Nanking, China.

Even though the study was carried out by a joint committee of global experts appointed by several Christian organizations, the study went to great lengths to assess as accurately as possible any limitation on religious freedom, without focusing on those related to restrictions on foreign missionaries. In Bates's words, "Truth has been sought in humility, and the results have been stated honestly – not sparing Christendom or its Protestant elements."[20]

The context of the war years of the 1940s is important because World War II was still underway as the study was completed. During that time period, several influential Christian-majority countries were committing some of the most egregious violations, including Nazi Germany, fascist Italy, and Communist Russia (the USSR).[21] Also, the reforms of Vatican II were still decades in the future, meaning that the Vatican had not yet recognized religious freedom as a human right.[22] At the same time, nearly every Muslim-majority country or territory was under the colonial rule of a European, Christian-majority country.

Using Bates's global investigation of religious liberty and relying on the same six questions we used for coding government restriction scores in the twenty-first century (see Table 3.1), we calculated a 1945 restriction score for each of the countries covered by Bates.[23] Comparing our coded data from 1945 with coded data from recent International Religious Freedom reports in Figure 6.4, we are able to see that the level of government restrictions has gone down in Christian-majority countries (from an average of 3.2 out of 10 in 1945 to 2.3 in 2005), while it increased in Muslim-majority countries (5.6 to 6.3) and "Other Majority" countries (3.7 to 4.6).

Although these historical trajectories are not completely surprising, the data indicate an important point: the level of religious regulation in Muslim-majority countries was much higher than in Christian- and "Other Majority" countries, even though Muslim-majority countries were under European colonial rule in the 1940s. This indicates that even during the period when Christian-majority countries reached a high level of government regulation of religion, the level of regulation was still higher in Muslim-majority countries.

---

[20] Bates (1945:xi).

[21] Although the Soviets were technically atheist, the rapid revival of Russian Orthodoxy suggests that nominal Christian identity continued throughout the Soviet period (Wanner 2007; Froese 2008).

[22] See Kwitny (1997) for a discussion of Pope John Paul II's involvement in the acceptance of the human right of religious freedom.

[23] Double-blind coded for 61 countries under the senior author's supervision.

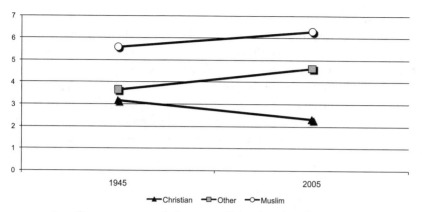

FIGURE 6.4. Government restrictions on religion (1945 and 2005)

Part of the drop in Christian-majority country scores may be attributable to the resolve in the West not to repeat twentieth-century atrocities such as the Holocaust. Many Christian-majority countries, for instance, enthusiastically supported the Universal Declaration of Human Rights, with article 18 recognizing religious freedom as a fundamental human right.

Within Muslim-majority countries, however, a different postwar process was at work.[24] Religious freedom was not a rallying cry – independence from the colonial powers was. With independence came the need to develop governing policies and legal codes as well as national identities for newly formed nations. Social and government restrictions on religion may thus have been seen as a strategic part of the nation-building process that occurred in these newly independent states as we saw with Turkey – a view that religion was not potent enough a force to withstand colonial powers.[25]

---

[24] There continues to be debate in Muslim-majority countries on how the Universal Declaration of Human Rights squares with Islam. As noted in a recent UN document, "Two conferences held at the Palais des Nations make this more than an intellectual exercise [sic]. In November 1998 the Office of the High Commissioner for Human Rights co-sponsored with the Organization of the Islamic Conference (OIC) a special seminar, entitled: Enriching the Universality of Human Rights: Islamic Perspectives on the Universal Declaration of Human Rights. On 14–15 March 2002, the OIC hosted alone a second seminar on Human Rights in Islam when many of the same issues were debated. The statement of the High Commissioner is noteworthy." See http://www.unhchr.ch/Huridocda/Huridoca.nsf/(Symbol)/E.CN.4.Sub.2.2002.NGO.19.En?Opendocument (accessed 6 August 2010).

[25] See Marx (2003).

Following independence movements, however, Islam gradually became (or reemerged as) the dominant social identity that began to define national identities, which helps to explain historical events such as Muslim-majority Pakistan and Bangladesh separating from Hindu-majority India. More important for our purposes, it sets a historical backdrop for current levels of religious restrictions: restrictions in Muslim-majority countries were not all driven by the events of the past several decades. High restrictions on religious freedoms have existed in Muslim-majority countries for some time.

Religion and Ethnicity

When attempting to understand the social context of religion, ethnicity quickly comes to mind. Some scholars have gone so far as to claim that ethnicity taps into the most significant differences across religions.[26] Even scholars proposing cultural explanations of social conflict often conflate ethnicity and religion, with some referring to "ethno-religious" activity.[27] We find this conflation of religion and ethnicity misleading because not all members of an ethnicity belong to the same religious group and vice versa. In some cases, religion does reinforce national and ethnic identities, such as during conflicts in Bosnia and Herzegovina and Kosovo between 1992 and 1995, which resulted in the deaths of hundreds of thousands.[28] But in other cases, religion and ethnicity have little overlap, and each remains a separate identity. In the religion-related violence in Iraq, for example, the conflicting sides share the same ethnicity. Although religion and ethnicity do overlap in some cases, they are not identical, and the degree of overlap will vary greatly by country and ethnic group.

The UK census, which asks detailed questions about both religion and ethnicity, illustrates the differences. Notice in Figure 6.5 that each ethnicity listed has some Christians, and most ethnicities contain substantial numbers of Muslims. Also, ethnicity is conflated with nationality, making ethnicity difficult to measure empirically, even by the sophisticated UK census. An additional difficulty is that ethnicity is composed of a variable

---

[26] Henderson argues against "conflating of religious variables in definitions of ethnicity" (1997:660).

[27] For instance, see Norris and Inglehart (2004).

[28] *2001 Report on International Religious Freedom*, http://www.state.gov/g/drl/rls/irf/2001/5570.htm (accessed 6 August 2010).

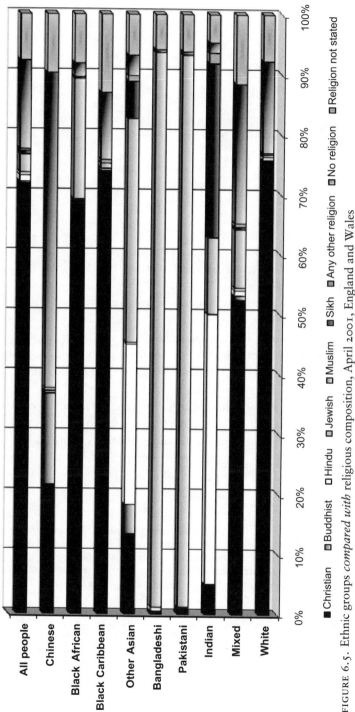

FIGURE 6.5. Ethnic groups *compared with* religious composition, April 2001, England and Wales

Legend: ■ Christian ■ Buddhist □ Hindu □ Jewish □ Muslim ■ Sikh ■ Any other religion ■ No religion ■ Religion not stated

Categories (top to bottom): All people, Chinese, Black African, Black Caribbean, Other Asian, Bangladeshi, Pakistani, Indian, Mixed, White

Axis: 0%, 10%, 20%, 30%, 40%, 50%, 60%, 70%, 80%, 90%, 100%

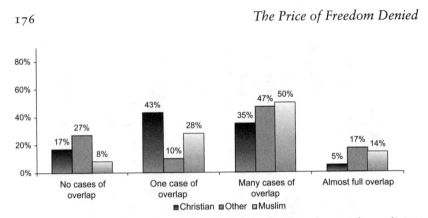

FIGURE 6.6. Level of Persecution *compared with* religion and cases where religion and ethnicity overlap (countries with populations greater than 2 million)

set of characteristics that overlap but are not coterminous with race.[29] In other words, ethnic boundaries are fluid and layered.[30] Even with imperfect measures, however, we can see that ethnicity alone does not capture religious differences.

Another source of information on the overlap of religion and ethnicity is the IRF reports. The reports go to some lengths to report abuses and restrictions that were clearly religious in nature and not ethnic. However, because religion and ethnicity do overlap, the reports indicated when this was clearly the case. We coded this at four levels for each country.[31] The lowest level was no reported cases of religion and ethnicity overlapping, and the highest was if all religions reported indicated a close overlap with ethnicity. There is some evidence that this overlap occurs in Muslim-majority countries more often than it does in other countries. Figure 6.6 shows that only 8 percent of Muslim-majority countries had no reports of overlap, compared with 17 percent of Christian-majority countries and more than 27 percent of other countries. Certainly, the higher level of

[29] The general idea of ethnicity is captured in the term *ethnic group*, which Marger defined as "a group within a larger society that displays a common set of cultural traits, a sense of community among its members based on a presumed cultural heritage, a feeling of ethnocentrism on the part of the group members, ascribed group membership, and, in some cases, a distinct territory. Each of these characteristics is a variable, differing from group to group" (1991:35).

[30] Cf. Okamoto (2003).

[31] In 48 percent of the cases, religion and ethnicity were not reported to be related, in 12 percent of the countries there was just one religious group for which religion and ethnicity were closely related, in 38 percent of the countries several ethnicities were related to specific religious affiliations, and in fewer than 3 percent of the countries did ethnicity seem inseparable from religious affiliation. See http://www.thearda.com/Archive/Files/Analysis/IRF2001/IRF2001_Var81_1.asp (accessed 6 August 2010).

association between Islam and ethnicity can reinforce loyalties, making any conflict that cuts across multiple sources of identity more severe; but even for Muslims there is seldom a complete overlap between religion and ethnicity.

In our analysis[32] of the cases, we find that persecution in Muslim-majority countries is less often associated with ethnic conflict and more often associated with such things as the vision that differing religious groups have for their society. The most lethal religion-related armed conflict in recent decades occurred during the Sudanese civil war, which resulted in more than six million people being killed or displaced between 1989 and 2005.[33] Religion played a central role in splitting the country into warring sides, primarily pitting government forces from the Muslim-majority north against an array of opposition forces from the south, which is largely Christian. The main dividing line was not ethnicity, but religion itself as the north sought to make the country an Islamic republic with Sharia as the law of the land.[34] The support of northern Muslim society reinforced this government direction, which was, of course, opposed by those in the south.

Ethnic context can shape the actions of Muslims just as ethnicity can shape the actions of others; yet it would be a grave error to reduce religion to ethnicity for Muslims – or for most other religious groups. Most ethnic groups show variation in religion, and Islam covers a diverse array of ethnicities – an ethnic diversity that reflects the regional diversity of Islam.

Regional Diversity

Contrary to popular perceptions, the majority of Muslims are *not* Arab, and they do *not* live in the Middle East. The combined total of Muslims living in Asia and Sub-Saharan Africa (estimated at 918 million) is more than two-and-one-half times as large as the total of Muslims living in the Arab-speaking Middle East and North Africa. This regional diversity has important implications for regional variations in religious persecution.[35]

Figure 6.7 displays the regional variation in religious persecution *among Muslim-majority countries*. The most noticeable difference is that,

---

[32] See Grim & Finke (2007).
[33] According to UN estimates.
[34] Toft (2007).
[35] See Johnson & Grim (2008).

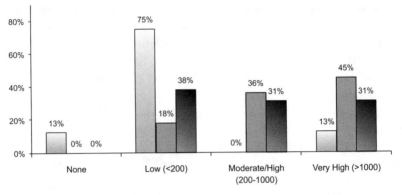

FIGURE 6.7. Religious persecution in Muslim-majority countries (countries with populations greater than 2 million)

on average between 2001 and 2005, 88 percent of the Muslim-majority countries in Sub-Saharan Africa (or 7 of 8) have no or low levels of persecution compared with only 18 percent of Muslim-majority countries in Asia/Eurasia (2 of 11) and 38 percent in the Near East/North Africa (6 of 16). A second difference is that only 13 percent (1 of 8) Muslim-majority countries in Sub-Saharan Africa have a moderate/high or very high level of persecution, compared with 81 percent in Asia and Eurasia (9 of 11) and 62 percent of Muslim-majority countries in the Near East and North Africa (10 of 16).[36]

Muslim-majority countries in Sub-Saharan Africa also have lower average levels of religious persecution when compared with the other countries in the region. As Figure 6.8 shows, 88 percent of Muslim-majority countries in Sub-Saharan Africa have no or low levels of persecution with 72 percent of Christian-majority in the same region. Thus, in Sub-Saharan Africa, the data indicate that Muslim-majority countries have slightly less-severe levels of religious persecution than do Christian-majority countries.

Sudan and Somalia are the only Muslim-majority countries in Sub-Saharan Africa with a very high level of persecution (see Table 6.1). Chad has a moderate persecution level (fewer than two hundred persons

---

[36] Once again, government restrictions of religion follow a similar pattern, with religious freedoms being far higher in Sub-Saharan Africa. Sub-Saharan Africa is the only region where Muslim-majority countries are present in the world's lowest-scoring 25 percent of scores on government regulation of religion.

TABLE 6.1. *Religious Persecution* Compared with *Government Restrictions on Religion (GRI) and Social Restrictions on Religion (SRI)*

Country	Persecution (0–10, 10 = high)	GRI (0–10, 10 = high)	SRI (0–10, 10 = high)	Outlier
Sudan	10.0	Very high	Very high	
Chad	4.0	Very high	Very high	
Somalia	[a]	Very high	Very high	
Mauritania	1.4	Very high	High	
Niger	1.4	High	High	
Mali	1.4	Low	Moderate	
Senegal	1.4	Low	Low	
Guinea	0.0	High	High	←

[a] General anarchy prevents accurate estimate.

persecuted), whereas Mauritania, Niger, and Mali have low levels of persecution. Senegal has low levels of restrictions and persecution.

In general, there is an observable pattern in Muslim-majority countries in which higher levels of religious persecution are associated with higher levels of government and social restrictions. Guinea, however, is an anomaly. The country reported no persecution from July 2000 through June 2005, despite high levels of government and social restrictions on religious freedom. But Guinea's exceptionalism didn't last. Looking at the IRF reports for July 2005 through June 2006 confirms this: several people were injured, and approximately fifty detained during religion-related violence after the reporting period ended.

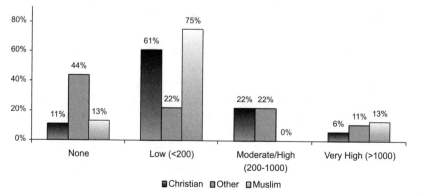

Christian (N=18), Other (N=9), and Muslim (N=8)

FIGURE 6.8. Persecution in countries of Sub-Saharan Africa (>2 million population)

In October 2005 there was religiously motivated violence between the predominantly Muslim Koniankes and the predominantly Christian Guerzes in N'Zerekore in the Forest Region. During Ramadan, violence erupted after the Koniankes complained that music from a Guerze baptism disturbed prayers at a nearby mosque. Several persons were injured and property destroyed, and police detained approximately fifty persons. Some of the detainees were held for approximately two weeks and charged with disorderly conduct.[37]

The one outlier now conforms to the expected pattern.

A few comments are useful on some of the factors that contribute to fewer religious restrictions in some Sub-Saharan countries. First, Islam itself has diverse forms, ranging from highly mystical Sufism practiced by a variety of groups to voluntary brotherhoods that cut across tribal and ethnic lines. Sufism, which focuses on the spirit above the law, is much more difficult to regulate centrally, resulting in opposition from Wahhabi groups, and even persecution in Saudi Arabia, though relative peace and harmony in western Africa.[38] Second, in Senegal,[39] in particular, where Sufism is strong, persecution occurs at lower levels. Senegal has policies that attempt to show equal respect for all religions, rather than showing favoritism only to Islam or one interpretation of Islam. Although this appears to contradict the concept of Dar al-Islam, it seems to have strengthened a moderate brand of Islam in Senegal. And, until recently, the situation appeared to be the same in Mali, which also has a strong historical presence of Sufism. When Sufism collaborated with the morally liberal stances of the secular governments in West Africa,[40] however, popular disillusionment resulted and other Muslims rallied support for a more conservative, Islamic norm-based society.[41] Thus, the developments in Guinea and Mali indicate that the levels of both are increasing.

Despite this important regional variation within Islam and the increase in religious restrictions since 1945, generally speaking, Muslim-majority countries have fewer religious freedoms and far higher rates of religious persecution. Merely identifying these results, however, is neither satisfying nor new. Our goal is to understand why.

---

[37] *2005 Report on International Religious Freedom, Guinea*, http://www.state.gov/g/drl/rls/irf/2006/71305.htm (accessed 6 August 2010).

[38] See Robinson (2004).

[39] For example, see Hunwick & Mbacke (2005).

[40] Lapidus (2002).

[41] See Soares (2005).

Understanding Religious Restrictions and Persecution

Based on data taken from Bates's 1945 global study of religious liberty, we know that any recent surge in Islamic fundamentalism is not the complete answer. And despite a tradition of toleration for other monotheistic religions, the data indicate that Muslim-majority countries had restricted religious freedoms for many years before the recent wave of violent fundamentalism. Likewise, we know that despite ethnicity overlapping with Islamic communities, this overlap falls far short of explaining the high rates of regulation and persecution. The historical and regional contexts of Islam, however, did point to the renewed importance of the concept of Dar al-Islam – defending and expanding the territory that is faithful to the tenets of Islam – a finding that returns us to our earlier explanation of religious persecution.

The general explanation or model reviewed in Chapter 3 found that social restrictions fueled a demand for increased government restrictions of religion and noted that for Muslim-majority countries both social and government restrictions were strong predictors of persecution. This same model identified civilization divides, percentage of Muslims, and religious law as strong predictors of social restrictions, with armed conflict having a direct impact on religious persecution. We want to take a closer look at this model as it applies to Muslim-majority countries.

Armed Conflict and Civil War

We saw in Chapter 3 that armed conflict had a direct influence on religious persecution that went above and beyond social and government restrictions. Because armed conflict has been common in Muslim-majority nations in recent history, and because many have been involved in severe and protracted armed conflict, we take a brief look at the extent of armed conflict in Muslim-majority countries.[42]

Figure 6.9 offers a summary of armed conflict for Muslim, Christian, and Other countries. From 1988 to 2002, armed conflict with battle deaths greater than one thousand occurred in 65 of 143 countries with populations greater than two million. Muslim-majority countries have been plagued both with more conflict – 58 percent of the countries (21 of 36) – and more lethality – 19 percent with more than one hundred thousand deaths since 1988. When limiting our attention to nations with

---

[42] Data coded by Grim (2005).

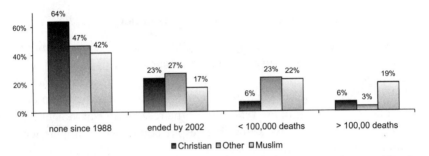

FIGURE 6.9. Armed conflict (countries with populations greater than 2 million)

an armed conflict costing more than one hundred thousand lives, the differences are especially pronounced. Whereas 19 percent of Muslim-majority nations fall into this category, only 6 percent of Christian and 3 percent of "Others" do.

The relationship between armed conflict and persecution was tested more rigorously in Chapter 3, but Figure 6.9 does make it clear that armed conflict alone is not sufficient to explain religious persecution. With religious persecution occurring in 97 percent of all Muslim-majority nations and armed conflict occurring in only 58 percent, it is obvious that armed conflict cannot fully explain religious persecution. Nevertheless, armed conflict occurs far more often in Muslim-majority countries than in Christian-majority countries and history has shown that religious persecution intensifies during wartime, especially when religion marks the opposing sides of the conflict.[43]

The war in Iraq is the most obvious recent example, one that we should note was initiated in 2003 by an invasion led by the United States. The many years of favoritism paid to Sunnis and other non-Shia minorities by Saddam Hussein's 1979–2003 regime created a religious pyre ready to ignite. Events such as the February 22, 2006, bombing of the Al-Askari mosque, one of the holiest sites in Shia Islam, resulted in Sunni–Shia violence and hundreds of deaths in the days that immediately followed. Although the thousands of sectarian revenge killings are not over religion per se, the opposing sides are identified by religion, and targets include religious leaders and mosques. Neighborhood after neighborhood was *religiously decimated*, to use a more accurate term than *religiously cleansed*.

---

[43] See Toft (2007) for a fuller discussion.

Another way of showing that armed conflict does not fully explain religious persecution is to look at the statistical relationship between the two and how it varies for major religions. If armed conflict were the driving force behind the higher levels of religious persecution for Muslim-majority countries alone, we would expect a substantially higher correlation between armed conflict and persecution for Muslim-majority countries. What we find, however, are only very small differences: the correlation is 0.43 for Muslim-majority countries, 0.38 for Christian-majority countries, and 0.34 for "Other Majority" countries. This suggests that armed conflict is associated with religious persecution for all nations and is not unique to Muslim-majority countries. This was earlier confirmed by the model tested in Chapter 3, including a test using only Muslim-majority nations that found armed conflict holds a direct relationship with persecution, but the relationship is much weaker than that of religious restrictions.

Clash of Civilizations

In Chapter 3 we discussed Huntington's clash of civilizations and how it is used to explain global conflict. Even prior to Huntington's thesis, one of the foremost Western historians of Islam, Bernard Lewis, argued that a clash between Islam and the West was in the offing. For Lewis, there has been an ongoing competition between Islam and the West for centuries, and current events are a manifestation of this potential clash between civilizations, which is likely as more Muslims return to their traditional roots. In Lewis's words:

In the classical Islamic view, to which many Muslims are beginning to return, the world and all mankind are divided into two: the House of Islam [Dal al-Islam], where the Muslim law and faith prevail, and the rest, known as the House of Unbelief or the House of War [Dar al-Harb], which it is the duty of Muslims ultimately to bring to Islam.[44]

The missionary vision of Islam – something necessary for any vital religion – is identified as a source of conflict by Lewis, in part due to the association of jihad (struggle that can include a so-called just war–type of armed conflict) with the task of bringing Islam to the Dar al-Harb.

---

[44] See Bernard Lewis, 1990, "The Roots of Muslim Rage," *The Atlantic Online*, September, http://www.theatlantic.com/past/issues/90sep/rage.htm (accessed 6 August 2010).

TABLE 6.2. *Being on a Fault Line* Compared with *High Levels of Religious Persecution*

	Christian	Other	Muslim
Percentage of countries located on a fault line	36	52	79
Percentage of countries with persecution >1,000	11	36	46
Percentage of fault line countries with persecution >1,000	25	62	46

Traditionally, the concept of Dar al-Islam has had clear geographic dimensions, not just spiritual dimensions. Dar al-Islam, as developed by classical theorists, is the physical territory within which society conforms to the precepts of Islam. This territory can accommodate other faiths (e.g., "People of the Book"), but it grants toleration only for their communities, not for their propagation beyond their own kin. Specifically, in the territory of Dar al-Islam, adherents of other faiths are free to convert to Islam, but Muslims dare not convert to other faiths. Muslims are to engage in the work of inviting all non-Muslims to submit to God and, when possible, to expand the geographic territory under submission to God.[45] For Lewis this clear distinction between Dal al-Islam (House of Islam) and Dar al-Harb (House of Unbelief or the House of War) resulted in an inevitable conflict between Islam and the West.

In Huntington's subsequent version, which is less focused on Islam, the clash of civilizations implies that tensions between nations with different civilizational loyalties are at the heart of conflicts. One way to see whether Muslim-majority countries are more likely to face pressure from neighbors of a different "civilization" is to compare who is more likely geographically to be bordered by a country of a different civilization. Put simply, are Muslim-majority countries more prone to lie on what Samuel Huntington called "fault lines"? The answer is yes. Although approximately the same number of Christian-majority (twenty-eight) and Muslim-majority (thirty) countries are located on these so-called fault lines, a higher percentage of Muslim countries (79 versus 36 percent) are located on a civilization divide (see Table 6.2). Do these fault lines explain persecution?

---

[45] See Hussein (2007).

Being located on a civilization fault line has a far greater impact on the level of religious persecution in non-Christian-majority countries. Looking at the second row in Table 6.2, we can see that the rates of persecution are generally far higher for Muslim-majority countries – 46 percent have high levels of persecution (more than a thousand cases). However, the rate is identical for Muslim-majority countries located on a fault line (46 percent), indicating that being on a fault line makes the level of persecution no higher than for Muslim-majority countries in general. However, more than twice the percentage of Christian-majority countries located on fault lines have high levels of persecution (25 percent) than Christian-majority countries in general. Perhaps the greatest surprise is the high level of persecution found in countries on fault lines from the "Other" category (62 percent). This rate is fueled, in part, by several Communist or former Communist nations with high levels of persecution. But the rate also included several Buddhist-majority and Hindu-majority nations. However, in Chapter 3 we were able to test the impact of this finding on religious persecution, controlling for the level of restrictions on religion as well as a host of other possible explanations. What we find is that, although being on these fault lines increases the likelihood of persecution, it is not a direct cause of persecution. The data in Table 6.2 show, however, that being on a fault line is not at all a likely explanation for the level of persecution in Muslim-majority countries.

Additional findings show that victims of religious persecution are often minority sects or coreligionists of the nation's dominant world religion. Specifically, in recent coding managed by Brian Grim, we are able to see that Muslims are more likely to be harassed (including verbal abuse) and violently persecuted by governments in Muslim-majority countries than by governments in countries where the populations are predominantly of other faiths (see Table 6.3). *Governments in more than seven in ten Muslim-majority countries harass Muslims* compared with Muslims being harassed in only three in ten Christian-majority countries. This is an important observation. The dominant religion of the country tends to harass and persecute minority sects or coreligionists of their own world religion as much as they do religions of another "civilization."[46]

---

[46] The findings are similar when considering social harassment and persecution. As with government harassment, Muslims are much more likely to be harassed by social actors in Muslim-majority countries than by social actors in countries where the populations are predominantly of other faiths. Social actors in nearly three in five Muslim-majority countries harass Muslims compared with fewer than than three in ten Christian-majority countries.

TABLE 6.3. *Government Harassment of Religious Groups* Compared with *Majority Religion of the Country*

Religious Group Harassed or Persecuted	Christian 122 %	Muslim (48) %	Mixed[b] (17) %	Buddhist (9) %	Other[c] (4) %
Christians	33.6	63.0	47.1	44.0	75.0
Muslims	30.0	71.0	41.0	22.0	25.0
Jews	7.4	6.3	0.0	0.0	50.0
Hindus	0.0	8.3	0.0	11.1	0.0
Buddhists	1.6	0.0	11.8	22.2	25.0
Baha'is	0.8	18.8	5.9	11.1	0.0
Other	22.1	39.6	11.8	33.3	0.0
Countries with at least one incident of harassment or persecution	58.0	90.0	71.0	89.0	100.0

[a] Religious composition of countries source: Johnson and Grim, *World Religion Database* (Leiden and Boston: Brill, 2008).
[b] No single religion makes up 50 percent of the population.
[c] Other includes Hindu (2 countries), Jewish (1), and agnostic (1).
Source: Pew Forum on Religion & Public Life (2009).

In short, the clash is often more from within than without, regardless of the dominant religion. Persecution in Muslim-majority countries is directed at Muslims as well as other faiths. Neither Lewis's nor Huntington's thesis would have anticipated this finding. For Muslims the clash is often over the extent of control religion should have over the workings of society as a whole. Once again, this returns us to Dar al-Islam and the importance of Sharia law.

Sharia Law

In Chapter 2 we noted that countries with provisions for Sharia law are less likely than other countries to make promises of religious freedom in their constitutions or other legal codes, and all but one of the countries with Sharia have *four* or more laws restricting religious practice in some way. We also found that the absence of strict Sharia law in much of Sub-Saharan Africa was associated with less persecution. When exploring the historical context of Islam, we found political movements calling for a revival of Dar al-Islam usually focus on a stricter application of Sharia, and when exploring clashes within Islam, we found differing interpretations of Sharia law to be a source of increased persecution. We also find that the growing implementation of and/or attempts to implement Sharia law are a form of religious regulation connected to persecution and conflict in Muslim-majority countries, as seen in the events at Pakistan's Red Mosque described earlier in this chapter.

As reviewed in Chapter 2, apostasy and heresy are examples of prohibitions that go to the core of Sharia law and often restrict the religious freedoms of non-Islamic religious groups. Rulings on apostasy prevent Muslims from freely changing their religion, and rulings on heresy prevent them from coming to and freely expressing new understandings of the teachings of Islam. Also, Sharia offers limited toleration of some non-Muslim religions but vehemently opposes others, especially any religion, such as Baha'i, that recognizes a prophet subsequent to Muhammed. The result is that non-Islamic groups hold limited religious freedoms, and some Muslims face harsh persecution under Islamic law, which in some countries goes as far as stoning for sexual transgressions and amputation for theft. What this doesn't explain, however, is why the harshest religious persecution is often directed at other Muslims, such as the Ahmadiyya sect in Pakistan and Indonesia. Once again, we return to Sharia law to understand this form of persecution. In particular, we try to understand how the importance of Sharia law can contribute to competition and conflict between Islamic groups.

The starting point for understanding why religious persecution arises between Muslim groups is to understand what Sharia law is and why its adoption is so important to religious leaders. At its core, Sharia law is a system of jurisprudence that is based on the sacred text of Islam (i.e., the Quran) and the additional moral teachings and behavior ascribed to the Prophet Muhammed, known as the Sunnah or *Hadīth*. For many, Sharia also includes a collection of legal arguments or decisions called the *qiyās*. Typically, there is a distinction drawn between those rulings that are the core teachings of the Quran and Sunnah and those that are based on interpretation. What is considered a "core teaching," however, can vary from one group to another.

When comparing Sharia law to most Western legal systems, two differences should be highlighted. First, Sharia typically has far greater scope, including prescriptive rulings on religious, political, and social spheres. Historically, Muslims have looked to Sharia law as a way to safeguard society from corruption, social ills, and colonial and foreign encroachments. Second, whereas the judicial systems of predominantly Christian countries in the West are typically subsumed within the larger state structure, the judicial system under Sharia law holds substantial independence from the state and is heavily swayed by religious leaders.[47] Thus, religious leaders hold substantially more power when the courts are based on religious teachings and hold independence from the state.

The movement that seems to be at the heart of many disputes within Islam today is the most conservative of the four schools[48] of Islam, the Hanbali school, a version of which is championed by the Wahhabi school that predominates in Saudi Arabia today. Wahhabism is a call to return to a purer faith of the early centuries of Islam that is not subject to the next millennium of accumulated opinion or to modern innovations that seek to reinterpret the Quran and *Hadīth* according to today's social norms. The rise of Wahhabism has been opposed by many countries, ranging from Uzbekistan to Montenegro, Pakistan to Indonesia, and Egypt to Mali. It is Wahhabism that motivated Osama Bin Laden and the Taliban, and it is Bin Laden's disdain for Saudi Arabia's acceptance of non-Muslim troops on Saudi soil that motivates his opposition to his homeland, which would otherwise seem open to him.

Such variation in the interpretation of Sharia law results in inevitable conflicts. Because the judiciaries are often not an arm of the state and their rulings are based on religious teachings, religious movements will seek to sway the extent to which Sharia law is imposed and the final interpretations that are rendered. This is especially the case in Sunni areas, where tradition allows for a variety of interpretations. Thus, one of the common ways by which Muslim groups pressure Muslim-majority societies to adhere more strictly to the precepts of Islam is by advocating for the more thorough adoption of Islamic law (the Sharia).

Our data confirmed that movements seeking the adoption of religious law are overwhelmingly in Muslim-majority countries, where 67 percent report such movements compared to 4 percent of the Christian-majority countries and 20 percent of "Other Majority" countries. Even

---

[47] Hallaq (2004).

[48] Sharia law is not a single body of law that is either adopted or not adopted, nor is it a judiciary system that either has full authority or none. Instead, the application of Islamic law varies from one Muslim-majority country to another. For example, most scholars point to four schools of jurisprudence in Sunni Islam, with each school tending to dominate different regions of Islam. Maliki focuses on the Hadīth, Hanafi on juridical analogy or opinion, Shaft'i on the classical science of Islamic law, and Hanbali reject analogy and precedent and reserve opinion (*qiyās*). Although the schools are viewed as complementary, and all look to the Quran and Sunnah for guidance, substantial variation remains both across and within each school. Likewise, the judiciaries vary in the range of decisions over which they have control.

when movements for the adoption of religious law occur in non-Muslim-majority countries, the movements are frequently Muslim groups seeking Sharia law for Muslim residents in those countries. This occurs, for example, in India, Kenya, Nigeria, the Philippines, Singapore, and Tanzania.

We propose that the battle between Muslims over the understanding and enactment of Sharia law is closely related to the religious restrictions and persecution that often follow. Although this may be in part a reaction against the centuries of Western domination, *we find that this is primarily a struggle within Islam rather than with the West*. In the example that follows we try to illustrate how the multiple sects within Sunni Islam compete over defining and interpreting Islamic law, and we point out important distinctions between the Sunni and Shia administration of Sharia. We return to the example of the Red Mosque mentioned at the beginning of this chapter.

At first glance, the conflict at the Red Mosque coincides with a global spike in anti-Americanism,[49] in which it is quite fashionable to express opposition to American icons such as the Hollywood video industry that depict and even glamorize lifestyles contrary to Islamic morality. Video burnings, however, are not just a protest against Hollywood. There is also a regional[50] video culture that rivals Hollywood – *Bollywood*.[51] Among the videos burned, as many or more may have come from Bollywood, which serves as an icon of the South Asian giant-next-door, Hindu-dominated India.

---

[49] See Kohut & Stokes (2006) and Pew Global Attitudes Project, 2006, "America's Image Slips, but Allies Share U.S. Concerns over Iran, Hamas," http://pewglobal.org/2006/06/13/americas-image-slips-but-allies-share-us-concerns-over-iran-hamas (accessed 6 August 2010).

[50] Looking at regional variation, for instance, is important in order to avoid one of the common mistakes Western observers make – viewing Muslim societies only through an Arabist's lens (e.g., Pakistanis are not Arabs and do not speak Arabic).

[51] *Bollywood* is the popular Mumbai-based Hindu- and Urdu-language film industry in India famous for its melodramatic musicals of love and social intrigue. See, for example, "Islamists Oppose Bollywood Film Screening," *Hindustani Times*, January 24, 2006, http://www.hindustantimes.com/Islamists-oppose-Bollywood-film-screening/Article-54877.aspx (accessed 6 August 2010). Also, according to the Lawdit Reading Room, Pakistan is "one of the major sources of illegal copies of popular Indian films and music and one of the largest manufacturers and exporters of pirate discs in the world, exporting tens of millions of pirate CDS and DVDS annually," http://www.lawdit.co.uk/reading_room/room/view_article.asp?name=../articles/Bollywood%20Piracy%20in%20Europe.htm (accessed 6 August 2010).

When the Islamic Republic of Pakistan divided from a predominantly Hindu British India in 1947, the Quran became recognized as the source of theological truth as well as the foundation for civil and criminal law. But the 1973 constitution openly acknowledged that multiple sects remained and many held different interpretations of Islamic law:

Article 227. Provisions relating to the Holy Quran and Sunnah. – All existing laws shall be brought in conformity with the Injunctions of Islam as laid down in the Holy Quran and Sunnah... the expression "Quran and Sunnah" shall mean *the Quran and Sunnah as interpreted by that sect.* [italics added][52]

Along with the multiple Sunni sects, Pakistan also has large numbers of Shia Muslims. Despite being predominantly Sunni (85–90 percent), Pakistan may have the largest number of Shia Muslims of any country other than Iran.[53]

The italicized part of article 227 is especially important: *the Quran and Sunnah as interpreted by that sect.* It specifically allows for sectarian divisions in the interpretation of personal law. While permitting diversity is a type of freedom, failing to address how the Quran and Sunnah should be applied to national and international policies opened the door to competing interpretations and attempts to regulate national affairs. Because divergent religious interpretations are approved by the constitution as the basis for society, the question is who will decide which Islamic interpretation is correct?

The case of the Red Mosque can be understood as an example of a particular Sunni group attempting to revise the scope, interpretation, and influence of Islamic law. The two leading clerics at the mosque, Maulana Abdul Aziz and his brother, Abdul Rashid Ghazi, were pursuing a mission to extend their Taliban-style interpretation of Sharia law to all of Pakistani society. They came by this mission naturally, since they are sons of the Red Mosque's previous leader, Maulana Abdullah, who was an avid supporter of the Taliban and evidently close to Osama Bin Laden.[54] Maulana Abdullah's leadership was abruptly ended in October 1998 by

[52] See http://www.pakistanconstitution-law.com/const_results.asp?artid=227&title= Provisions%20relating%20to%20the%20Holy%20Quran%20and%20Sunnah (accessed 6 August 2010).
[53] *Mapping the Global Muslim Population*, Pew Forum, 2009, http://pewforum.org/ Mapping-the-Global-Muslim-Population.aspx (accessed 6 August 2010).
[54] Declassified U.S. Army strategy paper prior to September 2001 viewed by the authors. This, in itself, is not remarkable given that Pakistani officials encouraged religious zeal as part of the U.S.-backed campaign in the 1980s to oust Soviet forces from Afghanistan.

assassins' bullets. Although the assassins were never apprehended, Shia militants are suspected.

But if the predominantly Sunni leadership of Pakistan was vague in defining who had authority in interpreting Islamic law, the Shia leadership of Iran was clear following the ousting of the secular shah Mohammad Reza Pahlavi in 1979. The Shia perspective on how the Islamic law and Islam in general are to be interpreted for society is seen in article 2(5) of the Islamic Republic of Iran's constitution.

Article 2. The Islamic Republic is a system based on belief in: 5. continuous leadership (imamah) and perpetual guidance, and its fundamental role in ensuring the uninterrupted process of the revolution of Islam... [55]

In Shia Islam, the final arbiter on Islamic questions is the *imamah*, which includes a hierarchy of Quranic and Sunnah scholars, with ayatollahs represented on the top tier. Shias look to recognized religious scholars for direction, whereas Sunnis emphasize that the Sunnah (traditional teachings) are the final arbiter and not particular religious clerics. Thus, Osama Bin Laden, a Sunni lay clergyman (so to speak), can claim to offer authoritative rulings, or fatwas, just as the ayatollahs of Iran and Iraq do. Although the grand imam of the Al-Askar mosque in Cairo is considered the foremost Sunni scholar, his position is one of tradition rather than hierarchical lineage.

Shias and other Muslim minorities in Pakistan, such as the millions of Ahmadis[56] who are considered heretics by many Muslims, worry that what the Muttahida Qaumi Movement (MQM) calls the Kalashnikov Sharia policy of the Red Mosque vigilantes could become state policy. Then the government guns that keep violence in check today would back up the "vice and virtue" squads and be turned on them. For now, the Pakistani armed forces stormed the mosque and took back control. Abdul Rashid Ghazi was killed in the siege on July 10, 2007, and Maulana Abdul Aziz, his brother, who attempted to leave the mosque prior to the siege wearing a burqa, is in prison in Pakistan.

[55] See http://www.iranonline.com/iran/iran-info/Government/constitution-1.html (accessed 6 August 2010).

[56] The *2006 Report on International Religious Freedom* states, "Specific government policies that discriminate against religious minorities include the use of the 'anti-Ahmadi laws,' the blasphemy laws, and the Hudood Ordinances. In 1984, the Government added Section 298(c), commonly referred to as the 'anti-Ahmadi laws,' to the penal code. The section prohibits Ahmadis from calling themselves Muslims or posing as Muslims, from referring to their faith as Islam, from preaching or propagating their faith, from inviting others to accept the Ahmadi faith, and from insulting the religious feelings of Muslims."

> ## THE MODERN GROWTH OF ISLAM, FROM A RELIGIOUS ECONOMIES PERSPECTIVE
>
> The religious economies model predicts that religious participation is higher either in societies with low levels of religious regulation or with high levels of conflict. Muslim-majority countries have a unique combination of both. First, Sunni Islam is not centrally regulated, requiring mosques and madressahs to compete for the loyalties of Muslims. The irony is that within a highly normative religion, there is a form of deregulation that promotes internal growth. Second, the conflict between Sunni and Shia Islam also stimulates participation, as do calls to rally to conservative interpretations of Islam as a way to counter aspects of Western culture that are seen as morally corrupting. Even in Shia Islam, local imams can compete for loyalties, as is seen with Muqtada al-Sadr in Baghdad during the years following the U.S. invasion in 2003.

The Pakistani case offers a few important illustrations. First, with pluralism built into the way Sunnis interpret Islamic law, conflict can occur between rival groups when they are competing for *official* social and judicial dominance, as is seen in the Red Mosque example. Second, there is a major divide between Sunnis and Shias on how Sharia should be implemented and administered. Pakistan struggles with both Sunni sects offering competing interpretations of Islamic law and the Shia–Sunni divide.[57]

The struggle over implementing more conservative versions of Sharia law is not limited to Pakistan. The Wahhabi movement has spread from Timbuktu to the Philippines to Kyrgyzstan, which borders China, and to China itself. Wahhabism is outlawed in a range of Muslim-majority countries including countries as different as Iraq and Montenegro. Violence toward Salafi groups (a designation similar to Hanbali and Wahhabi) is reported in Indonesia. In Azerbaijan, hostilities are directed toward Islamic Wahhabism and any new religious group making

---

[57] The conflict can become especially violent when it cuts across Sunni and Shia groups, as has been seen recently in Iraq. The February 22, 2006, bombing of the Al-Askari mosque, one of the holiest sites in Shia Islam, resulted in Sunni–Shia violence and hundreds of deaths during the days following, and arguably set off the bloodshed that continues to the present.

inroads into the population. In Africa, Chad has experienced some tensions between fundamentalist and moderate Muslims, Guinea has strong social pressure discouraging conversion from Islam, Mali experienced violence in 2003 between traditional Sunni practitioners and Wahhabi Sunnis, and Niger similarly saw mainstream Sunni youths demonstrating against the Wahhabist Izalay sect.

As shown by the data and the examples just given, increased religious persecution and conflict occur as rivalries form over both the enactment of Sharia law and the version that should be enacted. Not only do implementing and interpreting Sharia law contribute to increased religious restrictions and persecution for non-Islamic groups, such as Baha'is, they are also major sources of persecution of Muslims within Muslim-majority countries.

Muslims in Dar al-Harb (Muslims in Non-Muslim-Majority Countries)

Much of our attention has centered on Muslims in Dar al-Islam, but what about Muslims living outside the House of Islam? The classical Islamic view is that Muslims living in Dar al-Harb should consider migration back to Dar al-Islam, following the model of Muhammed's flight from Mecca to Medina.[58] This is not, though, practical in a globalized world, where, for example, economic circumstances in Europe create a situation that favors immigration from various Muslim lands to provide labor. Similar migration to the United States also occurred and continues to occur, to an increasing extent. Sizable populations of second-generation Muslims in Western countries are now rediscovering Islam through various means, including through contact with missionaries, the Internet, and, according to a recent poll, directly through the Quran itself. What is their response to life in Dar al-Harb? In particular, what is their response to a less-regulated religious environment?

Initial findings suggest that religious freedoms help Muslims positively integrate into Christian-majority societies. For example, a recent study by the Pew Research Center found that in the United States, which is more religiously deregulated than Europe, Muslims are overwhelmingly moderate and mainstream. The American dream has become their dream. Views toward the use of violence offer one indicator. Very few Muslim Americans – just 1% – say that suicide bombings against civilian targets are often justified to defend Islam; an additional 7% say suicide bombings

[58] Hussein (2007).

are sometimes justified in these circumstances. A summary report on the surveys concluded that "Muslims in France, Spain and Great Britain were twice as likely as Muslims in the U.S. to say suicide bombing can be often or sometimes justified. But the Muslims in Europe were far less accepting of the tactic than Muslims in Nigeria, Jordan and Egypt."[59] It may be that Muslims from places such as the United States and Europe will be the vanguard of a new approach to Islam – one that is more tolerant, and more vital.

TERRORISM AND PERSECUTION BY TERRORIST ORGANIZATIONS

Although most forms of religious persecution and conflict have received little public attention, one form has been the focus of daily attention: religion-related terrorism. Before concluding this chapter, we briefly address this specific form of religious persecution and conflict. Like persecution in general, we find higher rates of terrorist activity in Muslim-majority countries and a strong relationship between terrorism and a lack of religious freedoms. As we develop these points, however, we fully reject any argument that stereotypes Muslims as supporters of terrorism and recognize that there is a wide variety of opinions within any religious tradition on the proper role of force. As just noted, for example, there is wide variation across and within countries on Muslims' acceptance of violent tactics in promoting or defending Islam.[60] We also reject stereotypes that automatically link Islam and terrorism. Terrorist actors have come from a variety of religious backgrounds. One of the most protracted religion-related conflicts that involved terrorism in the twentieth century centered on the conflict between Protestants and Catholics in Northern Ireland. Despite rejecting these stereotypes, however, we feel it essential to understand terrorist acts in Muslim-majority countries.

One additional caveat: discussing terrorism involves a judgment call, because one person's terrorist may be another person's freedom fighter. Even before 9/11, Walter Laqueur evaluated more than one hundred definitions of terrorism and concluded that the "only general characteristic generally agreed upon is that terrorism involves violence and the threat of

---

59 Pew Research Center (2007:53).
60 Pew Research Center (2007).

violence."[61] Although most definitions of terrorism include violence and the threat of violence, several widely used definitions also focus on the motivation of terrorist actors. Jessica Stern defines terrorism as "an act or threat of violence against noncombatants with the objective of exacting revenge, intimidating, or otherwise influencing an audience."[62] Borrowing from multiple definitions and restricting our attention to religion-related acts, we will look at actions that are a calculated use of unlawful violence or threat of violence to sway governments or societies to succumb to their religious objectives.[63] Like our more general definition of religious persecution, we will focus on actions that result in religion-related physical abuse and displacement of people. For religion-related terrorism, however, we will limit our attention to unlawful violence that aims to influence the existing governments and the society more generally. Unlike many forms of religious persecution that we have discussed, where the persecution is targeted at specific religious groups or individuals to restrict their ability to worship, this form is typically aimed at a much larger audience in an attempt to achieve specific religious objectives of the group enacting the violence. Religiously motivated terrorist groups usually impose social restrictions on religion and religious practice when they control an area. These restrictions set up a situation in which persecution of those outside the terrorist fold is not only more likely, but can be given a religious blessing as well.

---

[61] Laqueur (1999).

[62] Stern (1999:11).

[63] Our definition draws heavily on the DoD's definition: "The calculated use of unlawful violence or threat of unlawful violence to inculcate fear; intended to coerce or to intimidate governments or societies in the pursuit of goals that are generally political, religious, or ideological." *The DOD Dictionary of Military and Associated Terms*, 2007, http://www.dtic.mil/doctrine/jel/new_pubs/jp1_02.pdf (accessed 6 August 2010). p. 540. The U.S. government's definition touches on similar themes, legally defining *international terrorism* as "activities that (A) involve violent acts or acts dangerous to human life that are a violation of the criminal laws of the United States or of any State, or that would be a criminal violation if committed within the jurisdiction of the United States or of any State; (B) appear to be intended (i) to intimidate or coerce a civilian population; (ii) to influence the policy of a government by intimidation or coercion; or (iii) to affect the conduct of a government by mass destruction, assassination, or kidnapping; and (C) occur primarily outside the territorial jurisdiction of the United States, or transcend national boundaries in terms of the means by which they are accomplished, the persons they appear intended to intimidate or coerce, or the locale in which their perpetrators operate or seek asylum," TITLE 18 – CRIMES AND CRIMINAL PROCEDURE, PART I – CRIMES, CHAPTER 113B – TERRORISM, Sec. 2331, http://frwebgate.access.gpo.gov/cgi-bin/getdoc.cgi?dbname=browse_usc&docid=Cite:+18USC2331 (accessed 6 August 2010).

SUNNI VS. SHIA TERRORISM

As noted earlier, theological differences between Shia and Sunni Islam result in important organizational differences. Because Shia Islam turns to a hierarchy of Quranic and Sunnah scholars for final authority and direction, they tend to be far more hierarchical in their administration of Sharia law. In contrast, because Sunni Islam looks to the Sunnah, and not specific religious offices for authoritative rulings, local officials hold far more authority and new religious movements and organizations arise with less resistance. These same differences result in important differences in the organizational structures of the groups involved in terrorism. Whereas Sunnis are often mobilized through loosely affiliated Al Qaeda–like cells, Shia groups respond to the calls of leading clerics such as Muqtada al-Sadr, in Baghdad or the Iranian government.[64]

We coded two levels of data on religion-related terrorism from the IRF reports. The first is terrorism that had any effect on religion or attitudes toward religion in a country. This includes violent incidents such as the March 11, 2004, and July 7, 2005, train terror bombings in Madrid and London, respectively, which were carried out by groups of individuals with loose or unclear connections to specific terrorist organizations. The second, a subset of the first, is terrorism that is clearly carried out by an organization motivated by a particular interpretation of religion or that directly targets members of certain religious groups.

The more general type of terrorism occurred in thirty-one different countries between 2001 and 2005, affecting eight of seventy-seven Christian-majority countries, seven of thirty "Other Majority" countries, and sixteen of thirty-six Muslim-majority countries. In raw numbers, twice as many Muslim-majority as Christian-majority countries had reported cases of terrorism. Again, the contrast is even greater when considering ratios: terrorism affected more than four times the percentage of Muslim-majority countries (44.4) as it did Christian-majority countries (10.4).

The more specific type of organized terrorist activity, which either is motivated by religious rhetoric or targets certain religious groups, has

---

[64] See "Sunni and Shi'a Terrorism: Differences that Matter," Thomas F. Lynch III, http://gsmcneal.com/wp content/uploads/2008/12/sunni-and-shia-terrorism-differences-that-matter.pdf (accessed 6 August 2010).

been monitored since 2004 in the IRF reports. The State Department refers to this as "persecution by terrorist organizations." This type of terrorism is usually supported by an organizational infrastructure that has an ongoing membership and support base. This particular form of persecution results from the direct actions of nongovernment groups that use violence to accomplish their aims, so it represents a particular security concern because it challenges the legitimacy of governments. In 2005, such persecution was reported in more than one in ten countries with populations greater than two million (15 of 143). Twenty-two percent of Muslim-majority countries were affected by such persecution (8 of 36), which is more than four times the incident rate of Christian-majority countries (3.9 percent, or 3 of 77) and a third more than the rate of "Other Majority" countries (13.3 percent, or 4 of 30). More than half of the reported cases were in Muslim-majority counties (8 of the 5).

Some of the terrorist organizations are primarily political in nature, where the victims are religionists who oppose their aims, such as clergy who speak out against the aims or tactics of groups such as the Revolutionary Armed Forces of Colombia (FARC), the United Self-Defense Forces of Colombia (AUC), the Maoists in Nepal, or the Liberation Tigers of Tamil Eelam (LTTE) in Sri Lanka. In Colombia during the first six months of 2006 alone, for instance, there were "29 assassinations of men, women and children linked to [Protestant] congregations, 84 cases of displacement, 21 civilian combat-related injuries, four arbitrary detentions and other human rights offenses."[65] FARC and the AUC were responsible for the vast majority of these offenses that affected members of Protestant congregations.

In contrast to countries where religious groups have been more politically targeted (as in Colombia, Nepal, and Sri Lanka), religious persecution by terrorist organizations is more often inspired by a militant revolutionary perspective *on religion* with the aim of obtaining power or dominion for a particular brand of religion. Table 6.4 provides a summary of all fifteen countries where the State Department reported cases of persecution by terrorist organizations. Of these, one is a Buddhist-majority country, two are Hindu-majority, one is Jewish-majority, three are Christian-majority, and eight are Muslim-majority.

---

[65] See the report by the Mennonite peace organization Justapaz and the Commission for Restoration Life and Peace of the Evangelical Council of Colombia on the period January 2006–July 2006, "A Prophetic Call: Colombian Protestant Churches Document Their Suffering and Their Hope," August 2006, http://www.justapaz.org/IMG/pdf/pcall_final.pdf (accessed 6 August 2010).

TABLE 6.4. *Terrorist Organizations' Aims and Identities (July 1, 2004–June 30, 2005)*

Country	Country's Majority Religion	Main Perpetrators	Terrorists' Aim	Terrorists' Identities
Sri Lanka	Buddhist	LTTE	Separate Tamil state	Mostly Hindu
India	Hindu	LET & BKI	Muslim and Sikh states	Muslim and Sikh
Nepal	Hindu	Communist Party of Nepal	Communist state	Atheist
Israel	Jewish	Hamas, PIJ, and the Al Aqsa Martyrs Brigades	Islamic/non-Jewish state	Muslim
Colombia	Christian	FARC, AUC & ELN	Marxist state and security	Mostly atheist
Philippines	Christian	Abu Sayyaf Group	Independent Islamic state	Muslim
South Africa	Christian	PAGAD	Islamic voice in S. Africa	Muslim
Afghanistan	Muslim	Al Queda & Taliban	Islamic states and caliphate	Muslim
Algeria	Muslim	AIG & SGPC	Islamic state	Muslim
Bangladesh	Muslim	Jamaatul Mujahideen	Islamic state	Muslim
Iraq	Muslim	Militias, insurgents, sects	Sectarian domination	Muslim
Indonesia	Muslim	Jemaah Islamiyah, etc.	S.E. Asian Islamic state	Muslim
Pakistan	Muslim	SSP, LJ, ST, SMP	Sectarian domination	Muslim
Palestine	Muslim	Kach, Hamas, PIJ	Jewish rule; Islamic state	Jewish; Muslim
Saudi Arabia	Muslim	Al Qaeda	Islamic caliphate	Muslim

Key: LTTE, The Liberation Tigers of Tamil Eelam; LET, Laskhar Toiba; BKI, Babbar Khalsa International; PIJ, Palestinian Islamic Jihad; FARC, Revolutionary Armed Forces of Colombia; AUC, United Self-Defense Forces of Colombia; ELN, National Liberation Army; PAGAD, People Against Gangsterism and Drugs; AIG, Armed Islamic Group; SGPC, the Salafist Group for Preaching and Combat; SSP, Sipah-i-Sahaba; LJ, Lashkar-e-Janghvi; ST, Sunni Tehrik; SMP, Sipah-i-Mohammad.

In twelve of the fifteen countries, there are terrorist organizations that aim to establish a more favored place for Islam in the country, and in thirteen of the sixteen countries, Muslims were among the perpetrators of violence. In this list there are currently no active organizations advocating for increased Christian domination, but there are organizations advocating increased favorability for Sikhism, Hinduism, and Judaism. Of course, the governments of Christian-majority countries use force of arms that target Islamist groups in response, such as in the Philippines, or the United States in its "preemptive" war in Iraq. The point of Table 6.4 is not to associate Muslims with violence and Christians with nonviolence; rather, it is to demonstrate that religious regulation is an aim of religion-related terrorist groups. The motivation of altering religious restrictions, support, and controls helps explain why religion-related terrorism is much higher in Muslim-majority countries and is instigated by Muslims in the majority of recent cases.

The fourth column of Table 6.4 reveals the specific motives or aims of the terrorist organizations and strongly supports the observation just made. In all eight of the Muslim-majority countries where there was religion-related terrorism, the aim of the organization was to establish either an Islamic state or domination for the organization's particular brand of Islam (e.g., Iraq and Pakistan). In Algeria, for example, the Armed Islamic Group (GIA) and its spin-off, the Salafist Group for Preaching and Combat (SGPC), want a stricter interpretation of Islam for the country, despite the fact that Islam is established as Algeria's state religion and its constitution requires that all institutional activities be compatible with Islamic morality. The same is even truer for the Kingdom of Saudi Arabia, which by all measures is one of the two most socially conservative and theologically fundamentalist Muslim-majority countries (Iran being the other). Al Qaeda opposes not only the close relationship of the Kingdom of Saudi Arabia with the United States but also the lifestyles of the royals.[66] In contrast, the case of Palestine is particularly revealing. Contrary to popular notions, Yasser Arafat's Palestinian Liberation Organization (PLO) was primarily a nationalist movement rather than an Islamic one. The Fatah Party is the political party in Palestine that includes Christian as well as Muslim delegates and emphasizes secular nationalism, whereas Hamas, which now controls Gaza, emphasizes Islam and nationalism. Hamas's struggle is to bring Islam to the fore in public life

---

[66] See Claire Miller, 2003, "SAUDI ARABIA: In al-Qaeda's Sights," Council on Foreign Relations, http://www.cfr.org/publication.html?id=7740#1 (accessed 6 August 2010).

and governance. The case of Hamas is one in which its designation as a terror organization is made by the United States but obviously not shared by the many Palestinians who voted them into leadership. Like many forms of religious persecution in Muslim-majority countries, terrorism is often the product of social movements calling for a revival of the house of Islam (Dar al-Islam) and a more conservative enactment of Sharia law.

These examples suggest that the aim of most terrorist organizations is not to launch attacks on the West, but rather to claim their country for a particular interpretation of Islam. Yet, attacks clearly do occur on the West. Once terrorist organizations are established, they can be mobilized to address global concerns. As global communication and transportation ease contact, religious persecution and conflict in the form of religion-related terrorism are easily exported.[67]

CONCLUSIONS

Understanding religious persecution in Muslim-majority countries requires us to understand differing views on how religion should be regulated – or not regulated. Social restrictions are higher within the Islamic tradition not only because it looks to the community of Muslims and its religious leaders to regulate religion, but also because there are movements throughout the Muslim world that advocate a greater role for Islam in the public sphere, including implementing a stricter version of Sharia. An analysis of the recent *World Value Surveys* shows that respondents in Muslim-majority countries "display greater support for a strong societal role by religious authorities" than do respondents from Western countries, even when controlling for strength of religiosity and other social factors.[68] Given strong public support, many countries have moved toward more strictly implementing Sharia law, though individuals themselves may have a fuzzy notion of what it means to more fully implement Sharia. Once religious leaders have the authority to regulate religious affairs in society, however, we find that the chance of religious persecution greatly increases.

---

[67] Education offers one of many examples on how diffusion of ideas and organizations has become global. See Baker & LeTendre (2005).

[68] Norris & Inglehart (2004:147) conclude that the most substantial cleavage between Islamic countries and others is gender equality and sexual liberalization. Our gender measure has a weak although significant effect on social regulation but no direct effect on religious persecution.

In this chapter we also addressed why Muslim-majority countries are more likely to turn to religious leaders and other sources outside of the state to regulate religion. We demonstrated that it is not primarily a product of the historical times, but rather an attempt to regulate socio-geographic territory within Dar al-Islam through the use of Sharia law.[69]

Finally, we agree with those who see the rise of militant religious fundamentalism in places such as Algeria, Egypt, Iran, and Syria as the result of a state (often associated with foreign influence) that was "zealously undermining the social functions and influence of religion."[70] The history of secularism among Muslim-majority countries during the twentieth century was not simply an attempt to separate church and state; the goal was to rid the state of all religious entrapments. This goal was intolerable for many Muslims in Dar al-Islam.

---

[69] Also, as we noted in Chapter 2, understanding how Sharia law is implemented is crucial for understanding why religious leaders play such a crucial role. Whereas the courts in predominantly Christian countries are typically subsumed within the larger state structure, the Sharia courts in predominantly Muslim countries frequently hold substantial independence from the state and are heavily swayed by religious leaders: (Hallaq 2004).

[70] Moaddel (2005:342).

7

Do Religious Freedoms Really Matter?

When reviewing human rights throughout European history, Michael Horowitz described Jews as the "canaries in the coal mine": nations persecuting Jews held less democratic commitment and were more likely to deny other freedoms as well. He later argued that vulnerable Christians are now the canaries, serving as a "litmus indicator of whether freedom exists not only for them – but for all others in their societies."[1] We expand the litmus test beyond a particular religious group to religious freedoms in general, and we agree that the violations of vulnerable religious liberties indicate potential threats to other liberties as well.

Using a wealth of new data, we have shown how denying religious freedoms so often leads to the physical abuse and displacement of individuals based on religion. But this relationship doesn't stand alone. Indeed, it is often embedded within a complex web of religious, social, ethnic, and political relationships. Religious persecution is often one part of a larger social conflict, and religious freedom is often one of many freedoms denied. The relationship between religious freedoms and persecution has implications that go far beyond the topic of religion. Later in this chapter we will briefly touch on the relationships religious freedoms hold that go beyond religious persecution and conflict. Before we introduce these relationships, however, we address a more basic question: Are religious freedoms, and religion as an issue in public life more generally, still topics in need of careful study?

---

[1] As quoted in Hertzke (2004:163–164).

PERSISTENCE OF RELIGION AND THE DESIRE FOR
RELIGIOUS FREEDOM

For some, there remains an ongoing hope that religion will soon dis-appear and that the concern over denying religious freedoms will fade away with it. Needless to say, this is not a new hope. Writing in 1710, Thomas Woolston predicted that religion would be gone by 1900,[2] and many scholars who followed Woolston thought the end would be much sooner. In the mid-1700s Voltaire gave religion another fifty years. These writers were followed by a long list of social scientists, including Comte, Freud, and Marx, who were equally convinced that religion would soon disappear.[3] Even today there is no shortage of scholars offering predic-tions of the secularizing effects of modernity and the imminent demise of religion.[4]

But the evidence has proved stubbornly uncooperative. Even with the full force of state support, Communist regimes couldn't eliminate reli-gion. Chairman Mao Zedong's Cultural Revolution was successful in annihilating most vestiges of organized religion, killing and imprisoning key religious leaders, and eliminating public religious gatherings; yet, the Cultural Revolution couldn't eliminate all beliefs in the divine. Ironically the cult of Mao soon arose, granting him divine qualities and making him an object of prayer and confession.[5] As we reviewed in Chapter 5, the Religious Affairs Bureau in China now acknowledges that atheism isn't working. Elsewhere the results have been similar. The efforts of the former Soviet Union were equally ardent and equally unsuccessful. Once the restrictions on religions were lifted, religious activities resumed.[6]

More recently, global surveys have shown the ongoing vitality of reli-gion. When the World Values Survey asked representative samples of people in countries around the globe if they believe in God, there was a slight increase over the past few decades. Comparing only those fifty coun-tries that are in both the most recent and older waves of the surveys (that is, comparing those taken in the early 2000s with those taken in the late 1980s and 1990s) shows that on average belief in God slightly increased from 73 to 79 percent. Western Europe is the only region that showed a slight decline, dropping from 74 to 73 percent, but Eastern Europe

[2] Woolston (1735).
[3] See Stark & Finke (2000).
[4] Bruce (2002).
[5] Zuo (1991).
[6] Froese (2008).

increased 16 percentage points, from 57 to 73 percent, and the rest of the world (Africa, the Americas, and Asia) consistently registered high levels of belief in God, averaging 92 percent in the most recent wave compared with 91 percent in the previous waves across the countries surveyed. An almost identical pattern is seen when looking at the importance people say religion has in their lives. Western Europe remains one of the few areas showing decline, whereas some of the largest countries are showing sharp increases. For example, in China there was a fourfold (400 percent) increase among those who considered religion either rather or very important in their lives from 1990 to 2007 (from 4 to 16 percent), with a corresponding sharp decrease among those indicating that religion was not at all important in their lives during the same time period, dropping from 76 percent in 1990 to 35 percent in 2007. In India, the percentage saying that religion was rather or very important rose from 78 percent in 1990 to 81 percent in 2006, with only 3 percent placing no importance on religion in 2006. These findings received additional support from surveys conducted by the Pew Global Attitudes Project in 2002 and 2007. Approximately 90 percent of the respondents interviewed placed at least some importance on religion in both years; on average across the countries, 55 percent considered religion to be very important in their lives.[7] Once again, the death of religion has been postponed.

But not only does religion remain vital; religious freedoms also remain important to the global population. As we noted in Chapter 2, the vast majority of respondents from the Pew Forum's ten-nation survey reported that it was very important to live in a country that protected their religious freedoms. This finding is further confirmed by the Pew Global Attitude Project's thirty-four-nation survey, where, on average, 93 percent report that "living in a country where I can freely practice my religion" is somewhat or very important and less than 2 percent indicate that it is not important at all. The level of importance of religious freedom was remarkably high across global regions, ranging from 84 percent in Eastern Europe to 98 percent in Africa.[8] Neither religion nor the desire for

---

7 See "World Publics Welcome Global Trade – but Not Immigration," Pew Global Attitudes Project, October 4, 2007, http://pewglobal.org/reports/pdf/258topline.pdf (accessed 6 August 2010).

8 See "World Publics Welcome Global Trade – but Not Immigration," Pew Global Attitudes Project, October 4, 2007, http://pewglobal.org/reports/pdf/258topline.pdf (accessed 6 August 2010). Question wording: "How important is it to you to live in a country where you can practice your religion freely? Is it very important, somewhat important, not too important or not at all important?" Countries covered: *The Americas*: Argentina,

religious freedoms is showing signs of abating. They remain topics in need of careful study.

RELIGIOUS FREEDOMS AND OTHER FREEDOMS

Although our focus has been on religious freedoms, these freedoms are embedded within a much larger bundle of civil liberties. At the core of religious expression is the freedom of speech and at the core of freedom to worship is the freedom to assemble. To claim freedom of speech without allowing for a freedom to express religious beliefs quickly erodes freedom of speech in other areas. Likewise, allowing for restrictions on the assembly of religious groups opens the door for curtailing the activities of other groups as well. The denial of religious freedoms is inevitably intertwined with the denial of other freedoms.

Because religious freedoms are intertwined with other civil liberties, the outcomes of these liberties are also closely associated. Harvard economist and Nobel laureate Amartya Sen[9] argues that human freedom is not just the *general* opportunity for freedom in the abstract, but the *specific* processes within a country that result in better lives. Our analysis of the most recent data[10] on religious freedom shown in Figure 7.1 graphically displays the relationships that religious freedoms hold with other civil liberties and the well-being of residents in various countries. The associations between religious freedoms and other civil liberties, press freedoms, and political freedoms are especially striking. The highly significant and strong correlations (exceeding 0.6) suggest that that the freedoms are closely intertwined.

There is also growing evidence that this group of freedoms, including religious freedom, is associated with the well-being of those in the society. Figure 7.1 points to a few of these relationships, but additional research confirms these findings. A recent study of 101 countries conducted by the Hudson Institute's Center for Religious Freedom – using entirely independent data from our own – also found that religious

---

Bolivia, Brazil, Chile, Mexico, Peru, Venezuela; *Eastern Europe*: Bulgaria, Czech Republic, Poland, Russia, Slovakia, Ukraine; *Middle East*: Egypt, Jordan, Kuwait, Lebanon, Morocco, Palestinian territories, Turkey; *Asia*: Bangladesh, India, Indonesia, Malaysia, Pakistan; *Africa*: Ethiopia, Ghana, Ivory Coast, Kenya, Mali, Nigeria, Senegal, South Africa, Tanzania, Uganda. The question was not asked in Western Europe.

[9] See Sen (1999, 2002).

[10] Our analysis of data coded for July 1, 2006, through June 30, 2008, at the Pew Forum under the supervision of the senior author. See http://www.PewForum.org (accessed 6 August 2010). for more details.

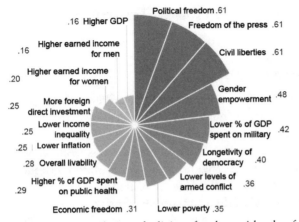

FIGURE 7.1. Correlation of religious freedom with other freedoms and well-being within countries

freedom in a country is strongly associated with other freedoms (including civil and political liberty, press freedom, and economic freedom) and with multiple measures of well-being.[11] They found that wherever the level of religious freedom is high, there tends to be fewer incidents of armed conflict, better health outcomes, higher levels of earned income, prolonged democracy, and better educational opportunities for women. Moreover, religious freedom is associated with higher overall human development, as measured by the human development index published by the United Nations Development Program.

We recognize, of course, that these are correlations and offer no claims on the causal order, but they do suggest that religious freedom is an integral part of a "bundled commodity" of human freedoms.[12] Both religious freedoms and this bundle of freedoms are associated with many positive outcomes. Yet the relationships that religious freedoms hold with other civil liberties and many positive outcomes are still poorly understood.

FREEDOMS, FAVORITISM, PERSECUTION, AND CONFLICT

Like all civil liberties, religious liberties must be consistently protected by the state if they are not to give way to discrimination, prejudice, persecution, and conflict. However, this does not suggest that the state must subsidize religion to avoid conflict or protect freedoms. Indeed, both

---

[11] Grim (2008) in Marshall (2008).
[12] The concept that human freedoms come as a bundled commodity is suggested by Sen (1999, 2002).

our data and our theory would suggest otherwise: favoritism toward select religions is associated with fewer religious freedoms and more religious persecution.

Although unexpected by many, our theory offers several reasons for these outcomes.[13] First, governments can use the carrot of support or the stick of restrictions to reduce religious freedoms and to control religious groups. For example, China's state subsidies and favoritism openly reward select religious groups who comply with their demands. Other religions face restrictions and potential persecution. Second, and closely related, when the state becomes the source of desired support and subsidy, religions may battle for its favor. Coalitions will form and alliances will be made that benefit some religions and not others. Third, as Anthony Gill has shown, the state will make alliances with select religions for political survival. Such alliances are especially common when the government is weak and a single religion is strong.[14]

Each of the reasons just listed assumes that favoritism is selective, with rewards being granted to some and withheld from others. We concede that in principle the state could choose to support or subsidize all religions with no strings attached. In practice, however, we found little evidence of this occurring. Our review of the International Religious Freedom reports and many other sources finds that a state's selectively choosing who is worthy of support consistently coincides with demands that the religions behave in the way the state desires in order for the support to continue. We also find that religious coalitions form in an attempt to gain resources and garner state support. Both the dominant religions and the state have incentives for selective favoritism.

The data confirm our expectations on the consequences of selective government favoritism of religion. As we showed in Table 1.3, when favoritism was shown to some or one religion, the level of violent persecution rose sharply. Table 7.1 illustrates the strong relationship between favoritism and a wide variety of measures that impinge on religious freedoms. Every type of government or social action shown in the table is significantly correlated with government favoritism, meaning that these restrictive actions are more likely to be present in a country when some religious groups receive government access, powers, or favors not provided to other groups. The strongest relationships between government favoritism and restrictions on religious freedoms not only involve government laws and policies that generally restrict religious freedoms, such

[13] Monsma & Soper (2009).
[14] Gill (2008).

TABLE 7.1. *Correlation of Government Favoritism of Religion with Government and Social Actions that Restrict Religious Freedom*

Favoritism's Strong and Significant Correlations		Favoritism's Less Strong but Still Significant Correlations	
Government laws and policies that restrict religious freedom	0.6	Government force used to control religious groups	0.3
Government restrictions on religious conversion	0.6	National government hostility toward minority or non-approved religious groups	0.3
Social hostility over conversions	0.6	Governments require religious groups to register	0.3
Acts of sectarian or communal violence between religious groups	0.5	Religion-related war or armed conflict	0.3
Religion-related terrorist groups active in the country	0.5	Crimes, malicious acts, or violence motivated by religious hatred or bias	0.3
Organized groups use force or coercion in an attempt to dominate public life with their perspective on religion	0.5	Religious groups attempted to prevent other religious groups from being able to operate	0.3
Government restrictions on foreign missionaries (of any religion)	0.5	Public preaching by religious groups was limited by some level of government	0.3
Government interference with worship or other religious practices	0.5	Some level of government formally banned one or more religious groups	0.3
National governmental organization that regulates or manages religious affairs	0.5	Harassment motivated by religious hatred or bias	0.3
		Physical assaults motivated by religious hatred or bias	0.3
Favoritism's Somewhat Strong and Significant Correlations		Instances when the national government attempted to eliminate an entire religious group	0.2
Instances when the national government did not intervene in cases of discrimination or abuses against religious groups	0.4	Violence resulted from tensions between religious groups	0.2
Individuals assaulted or displaced from their homes in retaliation for religious activities considered offensive or threatening to the majority faith	0.4		

Favoritism's Somewhat Strong and Significant Correlations		Favoritism's Less Strong but Still Significant Correlations	
Constitution does not specifically provide for freedom of religion	0.4	The wearing of religious symbols, such as head coverings for women and facial hair for men, was regulated by law or by any level of government	0.2
Constitution or basic law includes stipulations that qualify or contradict religious freedom	0.4	People were displaced from their homes due to religious hatred or bias	0.2
Proselytizing limited by some level of government	0.4	Killings motivated by religious hatred or bias	0.2
Social hostility over proselytizing	0.4	Mob violence related to religion	0.2
Intimidation of religious groups by some level of government	0.4	Detentions or abductions motivated by religious hatred or bias	0.2
Women harassed for violating religious dress codes	0.4		
Religious literature or broadcasting limited by some level of government	0.4		
Individuals or groups in society used violence or the threat of violence, including so-called honor killings, to try to enforce religious norms	0.4		

Note: Authors' analysis of data on 145 countries with populations of 2 million or more in 2009. Government favoritism and other measures used are from the Pew Forum's 2009 *Global Restrictions on Religion* report.

as the freedom to choose one's own religion (conversion), but also with acts of sectarian violence and religion-related terrorism. Although correlations are not the same as causation, it is impossible to ignore that in every measure considered, selective government favoritism is correlated with more restrictions on religious freedoms, not fewer.

Yet there are still many mysteries about this relationship, mysteries that we have only started to pursue. Despite the strong relationship between favoritism, freedoms, and persecution, our initial analysis suggests that the denial of religious freedoms has more explanatory power than government favoritism. When we placed favoritism measures into the statistical models presented in Chapter 3, favoritism was not a strong predictor of persecution once government restrictions were placed in the model. The associations are strong, but explaining the relationships between favoritism, freedoms, persecution, and conflict requires far more attention.

FREEDOMS, PERSECUTION, AND SOCIAL CONFLICT

Our research has taken an initial step in understanding the relationship between religious freedom and social conflict by focusing on violent religious persecution, but we don't view our thesis as being confined to persecution. As we noted in Chapter 1, three of the most prominent scholars of the eighteenth century, Voltaire, Adam Smith, and David Hume, laid bare the potential despotism of a lone dominant religion and forecast endless battles when two major religions fought for dominance. Building on their insights, we have demonstrated the pacifying consequences of religious freedoms. We have found that when social and government restrictions on religion are reduced, violent religious persecution is reduced.

The same arguments can be applied to many other forms of social conflict. Through both our analysis of the new data and our case studies of individual countries, it has been evident that violent religious persecution is often embedded within larger social conflicts, and that restricting religious freedoms is tied to the larger conflicts as well as religious persecution. Figure 7.2 displays by global regions the close relationship between legal restrictions on religion and broader religion-related violence, including terrorism and war.

Once again, we recognize that this is a correlation, and the strength of this relationship and our preliminary research in this area suggest that it shouldn't be ignored.

Both through the case studies reviewed in previous chapters and our own analysis of the new data, we have found that restrictions on religion have both direct and indirect effects on many forms of social conflict, especially religiously motivated conflict.[15] As with religious persecution, we expect that when social and governmental restrictions on religion increase, the probability of other forms of violence increases. Not only do these restrictions heighten tensions and increase grievances that potentially fuel violence, they also strengthen the identity and social bonds within the group facing restrictions and widen the chasm between groups.

---

[15] See Finke & Harris (forthcoming) for a review of several key findings.

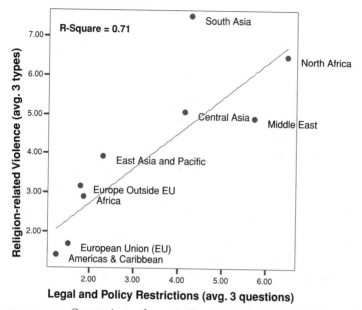

FIGURE 7.2. Comparison of average level of general legal/policy restrictions on religion (constitution, laws, policies) with average level of three types of religion-related violence (hate crimes, terrorism, and war) in regions of the world

Heightening the tension between groups and socially isolating them from other groups also serves to stimulate the growth of religious, social, and political movements that drive conflict. We have seen many examples of such movements in previous chapters. Regardless of the global region being studied or the dominant religion being reviewed, however, examples abound. This returns us to an irony we have explored throughout this book: attempts to reduce tensions by restricting religions often lead to more tension and potentially more conflict.

IN CONCLUSION

Governments often restrict religious freedoms in an effort to maintain order, protect the citizenry, and reduce potential violence. As we reviewed in earlier chapters, France reduced freedoms in an effort to protect citizens from the dangers of religious cults and sects; in China, increased restrictions on Falun Gong, Tibetan Buddhists, and Muslims in Xinjiang were justified as an effort for preserving social order. Many of the social restrictions on religion rely on similar justifications. The Hindu nationalist movements in India aggressively promote Hinduism above all other religions and cultures in an effort to preserve the unity of Hindus and India, and the Russian Orthodox Church views its battles against the new religions as an effort to preserve civic peace and protect the mental, physical, and spiritual health of Russians. No doubt some of the religious restrictions promoted by dominant religions have helped these groups to retain their dominance, but the data do not show that increased restrictions have necessarily helped to maintain order, protect the citizenry, or reduce potential violence.

The bitter irony is that in many places denying religious freedoms has resulted in less order and more violence. In particular, we have found that violent religious persecution and conflict rise as government and social restrictions on religion increase. This finding received strong confirmation from both our new sources of data as well as our six extended case studies and multiple other examples throughout. Even when we controlled for multiple other economic, demographic, and political influences in the statistical model in Chapter 3, the strong influence of denying religious freedoms remained. Whereas Huntington points to the clash of civilizations and the dangers of multiculturalism, our work implies that multiculturalism does not lead to violence, but the attempt to prevent multiculturalism does. More specifically, we found that it wasn't the plurality of religions that explained increased violent religious persecution, but rather it was the attempts to regulate and restrict these religions that led to increased levels of persecution and conflict.[16] Overall, our empirical test of the religious economies perspective shown in the Appendix finds that ensuring religious freedoms for all serves to defuse the potential volatility of religious plurality.

This returns us to our core thesis: *to the extent that governments deny religious freedoms, violent religious persecution and conflict will increase.* We propose that when religious freedoms are granted to all religions, the state has less *authority* and fewer *incentives* to persecute religion. The sharp contrast between China's response to Falun Gong and Japan's reaction to the Aum reviewed in Chapters 4 and 5 illustrates this difference. The perception of Falun Gong as a potential threat resulted in thousands being sent to prisons, labor camps, and mental hospitals. But the deadly attack of the Aum resulted in immediate action for the crimes

---

[16] In the time-lag model shown in the Appendix we note that religious homogeneity has a statistically significant but very weak relationship with religious persecution, confirming that the explanatory mechanisms underlying violent religious persecution are social and government restrictions, both of which have much stronger relationships with violent religious persecution.

committed but little collateral damage in the way of religious persecution of all members of the group or religious members outside the group. Rather than criminalizing the Aum religion, the government allowed it to continue and prosecuted only the individuals who engaged in criminal activities that hurt or aimed to hurt others. This action defused the violent side of the religion without further radicalizing the group.

When religious freedoms are ensured and no single religion holds special authority or privileges from the government, the incentives also change for social, political, and religious movements attempting to curtail the freedoms of other religions, leading to our closely related second thesis: *to the extent that social forces deny religious freedoms, physical persecution will increase.* As we saw in Chapter 6, having religious freedoms would give less incentive for extremist movements that arise within Muslim-majority communities using Sharia law as a way to place restraints on Muslims as well as other religions, as was seen in the case of Pakistan's Red Mosque. Religious freedoms would also give less fuel to the anti-cult movements that have arisen across Europe and to the Russian Orthodox Church's call for increased restrictions on minority religions. When religious freedoms are ensured, however, the state is more likely to protect freedoms of speech, assembly, and political choice.

The challenge, of course, is ensuring religious freedoms. Like other civil liberties, religious freedoms are both inconvenient and fragile. As we reviewed in Chapter 2, because religious freedoms are inconvenient, they are often conveniently overlooked. The most convenient action – and often the one with public support – is to restrict the actions of the religions perceived to threaten the state, the dominant religion, or both. Religious freedoms are fragile because restrictions placed on minority religions can easily be unseen, ignored, or even supported by those in the majority. Like any liberty, religious freedoms force those in power to protect the rights of minorities, even when the majority does not agree. Enforcing this liberty comes with a price, but the price of denying the freedom may be far higher.

Appendix

Testing the Competing Arguments

The statistical test we use – structural equation modeling – is not only appropriate for testing the competing arguments we have presented but it also provides a visual diagram of the relationships between the different measures we will describe. We hope that this will allow even statistical novices to visualize the argument and to see the strength of the relationships being tested. For those wanting more information on the models and the measures, please refer to our articles published in the *American Sociological Review*, the *Interdisciplinary Journal of Research on Religion*, and the *JSM Proceedings, AAPOR-Section on Survey Research Methods*, as well as the data at http://www.theARDA.com.[1]

To test the full model we begin by simplifying the measures. Whereas Tables 3.1 and 3.2 in Chapter 3 reviewed eleven different items measuring various restrictions on religious freedoms, we reduce these multiple measures into two summary indexes, neither of which includes instances of religious persecution. In other words, the indexes include only restrictions and do *not* include acts of physical persecution. For our statistical analysis, the six items on government restrictions in Table 3.1 are combined into a single measure called the *government restrictions index (GRI)* and the five items in Table 3.2 are combined into a single measure called the *social restrictions index (SRI)*.[2] The GRI measures *the restrictions placed on the practice, profession, or selection of religion by the official laws,*

---

[1] Grim & Finke (2006, 2007); Grim, Finke, Harris, Meyers, & VanEerden (2006:4120–4127); and http://www.thearda.com/Archive/CrossNational.asp (accessed 6 August 2010).
[2] In earlier publications we refer to these indexes as the Government Regulation Index and the Social Regulation Index. Here we have changed the titles, but the indexes remain unchanged.

policies, or administrative actions of the state, and the SRI measures *the restrictions placed on religion by other religious groups, associations, or the culture at large*. The total for each index is what we used as the government restrictions scores and the social restrictions scores in Chapters 3 through 6. Details on how the indexes were constructed can be found in previously published work,[3] which documents that the indexes are composed of reliably coded measures, have a high level of internal reliability, and are highly correlated with similar attempts to measure restrictions of religious freedoms. These indexes give us a single measure, ranging from 0 to 10, for each of our two key areas of restriction.

But the full model requires summary measures on far more than religious restrictions and persecution. The alternative arguments call for demographic, social, political, and economic measures not included in the International Religious Freedom reports. For these we turn to accepted international measures from sources such as the United Nations. Full details are provided online.[4] We also computed two measures for testing the clash-of-civilizations arguments. The first measures whether a country is located on a civilization divide or contains a divide within its borders; the second computes a level of religious homogeneity, that is, a *low* level of religious pluralism. The clash-of-civilizations argument implies that religious homogeneity should be associated with decreased conflict and civilization divides should increase conflict.

We offer two tests of the competing arguments. The first model highlights the religious economies argument (social and government restrictions on religion) and the clash-of-civilizations thesis (civilization divides and religious homogeneity), as well as adding a few measures on religion (religious law, religion–ethnicity tie, and the percentage Muslim and Christian). Figure A.1 displays this model and reports on all of the relationships that were statistically significant. In other words, the relationship of each measure to the level of violent religious persecution was tested, controlling for the other measures; the model shown in Figure A.1 presents only the statistically significant relationships among the measures that remained. Once again, additional details about the model and measures are reported in our previous publications.

As we reported in Chapter 3, the religious economies model offers the most complete explanation for religious persecution. The paths from

---

3 See Grim & Finke (2006).
4 See the *American Sociological Review* online supplement to Grim & Finke (2007): http://www2.asanct.org/journals/asr/2007/grim.pdf (accessed 10 August 2010).

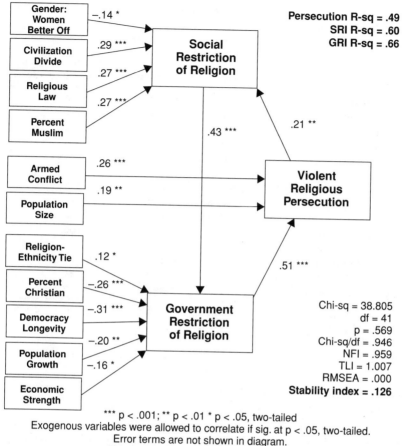

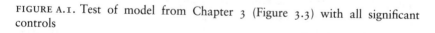

*** p < .001; ** p < .01 * p < .05, two-tailed
Exogenous variables were allowed to correlate if sig. at p < .05, two-tailed.
Error terms are not shown in diagram.
N = 143 countries > 2 million population

FIGURE A.1. Test of model from Chapter 3 (Figure 3.3) with all significant controls

social restrictions to government restrictions, from government restrictions to persecution, and from persecution to social restrictions hold the strongest coefficients and are all statistically significant. Government restrictions continue to have the strongest coefficient leading to persecution. Civilization divide does not directly predict persecution when the model includes *armed conflict*, which does, however, directly predict persecution (0.26). These findings indicate that civilization divides contribute only a very small amount to the level of violent religious persecution (0.066). Indeed, when taking into account the compounding effects of the cycle of violence (Table A.1), government restrictions on

TABLE A.1. *Standardized Total Effects for Structural Equation Model from Chapter 3 and Figure A.1*

Standardized Total Effects[a]	Restriction of Religion		Violent Religious Persecution (2003)
	Social	Government	
Women better off	−0.145	−0.062	−0.032
Religious law	0.279	0.119	0.061
Percentage Muslim	0.279	0.119	0.061
Civilization divide	0.302	0.129	0.066
Armed conflict	0.056	0.024	0.275
Population size	0.042	0.018	0.204
Religion–ethnic tie	0.013	0.123	0.063
Percentage Christian	−0.028	−0.267	−0.137
Democracy level	−0.034	−0.320	−0.164
Population growth	−0.022	−0.207	−0.106
Economic strength	−0.018	−0.167	−0.086
SRI: social restrictions	0.047	0.447	0.229
GRI: government restrictions	0.110	0.047	0.537
Religious persecution	0.215	0.092	0.047

[a] The total effects are slightly larger than the direct effects shown in the model due to the compounding effects of the nonrecursive loop.

religion are nine times as powerful (0.537) and social restrictions (0.229) are 3.5 times as powerful as civilization divides in predicting violent religious persecution. Overall, the model explains a substantial amount of violent religious persecution (R-sq = 0.49).

The model also shows how the religious economies model explains a key difference between the world's two largest religions – Islam and Christianity. The adoption of religious law (mostly Sharia law) and the percentage of Muslims in a country are *positively* associated with increased social restriction of religion (0.27 for each). Percentage of Christians, however, is associated with less government restriction of religion (−0.26). As expected, the longevity of democracy[5] (−0.31) and overall economic strength (−0.16) are negatively associated with government restrictions. One surprising result is that population growth is negatively associated with government restrictions (−0.20). Rather than offer a post hoc explanation, we will simply note that the effect of population growth may be different depending on the type of growth involved.

Population size does, however, directly predict the level of religious persecution (0.19). The best way to interpret the influence of population

---

[5] The length of time democracy has been the political typology of a country.

size in the model is by looking at its unavoidable scale relationship to the dependent variable. That is, the likelihood of having a large number of cases of persecution is higher in a larger country. Thus, the results hold when controlling for population size.

Table A.1 presents the standardized total effects of each variable with a significant regression path in Figure A.1 on social restrictions, government restrictions, and religious persecution. The main finding is that religious persecution is most powerfully explained by government restriction of religion (0.537), supporting the predictions made by the religious economies model. The level of democracy's longevity (maturity) contributed to the sharpest declines in government restriction of religion, and social restrictions contributed to the sharpest increases in government restrictions. As noted earlier, armed conflict had a direct relationship with religious persecution, but the "total effects" of armed conflict were far less than were government restrictions (0.275 versus 0.537).

To verify that our findings are not being driven by regions of the world where persecution is highest, we excluded the twenty-four countries from South Asia, the Near East, and North Africa (see Grim & Finke 2007) and ran the same model. This analysis shows *no change* in the substantive findings. In that analysis, the paths from social restrictions to government restrictions, from government restrictions to religious persecution, and from religious persecution to social restrictions show little change. Government restrictions increase in strength (from 0.51 to 0.56) and continue to have the strongest total effect on religious persecution. The nonrecursive stability index remains strong (0.127). Overall, the amount of variance in religious persecution remains at a high level and the model fit statistics all remain extremely strong.

We also conducted multiple other tests of our key hypotheses using alternate samples and recursive models. Most significantly, we find that the restriction → persecution model fits the data when we use only Christian-majority countries and when we use only Muslim-majority countries. We also find that a recursive model (one in which social restriction directly leads to religious persecution) provides a comparable R-square, but the fit of the model is lower than the model with the feedback from persecution to social restrictions. Although the path from social restriction to persecution in that model is significant, the coefficient is weaker and less significant than the persecution → social restriction path in the nonrecursive (feedback loop) model. Because the feedback loop model more effectively tests the proposed theoretical model and is a better statistical fit, we show only that model here, which is supported by

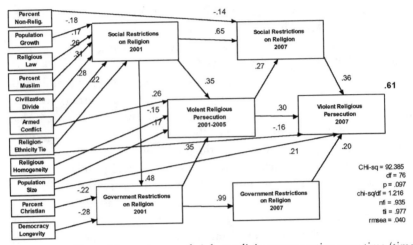

FIGURE A.2. Test of determinants of violent religious persecution over time (time lag) with all significant controls

a second model in which the feedback loop is modeled over time. All of the many models we tested, however, support the thesis that the restriction of religion results in higher levels of religious persecution, regardless of a country's majority religion or whether the model is *recursive* (no feedback loop) or *nonrecursive* (with a feedback loop).

Finally, using all of the same controls as well as a control for the level of secularism, we conducted a statistical test using measures from 2001, 2003, 2005, and 2007 to see if the same statistical relationship is present over time. The results, shown in Figure A.2, are strong and provide final supporting evidence that nonviolent social and government restrictions on religion lead to violent religious persecution and conflict. Using the time-lag model, we wanted to address the question posed by a reviewer: Does secularism substantially reduce violent religious persecution? Therefore, we also included in this model a measure for the percentage of the population in each country that is nonreligious. As shown in Figure A.2, the measure for secularism has only a weak negative relationship with social restrictions in 2007 and has no direct relationship with religious persecution. Of all of the predictors shown in the model, secularism had one of the lowest "total effects" (see Table A.2).

When looking at the two main types of restrictions in the time-lag model, social and government restrictions are the strongest overall predictors of persecution; however, social restrictions become a more powerful predictor of religious persecution than government restrictions in

TABLE A.2. *Standardized total effects for structural equation time-lag model (Figure A.2)*

Standardized Total Effects	Violent Religious Persecution (2007)
Percentage nonreligious	0.049
Religious law	0.092
Percentage Muslim	0.140
Civilization divide	0.165
Armed conflict	0.252
Population size	0.273
Religion–ethnic tie	0.038
Percentage Christian	−0.075
Democracy level	−0.094
Population growth	−0.096
Religious homogeneity	−0.060
SRI: social restrictions (2001)	0.536
GRI: government restrictions (2001)	0.335
SRI: social restrictions (2007)	0.360
GRI: government restrictions (2007)	0.198
Violent religious persecution (2001–2005)	0.398

the latter part of the first decade of the twenty-first century. This does not mean that government restrictions have decreased; rather, social restrictions are increasing. A possible implication is that decreases in the level of social restrictions appear to be critical to lowering the level of violent religious persecution and conflict. Government deregulation alone may not be sufficient.

In the time-lag model, the measure for civilization divides continues to have weak "total effects" (0.165 overall) on violent religious persecution, when compared with social restrictions (0.536 in 2001 compounded by 0.360 in 2007) and government restrictions (0.335 in 2001 compounded by 0.198 in 2007). In addition, in the time-lag model, religious homogeneity was statistically significant but very weak (−0.060), again confirming one of our main theses: restrictions placed on religion represent the explanatory mechanism underlying violent religious persecution; that is, social and government restrictions are more powerful explanations than either of the predictions made based on Huntington's civilization theory. Thus, at most we find only limited support for the civilization hypothesis. Therefore, rather than attributing persecution to irreconcilable differences between religious traditions or more general civilizations, our test of the religious economies perspective has found that ensuring religious freedoms for all serves to defuse the potential volatility of religious plurality.

The time-lag model also provides further evidence that restrictions precede persecution. When we tried running arrows both ways in the first model, the best fit was clearly with the arrow going from restrictions to persecution, including a feedback loop. The time-lag model confirms this finding. We acknowledge the short time frame, but we note that once again the best fit has the arrow running from restrictions to persecution, with a feedback path to social restrictions (in 2007).

In sum, the findings are robust and strongly supportive of the religious economies thesis. Once again, the core thesis holds: *to the extent that governments and societies restrict religious freedoms, physical persecution and conflict increase.*

Bibliography

Abou El Fadl, Khaled, 2002, *Rebellion and Violence in Islamic Law*, Cambridge: Cambridge University Press.

Adamczyk, Amy, John Wybraniec, and Roger Finke, 2004, "Religious Regulation and the Courts: Documenting the Effects of Smith and RFRA," *Journal of Church & State*, 46: 237–262.

Ahmed, Akbar, 1999, *Islam Today: A Short Introduction to the Muslim World*, London: I. B. Tauris.

2002, *Discovering Islam: Making Sense of Muslim History and Society*, rev. ed., New York: Routledge.

Ali, Farhana, 2005, "Muslim Female Fighters: An Emerging Trend," *Terrorism Monitor*, 3: 9–11.

Ali, Tariq, 2002, *Clash of Fundamentalisms: Crusades, Jihads, and Modernity*, London: Verso.

An-Na'im, Abdullahi Ahmed, 1996, *Toward an Islamic Reformation: Civil Liberties, Human Rights, and International Law*, Syracuse, NY: Syracuse University Press.

Aquinas, Thomas, 1952, *Summa Theologica*, Chicago: Encyclopedia Britannica, Great Books.

Arinori, Mori, [1872] 2004, "Religious Freedom in Japan," reprinted in Appendix of John E. Van Sant, 2004, *Mori Arinori's Life and Resources in America*, Lanham, MD: Lexington Books.

Armstrong, Karen, 2002, *Islam: A Short History*, rev. ed., New York: Modern Library.

Asad, Talal, 2003, *Formations of the Secular: Christianity, Islam, Modernity*. Stanford, CA: Stanford University Press.

Augustine, 1952, *City of God*, Chicago: Encyclopedia Britannica, Great Books.

Baker, David and Gerald LeTendre, 2005, *National Differences, Global Similarities: World Culture and the Future of Schooling*, Stanford CA: Stanford University Press.

Barker, Eileen, 1984, *The Making of a Moonie: Brainwashing or Choice*, Oxford: Basil Blackwell.

Barrett, David B., and Todd M. Johnson, 2001, *World Christian Trends*, Pasadena, CA: William Carey Library.

Barrett, David B., George T. Kurian, and Todd M. Johnson, 2001, *World Christian Encyclopedia*, 2nd ed., Oxford: Oxford University Press.

Bates, M. Searle, 1945, *Religious Liberty: An Inquiry*, New York: International Missionary Council.

Bearman, P. J., Th. Bianquis, C. E. Bosworth, E. van Donzel, and W. P. Heinrichs, 1960–2004, *Encyclopaedia of Islam*, new ed., Leiden, Netherlands: Brill.

Beckfield, Jason, 2003, "Inequality in the World Polity: The Structure of International Organization," *American Sociological Review*, 68: 401–424.

Beckford, James A., 1985, *Cult Controversies: The Societal Response to New Religious Movement*, London: Tavistock.

2004, "'Laïcité,' 'Dystopia,' and the Reaction to New Religious Movements in France," in J. T. Richardson, ed., *Regulating Religion: Case Studies from around the Globe*, New York: Kluwer Academic/Plenum Publishers, 27–40.

Berger, Peter, and Anton Zijderveld, 2009, *In Praise of Doubt: How to Have Convictions without Becoming a Fanatic*, New York: HarperOne.

Berry, Mary Elizabeth, 1982, *Hideyoshi*, Cambridge, MA: Harvard University Press.

1994, *The Culture of Civil War in Kyoto*, Berkeley: University of California Press.

Berry, Mary Frances, 2009, *And Justice for All: The United States Commission on Civil Rights and the Continuing Struggle for Freedom in America*, New York: Knopf.

Bhattacharji, Preeti, 2008, "Religion in China," Council on Foreign Relations, Backgrounder, http://www.cfr.org/publication/16272/.

Bin Sayeed, Khalid, 1995, *Western Dominance and Political Islam*, Albany: State University of New York Press.

Blakely, Rhys, 2009, "Indian Christians Caught up in Murderous Power Struggle," *Times* (London), April 14, http://www.timesonline.co.uk/tol/news/world/asia/article6087988.ece.

Bovingdon, Gardner, 2004, "Autonomy in Xinjiang: Han Nationalist Imperatives and Uyghur Discontent," East-West Center, Washington, DC: Policy Study 15. http://www.eastwestcenter.org/fileadmin/stored/pdfs/PS011.pdf.

Boxer, C. R., 1951, *The Christian Century in Japan*, Berkeley: University of California Press.

Bruce, Steve, 2002, *God Is Dead: Secularization in the West*, Oxford: Blackwell Publishers.

Brustein, William I., 2003, *Roots of Hate: Anti-Semitism in Europe before the Holocaust*, Cambridge: Cambridge University Press.

Chesnut, R. Andrew, 2003, *Competitive Spirits: Latin America's New Religious Economy*, Oxford: Oxford University Press.

Cleary, Edward L., 1992, "John Paul Cries 'Wolf,'" *Commonweal* (November 20): 119.

Cody, Edward, 2008, "China's Leader Puts Faith in Religious: Hu Sees Growing Spiritual Ranks as Helpful in Achieving Social Goals," *Washington Post* (Foreign Service), January 20, p. A21, http://www.washingtonpost.com/wp-dyn/content/article/2008/01/19/AR2008011902465.html.

Compilation Group for the History of Modern China Series, 1976, *The Taiping Revolution*, Beijing: Foreign Language Press.

Cragg, Kenneth, 1971, *The Event of the Quran: Islam in Its Scripture*, London: George Allen & Unwin.

Crenshaw, Edward M., Ansari Z. Ameen, and Matthew Christenson, 1997, "Population Dynamics and Economic Development: Age-Specific Population Growth Rates and Economic Growth in Developing Countries, 1965 to 1990," *American Sociological Review*, 62: 974–984.

Dadrian, Vahakn N., 2003, *The History of the Armenian Genocide: Ethnic Conflict from the Balkans to Anatolia to the Caucasus*, Oxford and New York: Berghahn Books.

Dasheng, Chen, 1984, *Islamic Inscriptions in Quanzhou (Zaitun)*, trans. Chen Enming, Yinchuan, Ningxia, and Quanzhou, Fujian: People's Publishing Society and Fujian People's Publishing Society.

Davie, Grace, 1990a, "Believing without Belonging: Is the Future of Religion in Britain?" *Social Compass*, 37: 455–469.

1990b, "'An Ordinary God': The Paradox of Religions in Contemporary Britain," *British Journal of Sociology*, 41: 395–420.

Dawidowicz, Lucy S., 1975, *The War against the Jews, 1933–1945*, New York: Holt, Rinehart, & Winston.

Dawson, Andrew, 2007, *New Era – New Religions*, Hampshire, UK: Ashgate.

De Groot, J. J. M., 1903, *Sectarianism and Religious Persecution in China: A Page in the History of Religions*, Amsterdam: Johannes Müller.

Demerath, N. J., III, 2002, *Crossing the Gods: Worldly Religions and Worldly Politics*, New Brunswick, NJ: Rutgers University Press.

Drinan, Robert F., 1997, "Reflections on the Demise of the Religious Freedom Restoration Act," *Georgetown Law Journal*, 89: 101, 115–116.

Durant, Will, and Ariel Durant, 1965, *The Age of Voltaire*, New York: Simon & Schuster.

Durham, W. Cole, Jr., 1996, "Perspective on Religious Liberty: A Comparative Framework," in J. D. van der Vyver and J. Witte, Jr., eds, *Religious Human Rights in Global Perspective: Legal Perspectives*, The Hague: Kluwer Law International, 1–44.

Duvert, Cyrille, 2004, "Anti-Cultism in the French Parliament," in J. T. Richardson, ed., *Regulating Religion: Case Studies from around the Globe*, New York: Kluwer Academic/Plenum Publishers, 41–52.

Dwyer, Arienne M., 2005, "The Xinjiang Conflict: Uyghur Identity, Language Policy, and Political Discourse," East-West Center, Washington, DC: Policy Study 15, http://www.eastwestcenter.org/fileadmin/stored/pdfs/PS015.pdf.

Ebisawa, Arimichi, and Saburo Ouchi, 1970, *Nihon Kirisutokyoshi* (History of Christianity in Japan), Tokyo: Nihon Kirisutokyodan Shuppan.

Eisenstein, Marie A., 2008, *Religion and the Politics of Tolerance*, Waco, TX: Baylor University Press.

El Guindi, Fadwa, 1999, *Veil: Modesty, Privacy, and Resistance*, New York: Berg.

Esposito, John L., 2002a, *Islam in Transition: Muslim Perspectives*, 2nd ed., Oxford: Oxford University Press.

—— 2002b, *Unholy War: Terror in the Name of Islam*, Oxford: Oxford University Press.

Esposito, John L., and François Burgat, eds., 2003, *Modernizing Islam: Religion in the Public Sphere in Europe and the Middle East*, New Brunswick, NJ: Rutgers University Press.

Esposito, John L., and John Obert Voll, 2001, *Makers of Contemporary Islam*, Oxford: Oxford University Press.

European Monitoring Centre on Racism and Xenophobia (EUMC), 2006, "Muslims in the European Union: Discrimination and Islamophobia," Vienna, Austria: European Monitoring Centre on Racism and Xenophobia, retrieved January 16, 2007, from http://eumc.europa.eu/eumc/material/pub/muslim/Manifestations_EN.pdf.

Evans, Malcolm D., 1997, *Religious Liberty and International Law in Europe*, Cambridge: Cambridge University Press.

Farr, Thomas F., 2008, *World of Faith and Freedom: Why International Religious Freedom Is Vital to American National Security*, New York: Oxford University Press.

Fearon, James D., and David D. Laitin, 2003, "Ethnicity, Insurgency, and Civil War," *American Political Science Review*, 17: 75–90.

Ferrari, Silvioa, 2003, "The European Pattern of Church and State Relations," *Comparative Law*, 20: 1–24.

Finke, Roger, 1990, "Religious Deregulation: Origins and Consequences," *Journal of Church and State*, 32 (3): 609–626.

—— 1997, "The Consequences of Religious Competition: Supply-side Explanations for Religious Change," in Lawrence A. Young, ed., *Rational Choice Theory and Religion*, New York: Routledge Press.

Finke, Roger, and Jaime Harris, forthcoming, "Wars and Rumors of Wars: Explaining Religiously Motivated Violence," in Jonathan Fox, ed., *Religion, Politics, Society and the State*, Boulder, CO: Paradigm.

Finke, Roger, and Rodney Stark, 1988, "Religious Economies and Sacred Canopies: Religious Mobilization in American Cities, 1906," *American Sociological Review*, 53 (1): 41–49.

—— 1992, *The Churching of America 1776–1990: Winners and Losers in Our Religious Economy*, New Brunswick, NJ: Rutgers University Press.

—— 2005, *The Churching of America: Winners and Losers in Our Religious Economy, Revised and Expanded Edition*, New Brunswick, NJ: Rutgers University Press.

Flora, Cornelia Butler, 1976, *Pentecostalism in Columbia: Baptism by Fire and Spirit*, Cranbury, NJ: Associated University Presses.

Foalola, Toyin, 2002, *Key Events in African History: A Reference Guide*, Westport, CT: Greenwood Press.

Ford, Peter, 2008, "Uighurs Struggle in World Reshaped by Chinese Influx," *Christian Science Monitor*, April 28.

Forrest, R. J., 1867, "The Christianity of Hung Tsiu Tsuen," *Journal of the Royal Asiatic Society, North China Branch*, N.S., 4: 187–208.

Fox, Jonathan, 2008, *A World Survey of Religion and the State*. New York: Cambridge University Press.

2009, "Separation of Religion and State in Constitutions and State Religion Policy in Practice: Do the Two Correlate?" paper presented at the Argoy Center Conference on Religion, Politics and the State, Bar-Ilan University, Israel, January 8, 2009.

Fox, Jonathan, and Ephraim Tabory, 2008, "Contemporary Evidence Regarding the Impact of State Regulation of Religion on Religious Participation and Belief," *Sociology of Religion* 69: 245–271.

Froese, Paul, 2001, "Hungary for Religion: Supply-side Interpretation of the Hungarian Religious Revival," *Journal for the Scientific Study of Religion*, 40 (2): 251–268.

2004, "After Atheism: Religious Monopolies in the Post-Communist World," *Sociology of Religion*, 65: 57–75.

2008, *The Great Secularization Experiment: What Soviet Communism Taught Us about Religion in the Modern Era*, Berkeley: University of California Press.

Froese, Paul, and Steven Pfaff, 2001, "Replete and Desolate Markets: Poland, East Germany, and the New Religious Paradigm," *Social Forces*, 80: 481–507.

Frykenberg, Robert Eric, 1989, "The Emergence of Modern 'Hinduism' as a Concept and as an Institution: A Reappraisal with Special Reference to South India." in G. D. Sontheimer and H. Kulke, eds., *Hinduism Reconsidered*, New Delhi: Monohar Publications, 29–50.

Gallwey, W. Timothy, 1974, *The Inner Game of Tennis*, New York: Random House.

Gaustad, Blaine, 2000, "Prophets and Pretenders: Inter-Sect Competition in Qianlong China," *Late Imperial China*, 21: 1–40.

Geertz, Clifford, 1966, "Religion as a Cultural System," in Michael Banton, ed., *Anthropological Approaches to the Study of Religion*, New York: Praeger, 1–46.

Gill, Anthony J., 1998, *Rendering unto Caesar: The Roman Catholic Church and the State in Latin America*, Chicago: University of Chicago Press.

2005, "The Political Origins of Religious Liberty: A Theoretical Outline," *Interdisciplinary Journal of Research on Religion*, 2 (1): 1–35.

2008, *The Political Origins of Religious Liberty*, New York: Cambridge University Press.

Gladney, Dru, 1996, *Muslim Chinese: Ethnic Nationalism in the People's Republic*, 2nd ed., Cambridge, MA: Harvard University Press.

2009, "Islam in China in the Post-Olympics and Post-9/11 World," Purdue Symposium on Religion and Spirituality in China Today, West Lafayette, IN, April 30, 2009, http://www.purdue.edu/crcs/itemConference/symposium/CRCSsymposium2009.html.

Goldman, Merle, 1986, "Religion in Post-Mao China," *Annals of the American Academy of Political and Social Science*, 483: 146–156.

Greeley, Andrew M., 1994, "A Religious Revival in Russia?" *Journal for the Scientific Study of Religion*, 33 (3): 253–272.

2002, "Religious Revivals in Eastern Europe," *Society*, 39 (2): 76–77.

Grim, Brian J., 2004, "The Cities of God versus the Countries of Earth: The Regulation of Religious Freedom (RRF)," paper delivered at the Association for Study of Religion, Economics, and Culture national conference, October 21, 2004, http://www.religionomics.com/old/erel/S2-Archives/REC04/Grim%20-%20Cities%20of%20God.pdf.

2005, "Religious Regulation's Impact on Religious Persecution: The Effects of De Facto and De Jure Religious Regulation," Ph.D. dissertation, Department of Sociology, The Pennsylvania State University, University Park, PA.

2008a, "An Exodus from Iraq," *Newsletter of the Peace, War & Social Conflict Section of the American Sociological Association* (July): 5–6.

2008b, "Religion in China on the Eve of the 2008 Beijing Olympics," Pew Forum on Religion & Public Life, May 2, http://pewforum.org/Importance-of-Religion/Religion-in-China-on-the-Eve-of-the-2008-Beijing-Olympics.aspx.

2008c, "Religious Freedom: Good for What Ails Us?" *Review of Faith & International Affairs*, 6 (2): 3–7.

Grim, Brian J., and Roger Finke, 2006, "International Religion Indexes: Government Regulation, Government Favoritism, and Social Regulation of Religion," *Interdisciplinary Journal of Research on Religion*, 2 (1): 1–40.

2007, "Religious Persecution in Cross-National Context: Clashing Civilizations or Regulated Economies?" *American Sociological Review*, 72 (4): 633–658.

Grim, Brian J., Roger Finke, Jaime Harris, Catherine Meyers, and Julie Van-Eerden, 2006, "Measuring International Socio-Religious Values and Conflict by Coding U.S. State Department Reports," In *JSM Proceedings of the American Association of Public Opinion Research, Survey Research Methods Section* [CD-ROM], Alexandria, VA: American Statistical Association.

Grim, Brian J., and Richard Wike, 2007, "Turkey and Its (Many) Discontents," Pew Research Center Analysis and Commentary, October 25. http://pewresearch.org/pubs/623/turkey.

2010, "Cross-Validating Measures of Global Religious Intolerance: Comparing Coded State Department Reports with Survey Data and Expert Opinion," *Politics and Religion*, 3: 102–129.

Hafez, Mohammed M., 2004, "From Marginalization to Massacres: A Political Process Explanation of GIA Violence in Algeria," in Q. Wiktorowicz, ed., *Islamic Activism: A Social Movement Theory Approach*, Bloomington: Indiana University Press, 37–60.

Hallaq, Wael B., 2004, *The Origins and Evolution of Islamic Law*, Cambridge: Cambridge University Press.

Hardacre, Helen, 1989, *Shinto and the State: 1886–1988*, Princeton, NJ: Princeton University Press.

Hayes, Daniel H., 2003, "Chinese Christian Protestant Christianity Today," in Daniel L. Overmyer, ed., *Religion in China Today: The China Quarterly Special Issues No. 3*, New York: Cambridge University Press, 182–198.

Hefner, Robert W., 2000, *Civil Islam: Muslims and Democratization in Indonesia*, Princeton, NJ: Princeton University Press.

Henderson, Errol A., 1997, "Culture or Contiguity: Ethnic Conflict, the Similarity of States, and the Onset of War, 1820–1989," *Journal of Conflict Resolution*, 41: 649–668.

2004, "Mistaken Identity: Testing the Clash of Civilizations Thesis in Light of Democratic Peace Claims," *British Journal of Political Science*, 34: 539–563.

Hertzke, Allen D., 2004, *Freeing God's Children: The Unlikely Alliance for Global Human Rights*, Lanham, MD: Rowman & Littlefield.

Hitti, Philip K., 1970, *Islam: A Way of Life*, South Bend, IN: Regnery/Gateway, University of Minnesota.

2002, *History of the Arabs: From Earliest Times to the Present*, 10th ed., London: Macmillan.

Huang, Jianbo, and Fenggang Yang, 2005, "The Cross Faces the Loudspeakers: A Village Church Perseveres under State Power," in Fenggang Yang and Joseph B. Tamney, eds., *State Market and Religions in Chinese Societies*, Leiden, Netherlands: Brill, 41–62.

Hume, David, (1907), *Dialogues concerning Natural Religion*. Edinburgh and London: William Blackwood and Sons.

Hunter, Shireen, and Huma Malik, eds., 2005, *Islam and Human Rights: Advancing a U.S.-Muslim Dialogue*, Washington, DC: Center for Strategic and International Studies.

Huntington, Samuel P., 1993, "The Clash of Civilizations," *Foreign Affairs*, 72: 22–49.

1996, *The Clash of Civilizations and the Remaking of World Order*, New York: Simon & Schuster.

2001, "Religious Persecution and Religious Relevance in Today's World," in Elliott Abrams, ed., *The Influence of Faith*, Lanham MD: Rowman & Littlefield, 55–64.

Hunwick, John, and Khadim Mbacke, 2005, *Sufism and Religious Brotherhoods in Senegal*, trans. Eric Ross, Princeton, NJ: Markus Weiner.

Hussein, Sohail, 2007, "Dal al-Islam (House of Islam) and Dar al-Harb (House of Unbelief or the House of War)," presentation at Harvard University, Kennedy School of Government, Religion and World Affairs Symposium, June 2007.

Iannaccone, Laurence R., Roger Finke, and Rodney Stark, 1997, "Deregulating Religion: The Economics of Church and State," *Economic Inquiry* 35: 350–364.

Introvigne, Massimo, 1998, "Blacklisting or Greenlisting? A European Perspective on the New Cult Wars," *Nova Religio*, 2 (1): 16–23.

Jaffrelot, Christophe, 2007, *Hindu Nationalism: A Reader*, Princeton, NJ: Princeton University Press.

James, Herman G., 1923, *The Constitutional System of Brazil*, Washington, DC: The Carnegie Institution of Washington.

Jefferson, Thomas, [1787] 1954, *Notes on the State of Virginia*, ed. William Peden, Chapel Hill: University of North Carolina Press for the Institute of Early American History and Culture, Williamsburg, Virginia.

2005, *The Autobiography of Thomas Jefferson, 1743–1790*, Philadelphia: University of Pennsylvania Press.

Jenkins, Philip, 2002, *The Next Christendom: The Coming of Global Christianity*, New York: Oxford University Press.

Johnson, Todd M., and Brian J. Grim, eds., 2008, *World Religion Database: International Religious Demographic Statistics and Sources*, Leiden, Netherlands, and Boston: Brill, http://www.worldreligiondatabase.org.

Kamali, Mohammad Hashim, 1997, *Freedom of Expression in Islam*, rev. ed., Cambridge: Islamic Texts Society.

Keddie, Nikki R., 1983, *An Islamic Response to Imperialism: Political and Religious Writings of Sayyid Jamāl ad-Dīn "al-Afghānī,"* Berkeley: University of California Press.

Khalidi, Rashid, 1998, *Palestinian Identity: The Construction of Modern Consciousness*, New York: Columbia University Press.

Khalidi, Rashid, et al., eds., 1993, *The Origins of Arab Nationalism*, New York: Columbia University Press.

Kinross, Lord, 1965, *Ataturk: A Biography of Mustafa Kemal, Father of Modern Turkey*, New York: Morrow.

Kitagawa, Joseph, 1966, *Religion in Japanese History*, New York: Columbia University Press.

Knox, Zoe, 2003, "The Symphonic Ideal: The Moscow Patriarchate's Post-Soviet Leadership," *Europe-Asia Studies*, 55 (4): 575–596.

Kohut, Andrew, and Bruce Stokes, 2006, *America against the World: How We Are Different and Why We Are Disliked*, New York: Henry Holt.

Krey, August C., [1921] 1958, *The First Crusade: The Accounts of Eye Witnesses and Participants*, Gloucester, MA: Peter Smith.

Kuhn, Philip A., 1977, "Origins of the Taiping Vision: Cross-Cultural Dimensions of a Chinese Rebellion," *Comparative Studies in Society and History*, 19: 350.

Kumar, Ann L., 1987, "Islam, the Chinese, and Indonesian Historiography – a Review Article," *Journal of Asian Studies*, 46: 603–616.

Kuo, Cheng-Tian, 2008, *Religion and Democracy in Taiwan*. Albany: State University of New York Press.

Kurien, Prema, 2007, *A Place at the Multicultural Table: The Development of an American Hinduism*, New Brunswick, NJ: Rutgers University Press.

Kuru, Ahmet T., 2009, *Secularism and State Policies toward Religion: The United States, France and Turkey*, New York: Cambridge University Press.

Kwitny, Jonathan, 1997, *Man of the Century: The Life and Times of Pope John Paul II*, New York: Henry Holt.

Lang, Graeme, 1988, "Religions and Regimes in China," in M. Cousineau, ed., *Religion in a Changing World*, Westport, CT: Praeger, 149–158.

Lapidus, Ira M., 2002, *A History of Islamic Societies*, Cambridge: Cambridge University Press.

Laqueur, Walter, 1999, *The New Terrorism: Fanaticism and the Arms of Mass Destruction*, Oxford: Oxford University Press.

Lattimore, Owen, 1950, *Pivot of Asia: Sinkiang and the Inner Asian Frontiers of China and Russia*, Boston: Little, Brown.

Lewis, Bernard, ed., 1992, *The World of Islam: Faith, People, Culture*, New York: Thames & Hudson.

Lu, Yunfeng, 2008, *The Transformation of Yiguan Dao in Taiwan: Adapting to a Changing Religious Economy*, Lanham, MD: Lexington Books.

Luca, Nathalie, 2004, "Is There a Unique French Policy of Cults?" in J. T. Richardson, ed., *Regulating Religion: Case Studies from around the Globe*, New York: Kluwer Academic/Plenum Publishers.

Lupu, Ira C., 1998, "The Failure of RFRA," *University of Arkansas Little Rock Law Review*, 20: 589.

Macartney, Jane, and Jeremy Page, 2008, "Dalai Lama Threatens to Stand Down over Violence as China Calls Him a Liar," *Times* (London), March 19, http://www.timesonline.co.uk/tol/news/world/asia/article3574672.ece.

Madsen, Richard, 2003, "Catholic Revival during the Reform Era," in Daniel L. Overmyer, ed., *Religion in China Today: The China Quarterly Special Issues No. 3*, New York: Cambridge University Press, 162–181.

Marger, Martin N., 1991, *Race and Ethnic Relations: American and Global Perspectives*, 2nd ed., Belmont, CA: Wadsworth.

Marshall, Paul, 1997, *Their Blood Cries Out*, Dallas: Word.

2008, *Religious Freedom in the World*, Landam, MD: Rowman & Littlefield.

Martin, David, 1990, *Tongues of Fire: The Explosion of Protestantism in Latin America*, Oxford: Basil Blackwell.

Marx, Anthony W., 2003, *Faith in Nation: Exclusionary Origins of Nationalism*, Oxford: Oxford University Press.

McConnell, Michael W., 1990, "Free Exercise Revisionism and the *Smith* Decision," *Chicago Law Review*, 57: 1109.

McFarland, H. Neill, 1967, *The Rush Hour of the Gods: A Study of the New Religious Movements in Japan*, New York: Macmillan.

McLoughlin, William G., 1971, *New England Dissent, 1630–1833: The Baptists and the Separation of Church and State*, vols. 1 and 2, Cambridge, MA: Harvard University Press.

Mead, Sidney E., 1956, "From Coercion to Persuasion: Another Look at the Rise of Religious Liberty and the Emergence of Denominationalism," *Church History*, 25: 317–337.

Mernissi, Fatima, 2002, *Islam and Democracy: Fear of the Modern World*, 2nd ed., Cambridge, MA: Perseus.

Metraux, Daniel A., 1995, "Religious Terrorism in Japan: The Fatal Appeal of Aum Shinrikyo," *Asian Survey*, 35 (12): 1140–1154.

Midlarsky, Manus I., 1998, "Democracy and Islam: Implications for Civilizational Conflict and the Democratic Peace," *International Studies Quarterly*, 42: 458–511.

Milosavljević, Boris, 2002, "Religious Freedom and the Relationship between the State and Religious Communities within the Framework of the Reforms Being Undertaken in the Federal Republic of Yugoslavia," *SouthEast Europe Review for Labour and Social Affairs*, 01: 41–59.

Minority Rights Group International, 2008, *World Directory of Minorities and Indigenous Peoples – China: Uyghurs*, July, http://www.unhcr.org/refworld/docid/49749d3c4b.html.

Miyazaki, Kentaro, 2003, "Roman Catholic Mission in Pre-modern Japan," in Mark R. Mullins, ed., *Handbook of Christianity in Japan*, Leiden, Netherlands: Brill.

Moaddel, Mansoor, 1986, "The Shi'I Ulama and the State in Iran," *Theory and Society* 15: 519–556.

　2005, *Islamic Modernism, Nationalism, and Fundamentalism: Episode and Discourse*, Chicago: University of Chicago Press.

　2008, "Religious Regimes and Prospects for Liberal Politics: Futures of Iran, Iraq, and Saudi Arabia," unpublished manuscript, used with permission (where available).

Moaddel, Mansoor, and Kamran Talattof, eds., 2002, *Modernist and Fundamentalist Debates in Islam: A Reader*, New York: Palgrave Macmillan.

Moffett, Samuel Hugh, 1998, *A History of Christianity in Asia*, vol. 2, *1500–1900*, Maryknoll, NY: Orbis Books.

Mohiuddin, Fasahat, 2007, "Altaf Demands Demolition of Lal Masjid, Jamia Hafsa," *The News*, April 16, http://www.thenews.com.pk/top_story_detail.asp?Id=7177.

Monsma, Stephen V., and J. Christopher Soper, 2009, *The Challenge of Pluralism*, 2nd ed., Lanham, MD: Rowman & Littlefield.

Mortimer, Edward, 1982, *Faith and Power: The Politics of Islam*, New York: Vintage.

Morton, W. Scott, 1995, *China: Its History and Culture*, 3rd ed., New York: McGraw-Hill.

Myers, W. David, 1985, "Jansenism," in Richard P. McBrien, ed., *Encyclopedia of Catholicism*, New York: HarperCollins.

Naquin, Susan, 1981, *Shantung Rebellion: The Wang Lun Uprising of 1774*, New Haven, CT: Yale University Press.

Nasr, Seyyed Vali Reza, 1996, *Mawdudi and the Making of Islamic Revivalism*, New York: Oxford University Press.

　2001, *The Islamic Leviathan: Islam and the Making of State Power*. Oxford: Oxford University Press.

　2006, *The Shia Revival: How Conflicts within Islam Will Shape the Future*, New York: Norton.

Nasr, Seyyed Hossein, 2002, *Islam: Religion, History, and Civilization*, San Francisco: HarperCollins.

Norihisa, Suzuki, 1996, "Christianity," in Noriyoshi Tamaru and David Reid, eds., *Religion in Japanese Culture: Where Living Traditions Meet a Changing World*, Tokyo: Kodansha International, 63–78.

Norris, Pippa, and Ronald Inglehart, 2004, *Sacred and Secular: Religion and Politics Worldwide*, Cambridge: Cambridge University Press.

Okamoto, Dina A., 2003, "Toward a Theory of Panethnicity: Explaining Asian American Collective Action," *American Sociological Review* 68: 811–842.

Paden, John, 2005, *Muslim Civic Cultures and Conflict Resolution: The Challenge of Democratic Federalism in Nigeria*, Washington, DC: Brookings Institution Press.

Page, Jeremy, 2007, "Sharia Gangs Roam Streets of Capital City to Enforce Their Law with Threats," *Times* (London), April 6. http://www.timesonline.co.uk/tol/news/world/asia/article1620554.ece (last accessed August 2010).

Pangi, Robyn, 2002, "Consequence Management in the 1995 Sarin Attacks on the Japanese Subway System," *Studies in Conflict & Terrorism*, 25 (6): 421–448.

Peters, Shawn Francis, 2000, *Judging Jehovah's Witnesses: Religious Persecution and the Dawn of the Rights Revolution*, Lawrence: University Press of Kansas.

Pew Forum. 2006, *Spirit and Power*, http://pewforum.org/surveys/pentecostal/. 2009, *Restrictions on Religion in the World: 2009*, http://www.PewForum.org.

Pew Research Center, 2007, *Muslim Americans: Middle Class and Mostly Mainstream*, http://pewforum.org/surveys/muslim-american/.

Philpott, Daniel, 2001, *Revolutions in Sovereignty: How Ideas Shaped Modern International Relations*, Princeton, NJ: Princeton University Press.

Potter, Pitman B., 2003, "Belief in Control: Regulation of Religion in China," in Daniel L. Overmyer, ed., *Religion in China Today: The China Quarterly Special Issues* No. 3, New York: Cambridge University Press, 11–31.

Raquette, G., 1939, "An Ordeal in Central Asia," *Muslim World*, 29: 271–274.

Reid, Anthony, 1993, "Islamization and Christianization in Southeast Asia: The Critical Phase, 1550–1650," in Anthony Reid, ed., *Southeast Asia in the Early Modern Era: Trade, Power, and Belief*, Ithaca, NY: Cornell University Press, 151–179.

Richardson, James T., and Bryan Edelman, 2004, "Cult Controversies and Legal Developments concerning New Religious Movements in Japan and China," in James T. Richardson, ed., *Regulating Religion: Case Studies from around the Globe*, New York: Kluwer Academic/Plenum Publishers, 359–380.

Richardson, James T., and Massimo Introvigne, 2001, "'Brainwashing' Theories in European Parliamentary and Administrative Reports on 'Cults' and 'Sects,'" *Journal for the Scientific Study of Religion*, 40 (2): 143–168.

Richardson, Sophie, 2009, "China's Religious (Re)Awakening: The Impact of Religion on Chinese Society," paper presented at the Brookings Institution, Washington, DC, April 8, 2009.

Robbins, Thomas, 1988, *Cults, Converts and Charisma: The Sociology of New Religious Movements*, Beverly Hills, CA: Sage.

Robinson, David, 2004, *Muslim Societies in African History*, Cambridge: Cambridge University Press.

Roulet, Jean-Michel, 2006, *Report to the Prime Minister, 2006*, Interministerial Mission of Vigilance and Combat against Sectarian Aberrations, http://www.miviludes.gouv.fr/-Guides-?iddiv=5.

Ruback, R. Barry, Neena Kohli, and Janak Pandey, 2009, "Hindus' Evaluations of Hindus and Muslims: Religious Leaders and Pilgrims at the Magh Mela," *Journal for the Scientific Study of Religion*, 48: 375–385.

Runciman, Steven, 1951, *History of the Crusades*, vol. 1, *The First Crusade and the Founding of the Kingdom of Jerusalem*, Cambridge: Cambridge University Press.

1952, *History of the Crusades*, vol. 2, *The Kingdom of Jerusalem*, Cambridge: Cambridge University Press.

1954, *History of the Crusades*, vol. 3, *The Kingdom of Acre and the Later Crusades*, Cambridge: Cambridge University Press.

Russett, Bruce M., John R. Oneal, and Michaelene Cox, 2000, "Clash of Civilizations, or Realism and Liberalism Déjà Vu? Some Evidence," *Journal of Peace Research*, 37: 583–608.

Ryan, James E., 1992, "Smith *and the Religious Freedom Restoration Act: An Iconoclastic Assessment*," *Virginia Law Review*, 78: 1417.

Ryskamp, George R., 1980, "The Spanish Experience in Church-State Relations: A Comparative Study of the Interrelationship between Church-State Identification and Religious Liberty," *Brigham Young University Law Review*, 616.

Sanasarian, Eliz, 2000, *Religious Minorities in Iran*, New York: Cambridge University Press.

Sanasarian, Eliz, and Avi Davidi, 2007, "Domestic Tribulations and International Repercussions: The State and the Transformation of Non-Muslims in Iran," *Journal of International Affairs*, 60: 55–69.

Scheitle, Christopher P., and Roger Finke, 2008, "Maximizing Organizational Resources: Selection versus Production," *Social Science Research*, 37: 815–827.

2009, "Pluralism as Outcome: The Ecology of Religious Resources, Suppliers and Consumers," *Interdisciplinary Journal of Research on Religion*, 5 (7), http://www.religjournal.com.

Seiwert, Hubert, 2003, "Freedom and Control in the Unified Germany: Governmental Approaches to Alternative Religions since 1989," *Sociology of Religion*, 64 (3): 367–375.

Sen, Amartya K., 1999, *Development as Freedom*, New York: Knopf.

2002, *Rationality and Freedom*, Cambridge, MA: Belknap Press of Harvard University.

Shakya, Tsering, 2009, "China's Religious (Re)Awakening: The Impact of Religion on Chinese Society," paper presented at the Brookings Institution, Washington, DC, April 8, 2009.

Shea, Nina, 1997, *In the Lion's Den*, Nashville: Broadman and Holman.

Shih, Vincent Y. C., 1967, *The Taiping Ideology: Its Sources, Interpretations, and Influences*, Seattle: University of Washington Press.

Shterin, Marat S., and James T. Richardson, 1998, "Local Laws Restricting Religion in Russia: Precursors of Russia's New National Law," *Journal of Church and State*, 40 (2): 319–341.

2000, "Effects of Western Anti-Cult Movement on Development of Laws concerning Religion in Post-Communist Russia," *Journal of Church and State*, 42: 247–271.

Shupe, Anson D., and David G. Bromley, 1980, *The New Vigilantes: Deprogrammers, Anti-cultists, and the New Religions*, Beverly Hills, CA: Sage.

Simmel, Georg, [1908] 1971, "The Stranger," in D. N. Levine, ed., *Georg Simmel: On Individuality and Social Forms*, Chicago: University of Chicago Press, 143–149.

Singh, Teja, and Ganda Singh, 1950, *A Short History of the Sikhs*, Bombay: Orient Long.

Smith, Adam, [1776] 1976, *An Inquiry into the Nature and Causes of the Wealth of Nations*, Chicago: University of Chicago Press.

Soares, Benjamin F., 2005, "Islam in Mali in the Neoliberal Era," *Africa Affairs*, 105 (418): 77–95.

Stark, Rodney, 2001, *One True God: Historical Consequences of Monotheism*, Princeton, NJ: Princeton University Press.

  2004, "SSSR Presidential Address, 2004: Putting an End to Ancestor Worship," *Journal for the Scientific Study of Religion*, 43: 465–475.

Stark, Rodney, and William Sims Bainbridge, 1985, *The Future of Religion: Secularization, Revival, and Cult Formation*, Berkeley: University of California Press.

Stark, Rodney, and Roger Finke, 2000, *Acts of Faith: Explaining the Human Side of Religion*, Berkeley: University of California Press.

Stern, Jessica, 1999, *The Ultimate Terrorists*, Cambridge, MA: Harvard University Press.

Stoll, David, 1990, *Is Latin America Turning Protestant?* Berkeley: University of California Press.

Storch, Tonya, 2000, "Law and Religious Freedom in Medieval China: State Regulation of Buddhist Communities," in J. Thierstein and Y. R. Kamalipour, eds., *Religion, Law, and Freedom*, Westport, CT: Praeger, 34–44.

Sumimoto, Tokihisa, 2000, "Religious Freedom Problems in Japan: Background and Current Prospects," *International Journal of Peace Studies*, 5 (2): 77–86.

Tamaru, Noriyoshi, and David Reid, eds, 1996, *Religion in Japanese Culture: Where Living Traditions Meet a Changing World*, Tokyo: Kodansha International.

Taylor, Paul M., 2005, *Freedom of Religion: UN and European Human Rights Law and Practice*, Cambridge: Cambridge University Press.

Tezcür, Günes Murat, and Taghi Azadarmaki, 2008, "Religiosity and Islamic Rule in Iran," *Journal for the Scientific Study of Religion*, 47: 211–224.

Tipson, Frederick S., 1997, "Culture Clash-ification: A Verse to Huntington's Curse," *Foreign Affairs*, 76: 166–169.

Tocqueville, Alexis de, 1945 [1835], *Democracy in America*, vol. 1, New York: Vintage.

Toft, Monica Duffy, 2007, "Getting Religion? The Puzzling Case of Islam and Civil War," *International Security*, 31: 97–131.

Treat, Payson J., 1918, "The Mikado's Ratification of the Foreign Treaties," *American Historical Review*, 23: 531–549.

Tsuyoshi, Nakano, 1987, "The American Occupation and Reform of Japan's Religious System: A Few Notes on the Secularization Process in Postwar Japan," *Journal of Oriental Studies*, 26 (1): 124–138.

  1996, "Religion and State," in Noriyoshi Tamaru and David Reid, eds., *Religion in Japanese Culture: Where Living Traditions Meet a Changing World*, Tokyo: Kodansha International, 115–136.

Van Sant, John E., 2004, *Mori Arinori's Life and Resources in America*, Lanham, MD: Lexington Books.

Vlekke, Bernard Hubertus Maris, [1959] 1960, *Nusantara, A History of Indone-sia*, Chicago: Quadrangle Books.

Voas, David, and Alasdair Crockett, 2005, "Religion in Britain: Neither Believing nor Belonging," *Sociology*, 39: 11–28.

Volkoff, Alex, and Edgar Wickberg, 1979, "New Directions in Chinese Histori-ography: Reappraising the Taiping: Notes and Comment," *Pacific Affairs*, 52: 479–490.

Voll, John Obert, 1994, *Islam: Continuity and Change in the Modern World*, 2nd ed., Syracuse, NY: Syracuse University Press.

Voltaire, [1733] 1980, *Letters on England*, trans. L. Tancock, Middlesex, UK: Penguin.

von Grunebaum, G. E., ed., 1955, *Unity and Variety in Muslim Civilization*, Chicago: University of Chicago Press.

Wald, Kenneth D., and Clyde Wilcox, 2006, "Getting Religion: Has Political Science Rediscovered the Faith Factor?" *American Political Science Review*, 100: 523–529.

Wanner, Catherine, 2004, "Missionaries of Faith and Culture: Evangelical Encounters in Ukraine," *Slavic Review*, 63 (4): 732–755.

2007, Communities of the converted, Ithaca: Cornell University Press.

Weede, Erich, 1998, "Islam and the West: How Likely Is a Clash of These Civi-lizations?" *International Review of Sociology*, 8: 183–195.

Wike, Richard, and Brian J. Grim, 2010, "Western Views toward Muslims: Evi-dence from a 2006 Cross-national Survey," *International Journal of Public Opinion Research* 22: 4–25.

Wiktorowicz, Quintan, 2001, *The Management of Islamic Activism: Salafis, the Muslim Brotherhood, and State Power in Jordon*, Albany: State University of New York Press.

Witham, Larry, 2001 "France Determines Jehovah's Witnesses Are Not a Reli-gion," *Washington Times* (national weekly edition), July 6–12, p. 21.

Wood, James E., Jr., 1991, "The Religious Freedom Restoration Act," *Journal of Church & State*, 33 (Autumn): 673–679.

Woolston, Thomas, 1735, *Works of Thomas Woolston*, London: J. Roberts.

World Missionary Conference, 1910, *Report of Commission VII: Missions and Governments*, Edinburgh and London: Oliphant, Anderson & Ferrier.

Wright, Robin B., 2001, *Sacred Rage: The Crusade of Modern Islam*, rev. ed., New York: Simon & Schuster.

Wunderink, Susan, 2008, "Worse Than Ever," *Christianity Today*. 52 (Novem-ber): 15.

Wybraniec, John, and Roger Finke, 2001, "Religious Regulation in the Courts: The Judiciary's Changing Role in Protecting Minority Religions from Majori-tarian Rule," *Journal for the Scientific Study of Religion*, 40: 427–444.

Yang, C. K., 1961, *Religion in Chinese Society*, Prospect Heights, IL: Waveland Press.

Yang, Fenggang, 2005, "Between Secularists Ideology and Desecularizing Real-ity: The Birth and Growth of Religious Research in Communist China," in Fenggang Yang and Joseph B. Tamney, eds., *State Market and Religions in Chinese Societies*, Leiden, Netherlands: Brill.

2006, "The Red, Black, and Gray Markets of Religion in China," *Sociological Quarterly*, 47: 93–122.

2009, "Religious Trends in China and Their Social Implications," *Freeman Report*, Washington, DC: Center of Strategic and International Studies, March, p. 2.

Yang, Fenggang, and Dedong Wei, 2005, "The Bailin Buddhist Temple: Thriving under Communism," in Fenggang Yang and Joseph G. Tamney, eds., *State Market and Religions in Chinese Societies*, Leiden, Netherlands: Brill.

Yang, Mayfair, 2008, "China's Religious Landscape," *Council on Foreign Relations*, June 11, http://www.cfr.org/publication/16385/symposium_on_religion_and_the_future_of_china.html.

Zubaida, Sami, 2003, *Law and Power in the Islamic World*, London: I. B. Tauris.

Zuo, Jiping, 1991, "Political Religion: The Case of the Cultural Revolution in China," *Sociological Analysis*, 53: 99–110.

Index

AAPOR-Section on Survey Research Methods, 215
Abdullah, Maulana, 190–1
About-Picard Law (France, 2001), 34–5, 36
Abrahamic religions. *See specific religions*
Afghanistan
  constitutional provisions, 25
  conversion to Christianity, penalties for, 1–2
  persecution level in, 19
  social power of clerics, 41
  U.S.-backed defeat of Soviets, 168, 190
Africa, 19
  see also specific countries and regions
Ahmadi Muslims, 191
Ahmadinejad, Mahmoud, xiii, 155–6
Ahmadiyya Muslims, 10–11
Aid to the Church in Need, 11
Al-Askari mosque (Iraq), 192
Albania, 167–8
Aleksii II, Patriarch, 47, 49
Aleph. *See* Aum Shinrikyo
Algeria, 9, 66, 197–200
Ali, Muhammad, 75–6
Allah, 31–2
al-Qaeda, 167–8, 197–200

al-Sadr, Muktada, 192
American Sociological Review, 215
Andrabi, Asiya, 160
Angola, 37
anti-Americanism, 189
anti-conversion laws, 1–2, 15–16, 148
anti-cult movement, 34, 44–5
Anti-Defamation League, 157–8
anti-Semitism, 9, 110
apostasy, in Shari's Law, 32, 116, 157, 163
Aquinas, Thomas, 31
Ardas (Sikh Prayer), xii
armed conflict
  civilization divides and, 217–18
  civil war and, 181–3
  comparison to restrictions, 216, 219
  religious freedoms and, 205–6
  religious persecution as collateral damage, 74–5, 80
  in Sudan, 177
Armed Islamic Group (GIA), 197–200
Armenians, xii–xiv
Arouet, Armand, 3
Arouet, François Marie. *See* Voltaire
Ashura celebration, xi–xii
Asia, 91, 177–80, 203–4
  see also specific regions and countries

Assembly of Experts (Iran), 154–6
Association of Religion Data Archives
    (ARDA), 2, 10–11, 17, 215
Atatürk, Mustafa Kemal, 166–7
atheism, 7–8, 50–1, 131–2, 135, 203
Augustine, on government use of
    physical force, 31
Aum Shinrikyo, 97–9, 101–2, 103,
    136–8
Azerbaijan, 192–3
Aziz, Maulana Abdul, 160–1, 190–1

Babri Masjid mosque attacks (India),
    146–7
Baha'i Faith/Baha'is, xii, 11, 71–2,
    156–9
Bahá'u'lláh, 157–9
Bangladesh, xv, 19, 174
Baptists, 37–9, 45, 52, 56
Barker, Eileen, 48
Bates, M. Searle
    on religious competition in Brazil,
        108
    on religious liberty in China, 171–4
    on secret societies in China, 127
    on Tibet under Chinese rule, 130–1
Belgium, 33–4
beliefs, exclusivity of, 46–50
Benedict XVI, Pope, 1–2
Berger, Peter, 68–9
Bharatiya Janata Party (BJP, India),
    145, 147
Bible, 31
Bin Laden, Osama, 188, 191
Black, Galen, 53
blasphemy, in Shari'a Law, 32, 116
Bollywood, 189
Bosnia, 61, 75
brainwashing, myth of, 47–8, 102,
    103
Brazil
    anti-Semitism, 110
    case study overview, 88–90,
        104–10
    Catholicism in, 7, 107–9
    comparison to Mexico, 104–5
    constitutional provisions, 107

freedom with tensions in, 85–6
    hate crimes, 59
    historical restrictions, 107–9
    immigration patterns, 108
    Judaism in, 107–9
    Pentecostalism in, 5–6, 7, 109
    as Portuguese colony, 107
    Protestantism in, 107–9
    religion census, 109
    religious economies model, 7
    social restrictions, 109–10
Brustein, William I., 9
Buddhism/Buddhists, xii, 15–16, 64,
    123–5, 133–4
    see also specific sects
Buddhist-majority countries, 169
building codes, 40, 54–7
Burma, 15–17, 20–1
burqa, banning of, 36
Burrows, Peter, 43
Byzantine Empire, 75–6, 165

Canada, 59
cartels, 8–9
case studies
    overview, 88–90, 120
    Brazil, 88–90, 104–10
    China, 120–40
    India, 120, 140–9
    Iran, 120, 150–9
    Japan, 88–104
    Nigeria, 88–90, 110–19
Catholicism/Catholics
    on About-Picard Law, 34–5
    in Brazil, 7, 107–9
    in China, 133–4
    conflict with Evangelicals in
        Mexico, 20, 105
    death toll of adherents, 11
    hate crimes against in U.S., 58–9
    in Japan, 96
    Jesuit theology/missionaries, 3, 96
    persecution of in Russia, 37–9, 45
    U.S. court rulings on, 57
Central Asia, 167–8
Chad, 178–9, 192–3
Chestnut, Andrew, 7

Chiapas region (Mexico), 20, 104–5
Chile, 42–3
China
  anti-religious ideology, xiii–xiv,
    84–5
  Buddhism in, 123–5, 133–4
  case study overview, 88–90,
    120–40
  Catholicism in, 133–4
  Christianity in, 123, 128–30
  constitutional provisions,
  Cultural Revolution, xiii–xiv, 50–1,
    70–1, 131–2, 203
  current religious persecution, xv
  Document 19 (toleration), 133
  Document 6 (noninterference), 133
  Falun Gong, persecution of, 101,
    136–8
  harmonious society through
    restrictions, 10
  historical restrictions, 123–7
  importance of religion, survey on,
    203–4
  Japanese occupation of, 131–2
  legal status of religions, 121
  legislative restrictions, 125–6
  Manchu Qing Dynasty, 125–7,
    128–32
  Ming Dynasty, 125, 132
  Muslims in, 66, 133–4
  national character, xiv
  oil reserves, 139–40
  Protestantism in, 123, 133–4
  reeducation-through-labor camps,
    136–8
  religious demography of, 121–3,
    133–4
  restrictions on Internet access, 43
  on role of government in religious
    restrictions, 10
  selective denial of religious
    freedoms, 135–40, 207
  selective granting of religious
    freedoms, 133–5, 207
  Shandong Rebellion, 127–8
  state alliances with religions, 125–6
  state restrictions and, 139–40

  on strategic control of religions,
    50–1
  Taiping Rebellion, 128–31
  Tibetan Buddhists, persecution of,
    67, 136
  Uygur Muslims, persecution of, 66,
    67, 136, 139–40
  Wahhabism, 127–8
  Western imperialism and, 131
  see also Communist Party
China Buddhist Association, 131–2
China Catholic Laity Patriotic
    Committee, 131–2
China Catholic Patriotic Committee,
    131–2
China Daily, on survey of religious
    population, 121–2
China Daoist Association, 131–2
China Islamic Association, 131–2
Chin ethnic group (Burma), 15–16
Christian Crusades, 165
Christianity/Christians
  in China, 123, 128–30
  death toll of adherents, xii, 11
  as dominant religion and
    persecution levels, 21–2, 81
  Easter celebration, xi–xii
  global locations of, 65
  on government use of physical
    force, 31
  in Japan, 95–9
  Jews as advocates for, 11–12
  in Nigeria, 113–16
  peace activitist deaths, xv
  persecution of in Burma, 15–16
  persecution of in India, 146–7,
    148
  prejudice against sects in Latin
    America, 46, 49–50
  religious freedom in early America,
    5–6
  spiritual vs. legal theology, 31
  in Turkey, xii–xiv
  see also specific sects
Christian-majority countries
  armed conflict and civil war, 181–3
  civilization fault lines and, 183–6

Christian-majority countries (*cont.*)
  comparison of persecution levels,
    178
  data analysis, 169, 171, 219–20
  harassment of co-religionists, 185
  religion-ethnicity overlap levels,
    174–7
  terrorism cases, 194–200
  tolerance of Muslims in, 193–4
  trends in state restrictions, 172–4
  during World War II, 171–4
  see also specific countries
Christian Persecution, xv, 11, 15–16,
    46, 49–50, 146–8
Church of Jesus Christ of Latter-day
    Saints, 37–9
Church of Scientology, 34–5, 37–9,
    41–2
City of Boerne v. Flores (1997), 54–6
civilization divides. *See* clash-of-
    civilizations argument
civilizations, Huntington's definition,
    63
civil liberties, 40, 71–2, 205–6
Civil Rights Division, U.S. (DOJ),
    58–9
civil rights movement (U.S.), 40, 71–2
civil war, 181–3
*Clash of Civilizations and the
    Remaking of World Order*
    (Huntington), 9–10, 61–2
clash-of-civilizations argument
    (Huntington)
  actions/behaviors vs. general
    religious traditions, 75–6
  on Buddhism, 64
  civilization divides and persecution
    rates, 64, 216–22
  civilization fault lines and, 183–6
  civilizations, defined, 63
  data analysis, 80
  implications of, 65–8
  limitations of, 65–8, 72–4
  listing of civilizations, 64
  premise of, 62–5
  religious conflict within
    civilizations, 67

religious explanation problems in,
    66, 72–4, 75–6
religious homogeneity, 68, 212,
    216–22
on threat of multiculturalism, 62,
    63–4, 76
see also religious economies
    argument
Clay, Cassius, 75–6
colonial empires
  in Japan, 96
  Muslim-majority countries, 165–8,
    171–4
  in Nigeria, 113–15
  Shari'a Law and, 31, 187
  Taiping Rebellion and, 128–30
Columbia, 49
Commission on International
    Religious Freedom, U.S., 12
Communication and Information
    Technology Commission (CITC,
    Saudi Arabia), 43
Communist Party (China)
  approved religions, 135
  atheism, 131–2, 135
  on Christian social service, 130–1
  Document 19 (toleration), 133
  interest in religion and, 134–5
  on Taiping Rebellion, 129, 130
compelling interest test, 53–7
conflicts
  ethnic conflicts, 15–16, 20–1, 75
  persecution as collateral damage,
    74–5, 80
  religious freedom and reduction of,
    8
  social conflicts, 210–11
  see also armed conflict; *specific
    conflicts*
Constitutional Court (Russia), 37–9
constitutions
  Afghanistan, 25
  Brazil, 107
  China,
  India, 147–8
  Iran, 191
  Japan, 91–3, 98, 100

Nigeria, 116–18
Pakistan, 190–1
religious freedom protections,
27–30
state restrictions in opposition to,
27–30, 32
conversion, legal penalties, 1–2,
15–16, 148
Cooney, Daniel, 1–2
Council of Europe, 34–5
Country of Particular Concern status,
16–17
Country Reports on Human Rights
(2007)
on Chinese labor camps, 136
on house arrest, 136
cults/sects
anti-cult movement in France, 34–5
brainwashing myth and, 47–8,
102–3
U.S. court rulings on, 57
see also specific cults/sects
cultural identity, 49
see also clash-of-civilizations
argument
cultural restrictions. *See* restrictions
(social/cultural)
Cultural Revolution (China), xiii–xiv,
50–1, 70–1, 131–2, 203
cycle of persecution, 70–2, 79–80,
86
see also religious persecution,
violent

Dal, Bajrang, 146–7
Dalai Lama, 136, 138–9
Dar al-Harb, 163, 183–6, 193–4
Dar al-Islam, defined, 161
see also Muslim-majority countries;
Shari'a Law
Daughters of Faith, 160
Declaration on the Elimination of All
Forms of Interference and of
Discrimination Based on Religion
or Belief (UN), 27, 29–30
Defense Department, U.S., 195
De Groot, J.J.M., 128

Demerath, N.J., III, 69–70
democracy, longevity of, 216, 218,
220
Democratic Republic of Congo, xv
Deng Xioaping, 132
denial of religious freedom
overview, 212–13
based on exclusivity of religious
beliefs, 46–50
based on preservation of cultural
identity, 49
process of, 25–60
registration requirements as, 36–7,
39
state interference with property
rights as, 40
state interference with right to
workship, 39–40
state motivations for, 46–51
through complacency in protection
of minority religions, 45
see also religious freedoms;
restrictions (social/cultural);
restrictions (state/government)
deregulation of religion. *See* religious
freedom
dhimmi status, 32
displacement
based on religious bias, 118–19,
146–7
examples of, xi–xv
levels of, 20–1
in Sudan, 177
see also religious persecution,
violent
Diwali celebration, xii
dominant religions
alliances with states, 6, 50–1,
70
cultural restrictions by, 8–9
despotism of, 3–6, 67–8
discrimination against new
religions, 40–1
harassment of co-religionists, 185
motivations for restrictions, 46–50
threat of religious competition,
49–50

dominant religions (*cont.*)
    violent religious persecution and,
        75
    see also power partition, religion/
        state typology; *specific religions
        and countries*
Drinan, Robert F., 58
Dukhtaran-e-Millat, 160
Duvert, Cyrille, 44–5

East Asia, 19, 99, 109, 131
East China Normal University, 121–2
Easter celebration, xi–xii
Eastern Europe, 50–1
East Turkestan Islamic Movement
    (ETIM), 136, 139–40
Economist, The, on Red Mosque
    conflicts, 161
Edelman, Bryan, 103
Egypt, 167–8
embassy officials, U.S., 13, 17, 20–1
*Employment Division of Oregon,
    Depart. of Human Resources of
    Oregon v. Smith* (1990), 53–5,
    56, 57
Equal Employment Opportunity
    Commission, 58
ethnic cleansing, 61, 118–19
ethnic conflicts, 15–16, 20–1, 75
ethnic group, defined, 176
ethnicity. *See* religion-ethnicity tie
Europe, 9, 19, 44–5, 48, 166
    see also specific countries
European Court of Human Rights
    (ECHR), 26–7, 37–9
Evangelicalism/Evangelicals, 7, 20, 46,
    49, 105

Fagan, Geraldine, 38–9
Falun Gong (Falun Dafa), xv, 103,
    136–8
Farr, Thomas F., 5–6
Fatah Party, 67, 197–200
favoritism, toward select religions,
    22–4, 206–10
Federal Bureau of Investigation (FBI),
    58–9

First Amendment (U.S.)
    analysis of court claims, 54–7
    Free Exercise Clause, 54, 56–7
    protections of, 6
    testing of boundaries, 52–4
First Amendment Center, 59–60,
    86
Flores, City of Boerne v. (1997), 54–6
Foreign Contribution Regulation Act
    (FCRA) (India, 1976), 148
Foreigners Act (India, 1946), 148
Forum 18 reports, 10, 38–9
Fourth General Conference of Latin
    American Bishops (CELAM), 46
Fox, Jonathan, 8, 14, 28–9
France
    About-Picard Law (2001), 34–5,
        36
    anti-cult movement, state subsidies
        for, 44–5
    attitudes toward minority religions,
        survey on, 41–2
    on banning of burqa, 36
    constitutional provisions, 48
    Gest Commission report, 34–5
    hijab, banning of, 36
    international monitoring agency,
        34
    Jansenists, persecution of, 3
    local authority, violations by, 36
    media influence on anti-cult
        movement, 44–5
    MIVILUDES on cults and sects,
        34–5, 47–8
    power partition, 85
    Special Rapporteur on French
        school violations of religious
        freedom, 35–6
    state monitoring of religious groups,
        33–6
    use of brainwashing myth in policy,
        48
freedom of speech, 46, 205–6
freedom of the press, 20–1
freedom to assemble, 205–6
freedom to worship, 39–40, 59–60,
    77–80, 205–6

freedom with tensions typology
 explanation of, 85–6
 listing of countries, 91–3, 104–5
 see also Brazil
Free Exercise Clause, 54, 56–7
Froese, Paul, 7–8

Gambira, U, 15–16
genocide
 in Bosnia, 61
 Nazi mass murder of Jews, xiii, 9
 Turkish massacre of Armenians,
  xii–xiv
Germany, xiii, xiv, 9, 33–4, 112
Gest, Alain, 34–5
Ghazi, Abdul Rashid, 190–1
Gill, Anthony, 7, 51, 207
Golden Temple (Sikh), xii
government. *See* restrictions
 (state/government)
Government Restrictions Index (GRI),
 77–8, 82–6, 178–9, 215–22
Grim, Brian, 17, 43, 185
Guatemala, 49
Guerzes Christians (Guinea), 179–80
Guinea, 179–80, 192–3

Hadīth. *See* Sunnah
Hafez, Mohammed M., 9
Hamas, 67, 197–200
Hanbali school. *See* Shari'a Law
Hardacre, Helen, *Shinto and the State,
 1868–1988,* 100
harmonious society (China), 10
hate crimes, religion based, 58–9,
 86
hegemony, religious, 66, 75–6
heresy laws, 125–7, 132
 see also Shari'a Law
Hertzke, Allen D., 11–12
high religious freedom typology
 explanation of, 86
 listing of countries, 91–3
 see also Japan
hijab, banning of, 36
Himachal Pradesh state (India),
 148

Hinduism/Hindus, xii, xv, 145–6,
 149, 211
Hindu-majority countries, 169
Hindutva movement (India), 145–6,
 149, 211
Hitti, Philip K., 31
Holocaust, xiii, 9
homogeneity, cultural, 63
homogeneity, religious
 Huntington on, 67–8, 216–22
 increases in persecution due to,
  67–8, 212, 216–22
Hong Xiuquan, 128–30
Horowitz, Michael, 11–12, 202
House of Unbelief/War, defined,
 183–6
Howard, John, 1–2
Hudson Institute's Center for
 Religious Freedom, 205–6
Hui Muslims, 66
Hu Jintao, 134–5
Human Rights Commission (UN),
 157–8
Human Rights Committee (ICCPR),
 26–7
Human Rights League (France), 34–5
Hume, David, 2, 4, 50
Huntington, Samuel P.
 *Clash of Civilizations and the
  Remaking of World Order,* 61–2
 on single civilization, 9–10
 on toleration of non-national
  religions, 68
 see also clash-of-civilizations
  argument
Hussain, Altaf, 161
Hussein, Imam, xi–xii, 154–6

immigration patterns, 9–10, 108
indexes. *See* Government Restrictions
 Index; Social Regulation of
 Religion Index
India
 Babri Masjid mosque attacks,
  146–7
 as birthplace of religions, 141–4
 BJP political strength, 145, 147

India (*cont.*)
  Buddhism in, 66
  case study overview, 88–90, 120,
    140–9
  Christians, persecution of, 146–8
  constitutional provisions, 147–8
  importance of religion, survey on,
    203–4
  inclusion on USCIRF Watch List,
    149–50
  legislative restrictions, 148
  Muslims, persecution of, 146–7
  nationalist Hindutva movement,
    145–6, 149, 211
  persecution levels in, 19
  personal vs. universal religious
    freedom, survey on, 42–3
  political history, 140–1
  religious demography of, 144–5
  religious freedoms, survey on, 145
  religious intolerance gap in, 43
  Shari'a Law movements, 188–9
  see also Hinduism/Hindus
Indian Divorce Act (2001), 148
Indonesia, 29–30, 167–8, 192–3
*Interdisciplinary Journal of Research
  on Religion*, 215
Intermedia survey (2005), on
  communists' interest in religion,
  134–5
Interministerial Monitoring Mission
  against Sectarian Abuses
  (MIVILUDES)
  scope of, 34–5
  on threat of sects, 47–8
  use of brainwashing myth in policy,
  48
International Covenant on Civil and
  Political Rights (ICCPR, UN),
  26–7
International Religion Data Initiative,
  10–17
International Religious Freedom Act
  (U.S., 1998), 12, 14
International Religious Freedom
  Office, 12

*International Religious Freedom
  Reports*, 11–17
  bias and, 14–17
  Burma report (2009), 15–16
  on Chinese labor camps, 136
  coding of promises vs. practices, 12,
    27–30
  on conflicts due to power partition
    in, 105
  embassy officials and, 13, 17, 20–1
  Interim Report on Saudi Arabia
    abuses (1998), 16–17
  Legal/Policy Framework, 27–30
  limitations of, 17
  on local authority violations in
    France, 36
  ongoing implications of reports, 20
  on persecution levels in Guinea,
    179–80
  reliability of reports, 13, 14
  on religion-ethnicity overlap, 176–7
  on right to worship, 39–40
  on selective favoritism and
    persecution, 207–10
  on Shi'a vs. Sunni conflict in Iraq,
    xiv–xv
  on societal attitudes, 12
  on state employment
    discrimination, 144
  on state requirement for
    registration, 36–7, 39
  on terrorism, 196–200
  on trends in state restrictions,
    172–4
International Taoism Forum (2007),
  135
Internet access, 43
inter-religion alliances, 11–12
intolerance gap, 43
Introvigne, Massimo, 48
Iran
  Baha'i, persecution of, 71–2, 156–9
  case study overview, 88–90, 120,
    150–9
  constitutional provisions, 191
  Jews, persecution of, 156

mass exodus of religious minorities,
156–7
overthrow of Shah (1979), 168
presidential oath, 155–6
religious demography of, 150–1,
156–7
Shi'a vs. Sunni Muslims, 154–6,
191
socio-political monopoly, 83–4
state Islamic religion, 154–6
state restrictions, 156
Supreme Leader, 154–6
Iraq
alignment with Soviets, 167–8
bombing of Al-Askari mosque,
192
Christians, persecution of, xv
Shi'a vs. Sunni Muslims, xiv–xv, 67,
182, 192
socio-political monopoly, 83–4
Wahhabism, 192–3
Ireland, 67
Islam/Muslims
Ashura celebration, xi–xii
in Asia, 177–80
banning of burqa in France, 36
in Burma, 15–16
in China, 66–7, 133–4, 136,
139–40
Dar al-Islam concept, 161
death toll of adherents, xii
as dominant religion and
persecution levels, 21–2, 81
ethnic cleansing in Bosnia and, 61
in Europe, 193–4
on inclusion of legal in spiritual
theology, 31, 187–8
in India, 146–7
in Iran, 154–6, 191
in Iraq, xiv–xv, 67, 182, 192
in Nigeria, 113–16
origins of, 31
in Pakistan, 174
registration requirements in Russia,
37–9
role of Imams, xi–xii, 154–6

in Saudi Arabia, xv
social/cultural restrictions on
minority religions, 44–6
in Sub-Saharan Africa, 177–8,
180
suicide bombings, survey on,
193–4
supremacy of Islam in Afghan
constitution, 25
in Turkey, 166–7
in U.S., 57, 58–9, 193–4
see also Muslim-majority countries;
Quran; Shari'a Law; *specific sects*
Israel, xiii, 167–8
Italy, 85–6

Jahangir, Asma, 29–30
Jainism/Jains, xii
James, Herman G., 108
Jansenism/Jansenists, 3
Japan
Aum Shinrikyo and, 101, 104
case study overview, 88–90,
91–104
Christianity in, 95–9
constitutional provisions, 91–3, 98,
100
historical restrictions, 93–9
increase in religious freedoms,
99–101
League of Religions, 131
legislative restrictions, 99
non-use of brainwashing myth, 102,
103
occupation of China, 131–2
opening of ports to foreigners, 97
post-WWII, U.S. influence on, 91–3
social receptivity period, 95
State Shinto religion, 99–101,
131
Warring States' period, 95–6
Jefferson, Thomas
on First Amendment protections, 6,
52
on religious disputes, 71–2
on religious plurality, 5, 9

Jehovah's Witnesses
  listed as dangerous group in France,
    34–5
  persecution of through state
    restrictions, xv, 11, 37–9, 45
  Supreme Court rulings and, 52–3
Jenkins, Philip, *The Next
    Christendom*, 65
Jesuit theology/missionaries, 3,
    96
Jews. *See* Judaism/Jews
Jiang Zemin, 134–5
John Paul II, Pope, 46
John Templeton Foundation, 11
JSM Proceedings, 215
Judaism/Jews
  as advocates for persecuted
    Christians, 11–12
  anti-Semitism, 9, 110
  death toll of adherents, xii
  hate crimes against in U.S., 58–9
  Holocaust genocide, xiii, 9
  Horowitz on, as litmus indicator,
    202
  Passover celebration, xi–xii
  persecution of in Brazil, 107–9
  persecution of in Iran, 156
  U.S. court rulings on, 57
Justice Department, U.S.,
    58–9

Kalashnikov Shari'a, 161, 191
Kamali, Mohammad Hashim, 30–1,
    32
Kanagawa Treaty (1854), 97
Karzai, Hamid, 1–2
Kennedy, Anthony M., 55–6
Kenya, 188–9
Khamenei, Ali, 157–8
Khatami, Mohammad, 155–6
Khomeini, Ayatollah, 168
Koniankes Muslims (Guinea),
    179–80
Konovalov, Aleksandr, 38–9
Korea, 65, 131
Kurien, Prema, 145
Kuwait, 83–4
Kyrgyzstan, 192–3

Lacquer, Walter, 194–5
Lal Masjid. *See* Red Mosque conflicts
Latin America, 7, 46, 49–50, 66
  see also specific countries
Law on Civic Organizations (Taiwan),
    7
Law on Freedom of Conscience and
    Associations (Russia, 1997),
    37–41
Law on Freedom of Religions (Soviet
    Union, 1990), 37, 40–1
Legal/Policy Framework (IRF), 27–30
Lewis, Bernard, 183–6
Liberation Tigers of Tamil Eelam
    (LTTE), 197
Lu, Yungfeng, 7
Lula da Silva, Luiz Inácio, 110
Lun, Wang, 127–8

Madison, James, 5–6
Magellan, Ferdinand, 165
Makiguchi Tsunesaburo, 101
Mali, 178–9, 180, 192–3
Manchuria region, 131
Maoists (Nepal), 197
Mao Zedong, xiii–xiv, 203
  see also Cultural Revolution
Marger, Martin M., 176
Mauritania, 178–9
Mawdudi, Sayyid Abul Ala, 141–4
McConnell, Michael W., 54
media, influence of, 11, 44–5, 47–8
"Memorial and Remonstrance against
    Religious Assessments"
    (Madison), 5–6
mental manipulation, myth of, 47–8
Merkel, Angela, 1–2
methodology
  arguments, testing of, 215–22
  data analysis, 76–82
  nonrecursive/recursive models,
    219–20
  plotting of countries, 82–6
  region samples, 81, 219
  structural equation modeling, 215,
    216–22
  time lag model, 81–2, 220, 222
Mexico, 20, 85, 104–5

Middle East, 10–11, 19
  see also specific countries
mind control, myth of, 47–8
Ministry of Home Affairs (India),
  146–8
Ministry of Justice (Russia), 38–9
minority religions
  complacency in protections for, 45
  in court systems, 40, 53–7, 58
  First Amendment (U.S.) protections,
    6
  grievance reduction among, 72–4
  state monitoring of, 33
  see also specific religions
MIVILUDES *see* Interministerial
    Monitoring Mission against
    Sectarian Abuses
Mohammed, Prophet, xi–xii, 32,
    154–6, 163, 187
Mohiuddin, Fasahat, 161
monopolistic social pressures typology
  explanation of, 85
  listing of countries, 140–1
  see also India
Montenegro, 192–3
Moonies, 48
moral entrepreneurs, 44–5
Mori, Arinori, *Religious Freedom in
    Japan*, 98, 100
Mormons. *See* Church of Jesus Christ
    of Latter-day Saints
Moses, xi–xii
multiculturism, 62–4, 76
Muslim-majority countries, 160–2
  armed conflict and, 177, 181–3
  civilization fault lines and, 183–6
  communism and, 167–8
  data analysis, 169, 171, 219–20
  gender equality/sexual
    liberalization, 200
  geographical spread of Islam, 165
  harassment of co-religionists,
    181–3, 185
  historical restrictions, 171–4
  historical/social/geographical
    context, 162–8
  nationalism and, 167–8

pan-Arabism, 167–8
regional diversity, 177–80
religion-ethnicity overlap levels,
  174–7
restrictions and persecution
  overview, 169–94
  during twentieth century, 165–8
  women and, 160–61
  see also Shari'a Law; *specific
    countries*
Muttahida Qaumi Movement
  (MQM), 161, 191

Naga ethnic group (Burma), 15–16
Nassr, Vali, *The Shi'a Revival*, 65–6
National Commission for Minorities
  (India), 144
national security, 72–4
Native American Church, 53
Native American religions, 57
Nazi genocide, xiii, 9
Near East, 177–80
Nepal, 19
Next Christendom, The (Jenkins), 65
Niger, 178–9, 192–3
Nigeria
  case study overview, 88–90,
    110–19
  Christianity in, 113–16
  colonial empires and, 113–15
  constitutional provisions, 116–18
  Muslims in, 113–16
  power partition, 85
  religious demography of, 113–15
  religious riots, 118–19
  Shari'a Law in, 113–19, 188–9
  social restrictions, 113–18
  state restrictions, 113–15
North Africa, 177–80
North America, 44–5
  see also specific countries
North Korea, 17, 20–1, 84–5
N'Zerekore (Guinea), 179–80

Observatory on Sects/Cults (France).
    See Interministerial Monitoring
    Mission against Sectarian Abuses

O'Connor, Sandra Day, 54, 56–7
Omotokyo Shinto sect, 98–9
one true faith premise, 46–50
Open Doors, 11
Order of the Solar Temple, 33–4, 41–2
Orissa attacks (India), 146–7
Ottoman Empire, 75–6, 165

Page, Jeremy, 160
Pahlavi, Mohammad Reza, 191
Pakistan
  constitutional provisions, 190–1
  Dar al-Islam and, 174
  persecution level in, 19
  Red Mosque conflicts, 160–1,
    189–92
  religious demography of, 190
  video piracy, 189
Palestine, 67, 168, 197–200
Palestinian Liberation Organization
  (PLO), 167–8, 197–200
Pancasila philosophy (Indonesia),
  167–8
panel data. *See* time lag model
Passover celebration, xi–xii
Pentecostalism/Pentecostalists
  in Brazil, 5–7, 109
  groups on Gest Commission list,
    34–5
  growth of in Latin America, 46, 49,
    50
  lack of government protection of in
    Russia, 45
  registration requirements in Russia,
    37–9
Perry, Matthew, 97
persecution. *See* religious persecution,
  violent
Persecution.org, 10–11
Pew Forum on Religion & Public Life
  on growth of Pentecostalism in
    Brazil, 109
  hate crime in Western Hemisphere,
    study on, 59
  importance of religion, survey on,
    204
  Muslim/Christian attitudes in
    Nigeria, survey on, 115–16

personal vs. universal religious
  freedom, survey on, 42–3, 58
  similarity of cross-national reports,
    14
Social Regulation of Religion Index
  (SRI), 14, 169
Pew Global Attitudes Project, on
  importance of religion, 122,
  204
Pew Research Center
  attitudes of Muslims in U.S., survey
    on, 193–4
  religious freedoms, survey on, 204
Philippines, 188–9, 192–3, 197–200
physical abuse, xii–xiv, 20–1
  see also religious persecution,
    violent
Plassnik, Ursula, 1–2
plurality, of religion. *See* religious
  freedom
population growth, 216, 218, 220
population size, 80, 216, 218–20
Portugal, 107
power partition, religion/state
  typology
  explanation of, 85, 110–12
  listing of countries, 91–3, 112
  see also Nigeria
property damage, 58–9
property rights, 40
*Protestant Ethic and the Spirit of
  Capitalism* (Weber), 66
Protestantism/Protestants
  in Brazil, 107–8, 109
  in China, 123, 133–4
  as dominant U.S. religion, 54–7
  growth of in Latin America, 49–50
  terrorist activity against, 197
  see also specific sects
Protestant Three-Self Patriotic
  Movement, 131–2
Public Security Bureau (China),
  136
Public Security Investigation Agency
  (Japan), 102
Public Security Preservation Law
  (Japan, 1941), 99
Puritans, 57–60

Qigong, 136–8
quiyās. *See* Shari'a Law
Quran
on fighting persecution, 31
on freedom of religion, 30–1
as legal foundation for Pakistan,
190
Sunni vs. Shi'a tenets on, 154–6,
164
tenets of, 187
see also Islam/Muslims; Shari'a
Law

Raffarin, Jean-Pierre, 34–5
Rahman, Abdul, 1–2, 25, 41
Red Cross, 118–19
Red Mosque conflicts (Islamabad),
160–1, 189–92
reeducation-through-labor camps
(China), 136–8
registration, of religions, 36–9
regulation of religion. *See* restrictions
(state/government)
Religion and State Project, The
(ARDA), 14
religion as threat typology
explanation of, 84–5
listing of countries, 121–2
see also China; India; Iran
religion-ethnicity tie
ethnic diversity and, 174–7
ethnic group, defined, 176
persecution levels and, 75, 81,
216–22
see also ethnic conflicts
Religion in Chinese Society (Yang),
123–5
Religious Affairs Bureau (China),
50–1, 120, 133, 135, 136
religious cartels, 8–9, 71–2
"Religious Charter of the Empire of
Dai Nippon, The" (Arinori),
98
Religious Corporation Ordinance
(Japan), 99, 102
religious discrimination, U.S., 58–9
religious economies argument,
68–70

actions/behaviors vs. general
religious traditions, 75–6
defined, 6–7
in early America, 7
explanation of, 6–10
globalization and religious plurality,
68–9, 75–6
on growth of Islam, 192
testing of argument, 216–22
threat of multiculturalism vs., 62,
63–4, 76
see also clash-of-civilizations
argument; *headings at
restrictions*
religious explanation problem,
defined, 66, 75–6
Religious Freedom in Japan (Arinori),
98, 100
Religious Freedom Restoration Act
(RFRA) (U.S., 1993), 54–7,
58
religious freedoms, 202–13
civil liberties and, 205–6
consequences of restrictions on,
6–10
despotism of dominant religions,
3–6, 40–1
differing definitions of, 30–3
explanation of, 212–13
freedom to worship, 39–40, 59–60,
77–80, 205–6
Hume on, 2
Jefferson on, 5–6
pacifying consequences of, 2–10
process of denial and, 25–60
reduction of conflict and, 8
reduction of persecution and, 70–1
selective state favoritism vs.,
206–10
social conflict and, 210–11
surveys on, 42–3, 58, 204
Voltaire on, 2, 3, 50, 203
see also denial of religious freedom;
restrictions (social/cultural);
restrictions (state/government);
United Nations
Religious Institutions Act (India,
1988), 148

religious intolerance gap, 43
Religious Land Use and
    Institutionalized Persons Act
    (U.S., 2000), 58
religious law, 75, 81, 216–22
    see also Shari'a Law
Religious Organizations Law (Japan,
    1939), 99
religious persecution, violent, 16,
    18–86
    of Abrahamic religions, xi–xii
    armed conflict and, 74–5, 80
    of Armenians in Turkey, xii–xiv
    as collateral damage from larger
        conflicts, 74–5, 80
    cycle of persecution, 70–2, 79–80,
        86
    data analysis, 76–86
    defined, xiv, 77
    displacement as, xi–xv, 20–1,
        118–19, 146–7, 177
    favoritism to religions as,
        22–4
    historical overview, xi–xv
    human death toll, xii, xiv, 11
    increases in, 79–80
    interference levels and persecution,
        22–4
    Nazi genocide, xiii, 9
    patterns of, 21
    pervasiveness of, 18–21
    physical abuse, xii–xiv, 20–1
    population data collection, 18
    population growth and, 216, 218,
        220
    population size and, 80, 216,
        218–19, 220
    religious homogeneity and, 67–8,
        212, 216–22
    religious majority and, 21–2
    restrictions and persecution levels,
        77–8
    socio-political monopoly and, 83–4
    see also restrictions (social/cultural);
        restrictions (state/government);
        *specific religions, countries and
        typologies*

religious plurality. *See* religious
    freedom
religious restrictions. *See* restrictions
    (social/cultural); restrictions
    (state/government)
Report on Enforcement of Laws
    Protecting Religious Freedoms
    (DOJ, 2006), 58
restrictions (social/cultural)
    comparison to state restrictions,
        82–6
    data analysis, 82–6, 169–71
    denial of religious freedoms and,
        40–6
    impact on legal restrictions, 9–10
    increases in persecution due to,
        78–80
    influence on state restrictions, 9–10,
        40–6, 79–80
    on Internet access, 43
    listing of countries, 140–1
    on minority religions, 44–6
    motivations for restrictions, 46–50
    multiculturism and,
    neutralization of, 71–2
    personal vs. universal religious
        freedom, survey on, 41–2
    by religious cartels, 8–9
    under-reporting of, 17
    state restrictions, influence on,
        9–10, 40–6, 79–80
    on U.S. civil rights movement, 40,
        71–2
    vigilante policing actions and, 71–2
    see also religious economies
        argument; religious persecution,
        violent; *specific countries*
restrictions (state/government), 33–40
    alliances with dominant religions, 6,
        50–1, 70, 207
    anti-cult movements and, 44–5
    based on brainwashing myth, 47–8
    coercion tactics, 33
    comparison to social restrictions,
        82–6
    cycle of persecution and, 70–2,
        79–80, 86

data analysis, 82–6, 169–71
enforcement of freedoms vs.,
    71–2
favoritism to religions as, 22–4,
    206–10
increases in persecution due to,
    77–8
interference levels and persecution,
    22–4
mobilized support for, 72–4
monitoring bureaus, 33
motivations for restrictions, 50–1
multiculturism and,
national security and, 72–4
in opposition to constitutions,
    27–30
protection complacency as, 45
registration requirements as, 36–7,
    39
religion-ethnicity alliances and, 81
selective favoritism and persecution,
    206–10
social restrictions, influence on,
    9–10, 40–6, 79–80
threats to social order, 6
see also religious economies
    argument; religious persecution,
    violent; *specific countries*
Revolutionary Armed Forces of
    Columbia (FARC), 197
Richardson, James T.
    on Aum vs. Falun Gong, 103
    on media influence on anti-cult
        movement, 44–5
    on social restrictions in Russia,
        40–1
    on use of brainwashing myth in
        policy, 48
Royal Exchange (London), 3
Ruback, R. Barry, 145
Russia Federation
    complacency in protection of
        minority religions, 45
    dissolution of religious groups,
        37–9
    expansion of state investigative
        powers, 38–9

Law on Freedom of Conscience and
    Associations, 37–9, 40–1
monopolistic social pressures in, 85
refusal of Special Rapporteur visits,
    29–30
religion registration requirements,
    37–9
Russian Orthodox Church
    alliance with state, 37–9, 40–1, 51
    anti-cult movement within, 44–5
    on attempts to preserve cultural
        identity, 49
    on rationale for restrictions, 47
    religious competition and, 37

Saladin, 165
Salafi Muslims, 192–3, 197–200
Salafist Group for Preaching and
    Combat (SGPC), 197–200
Salvation Army, 37–9
Sanasarian, Eliz, 156–8
Sarkozy, Nicolas, 36
Saudi Arabia
    as ally of U.S., 167–8
    Country of Particular Concern
        status, 16–17
    restrictions on Internet access, 43
    socio-political monopoly, 83–4
    Sufis, persecution of, 180
    terrorism and, 197–200
    Wahhabism, 188
scientific atheism, 37–9, 70–1
sectarian hold, myth of, 47–8
secularization, 104–5, 166–7, 168,
    203
Seiwert, Hubert, 33–4
Sen, Amartya, 205
Senegal, 178–9, 180
Seventh-day Adventists, 53
Shah of Iran, 168
Shandong Rebellion (China), 127–8
shari'ah, defined, 31
Shari'a Law (Islam)
    alliances with states, 51, 70
    apostasy, 32, 116, 157, 163
    blasphemy, 32, 116
    colonial empires and, 31, 187

Shari'a Law (Islam) (*cont.*)
dhimmi status, 32
differing interpretations of, 154–6,
  164, 186–8, 193, 196
heresy laws, 125–6, 127, 132
in India, 188–9
in Nigeria, 113–19, 188–9
persecution levels and, 81
quiyās,
Red Mosque conflicts and, 160–1,
  189–92
religious freedom and, 30–3
restrictions on minority religions,
  44–6
state monitoring bureaus and, 33
tenets of, 164
in Turkey, 32
see also Quran
Sherbert v. Verner (1963), 53, 57
Shi'a Muslims
divisions within, 65–6
Imam Hussein and, xi–xii, 154–6
interpretation of Quran, 154–6,
  164, 196
persecution of in Saudi Arabia,
  16–17
Red Mosque conflicts and, 160–1,
  189–92
Sunni Muslims vs. (Iran), xiv–xv,
  154–6, 191
Sunni Muslims vs. (Iraq), xiv–xv,
  67, 182, 192
Shi'a Revival, The (Nassr), 65–6
Shiites. *See* Shi'a Muslims
Shinto and the State, 1868–1988
  (Hardacre), 100
Shoko Asahara, 102, 103
Shterin, Marat S., 40–1, 44–5
Sikhism/Sikhs, xii
Singapore, 188–9
Singh, Bhai Mani, xii
Smith, Adam, 2
on religious monopolies, 50
on religious plurality, 3–4, 70–1
Smith, Alfred, 53
*Smith, Employment Division of
  Oregon, Dept. of Human*

Resources of Oregon v. (1990),
  53–7
social conflict, 210–11
see also restrictions (social/cultural)
Social Regulation of Religion Index
  (SRI), 14, 169, 178–9, 215–22
social restrictions. *See* restrictions
  (social/cultural)
social restrictions index. *See* Social
  Regulation of Religion Index
  (SRI)
socio-political monopoly typology
explanation of, 83–4
listing of countries, 150–1
see also Iran
Soka Gakkai, 34–5, 101
Somalia, 168, 178–9
South Asia, 10–11, 19, 131,
  219
South Korea, 42–3
Soviets
religious persecution in, 10
scientific atheism, 37–9, 70–1
social pressure, 84–5
state religious registration
  requirement, 37, 39
see also Russia Federation
Spain, 66
Special Rapporteur (UN), on Freedom
  of Religion or Belief
on About-Picard Law, 34–5
appointment of, 27
differing definitions of religious
  freedom, 30–3
on French school violations of
  religious freedom, 35–6
on Iranian persecution of Baha'is,
  157–8
reports, 11
Sri Lanka, 19
state, Hume on role of, 4
State Department, U.S.
Country of Particular Concern
  status for Saudi Arabia, 16–17
on Indian state response to violent
  persecution, 147
IRF reports and, 13–14

on persecution by terrorist
organizations, 196–200
reports on socio-political
monopolies, 83–4
State Shinto religion (Japan), 98–100,
101, 131
Stavropol region (Russia), 38–9
Stern, Jessica, 194–5
Stone, Harlan Fiske, 52–3
Sub-Saharan Africa, 177–8, 180
Sudan, 83–4, 168, 177–9
Sufism/Sufis, 180
suicide bombings, 160, 193–4
Sunnah, 187–8, 190–1, 196
see also Islam/Muslims
Sunni Muslims
interpretation of Quran, 154–6,
164, 196
Red Mosque conflicts and, 160–1,
189–92
Saudi Arabia government and,
16–17
Shi'a Muslims vs. (Iran), 154–6,
191
Shi'a Muslims vs. (Iraq), xiv–xv, 67,
182, 191–2
supply side model. *See* religious
economies argument
Supreme Court, U.S.
analysis of First Amendment claims,
54–7
on compelling interest test and
religious freedom, 53, 55–7
on Jehovah's Witnesses and
religious freedom, 52–3
on unconstitutionality of RFRA,
54–8
see also specific cases
Supreme Leader (Iran), 154–6
Syria, 167–8

Tabory, Ephraim, 8
Taiping Rebellion (China), 128–30,
131
Taiwan, 131
Taliban, 188
Tanzania, 188–9

Tawain, 7
terrorism
in Christian-majority countries,
194–200
defined, 194–5
in Muslim-majority countries,
194–200
religious affiliation and support for
U.S. efforts against, 116
sarin nerve agent attack in Japan,
101
state monitoring of religious groups,
33–6, 139–40
state restrictions and, 210–11
see also specific terrorist groups
terrorist organizations, 197–200
Theravada Buddhism, 15–16
Tibetan Buddhists, 130–1, 136, 138–9
Timbuktu, 192–3
time lag model, 81–2, 220, 222
see also methodology
Tocqueville, Alexis de, 60
Toyotomi Hideyoshi, 96
Turkey
Armenians, persecution of, xii–xiv
Christianity in, xii–xiv
monopolistic social pressures in,
85
national character, xiv
secularization of, 166–8
Shari'a Law in, 32
Turkmenistan, 20–1
Twelver Ja'fari (Islam), 154–6
typologies. *See specific typologies*
tyranny of the majority, 60, 71–2,
102, 103

Uganda, 20–1
Unification Church (Moonies), 48
United Kingdom, census data, 174–6
United Nations
Declaration on the Elimination of
All Forms of Interference and of
Discrimination Based on Religion
or Belief, 27, 29–30
International Covenant on Civil and
Political Rights, 26–7

United Nations (*cont.*)
  Lula on anti-Semitism resolution,
    110
  *Universal Declaration of Human
    Rights*, 26–7, 171–4
  see also Special Rapporteur (UN)
United Self Defense Forces of
    Columbia (AUC), 197
United States
  Afghanistan campaign to oust
    Soviets (1980s), 168, 190
  civil rights movement, 40, 71–2
  dominant religion in, 54–7
  early growth in religious activity, 7
  embassies and IRF reports, 13, 17,
    20–1
  exclusion from IRF reports, 17, 19
  First Amendment, 6, 52–4, 56–7
  freedom with tensions category, 86
  growth of religious discrimination,
    58
  hate crimes, 59
  invasion of Iraq, 197–200
  Judeo-Christian principles, 166
  majority rule, 57–60
  Middle East allies, 167–8
  minority religions in court system,
    53–8
  Muslim moderation, survey on,
    193–4
  post-WWII influence on Japan,
    91–3
  Protestantism as dominant religion,
    54–7
  religious liberties, 52–60
  right to worship, survey on, 59–60
  separation of religion and state, 14
  see also Supreme Court, U.S.
Universal Church of the Kingdom of
    God, 109
*Universal Declaration of Human
    Rights* (UN), 26–7, 171–4
Unlawful Activities Prevention Act
    (India, 1967), 148
US Commission on International
    Religious Freedom (USCIRF),
    118–19, 149–50

Uygur Muslims, 66–7, 136, 139–40

Vatican, 171–4
Verner, Sherbert v. (1963), 53, 57
video industry, 189
Vietnam, 20–1, 84–5
vigilante actions, 71–2
violent religious persecution. *See*
    religious persecution, violent
Voice of the Martyrs, 11
Voll, John, 14
Voltaire, 2–3, 50, 203
Vyver, Johan van der, 13

Wahhabism, 127–8, 167–8, 186–8,
    193
Washington Post, on Afghani clerics'
    extreme social power, 41
Weber, Max
  on major world religions, 64
  *Protestant Ethic and the Spirit of
    Capitalism*, 66
Western Hemisphere, 19, 59, 91,
    104–5
  *see also specific regions and
    countries*
White Lotus sects, 127–8
Wike, Richard, 14, 43
Woolston, Thomas, 203
World Buddhist Forums (2009), 135
World Christian Database (WCD),
    123
World Jewish Congress (2004), 110
World Missionary Conference (1910),
    98
World Religion Database, 144–5,
    150–1
World Values Surveys
  on belief in God, 203–4
  on favorable qualities for children
    in Iran, 151–4
  on importance of religion, 203–4
  on religion in India, 141
  on role of religious authorities,
    200
World War II, 91–3, 131, 171–4
Wybraniec, John, 54

Xavier, Francis, 96, 165
Xinjiang province (China). *See* Uygur
  Muslims
Xizang (Tibet). *See* Tibetan Buddhists

Yang, C.K.
  on fear of rebellion in China, 127
  Religion in Chinese Society, 123–5

Yang, Fenggang, 123
Yang, Mayfair, 125–6
Ye Xiaowen, 133
Yoido Full Gospel Church (Korea),
  65

Zijderveld, Anton, 68–9
zoning codes, 40, 54–8